*From the Gaz... ...heart of Africa, Israel's secret commandos strike behind the front lines of terrorism . . .*

**Operation Isotope 1:** The commandos approach hijacked Sabena Airlines Flight 751 disguised as El Al mechanics. In ninety terrifying seconds they use .22s to kill the terrorists and liberate their hostages.

**Operation Spring of Youth:** Next to Entebbe, it is Sayeret Mat'kal's most extraordinary *known* mission—a daring sortie into the heart of Beirut, a precision execution of some of the PLO's most important terrorist leaders.

**Operation Crate 3:** Desperate for leverage in the Middle East bazaar of prisoner swapping, Israel sends its secret commandos across the border into Lebanon, where they stop a column of Syrian military vehicles—and bring home five top Syrian military officers.

**The Death of Abu Jihad:** In a mission designed for total deniability by the Israeli government, a thirty-man commando force is ferried to Tunis on four missile boats. Guided by Mossad agents, they "terminate" the number-two man in the PLO—in a thirteen-second attack!

# THE ELITE

## THE TRUE STORY OF
## ISRAEL'S SECRET
## COUNTERTERRORIST UNIT

# SAMUEL M. KATZ

**POCKET BOOKS**

New York   London   Toronto   Sydney   Tokyo   Singapore

An *Original* Publication of POCKET BOOKS

 POCKET BOOKS, a division of Simon & Schuster Inc.
1230 Avenue of the Americas, New York, NY 10020

ISBN: 0-671-72478-9

First Pocket Books printing May 1992

10  9  8  7  6  5  4  3  2  1

# Author's Note

This is the story of a top-secret commando and intelligence unit so important to Israeli security the Israeli government does not even acknowledge the unit's existence. This unit carried out the daring raid against Beirut in 1973 and the famed raid at Entebbe in 1976. According to foreign reports, the unit also assassinated Abu Jihad, Yasir Arafat's military commander, in Tunis in 1988, and the unit kidnapped Sheikh Obeid, Hizbollah's Southern Lebanon commander, in July 1989. If Israel enjoys an international reputation for lightning-quick military strikes against terrorist targets—and it does—this unit is largely responsible for that esteemed stature. But despite these and other exploits, the Israeli government has for years continued to deny the unit's existence. Even the very vocal and very independent Israeli press, restricted by military censorship, is forbidden to publish the almost sacred words Sayeret Mat'kal unless they are quoting foreign press reports.

Despite the government's hush-hush attempts, the existence of Sayeret Mat'kal, or the General Staff Reconnaissance Unit, is one of the worst-kept secrets in Israel, a nation where secrecy and security are inextricably linked. In a region where Byzantine double-talk is an art form, Sayeret Mat'kal has proven that actions truly speak louder than words; the actual title of this force is really unimportant.

The name, numeric designation, and unit insignia are insignificant. Whether the unit is called Sayeret Mat'kal, the Chief of Staff's Boys, Unit X, or whatever, its spectacular exploits in enemy territory place the unit a cut above all other fighting formations. Its history is, in fact, its calling card; its potential exploits make the enemies of Israel respect the group and fear it greatly. It has operated, it is believed, on three continents and in a dozen nations; the effects of its operations have been felt from the halls of the Pentagon to the terrorist training facilities in Lebanon and Syria. It is the tool the State of Israel must employ when the rules of conventional combat or intelligence gathering just will not do.

The purpose of this book is not to expose any great secrets, nor to promulgate controversy, conflict, and scandal. Many books on alleged top-secret units and personalities tend to fictionalize fact in order to transform the sometimes mundane activities of espionage and unconventional warfare into a spellbinding, best-selling chronicle. Sayeret Mat'kal is one of the world's best and most mysterious commando units; this book is a study of its history, of several personalities involved and of its known exploits—actions credited to the unit in various sources. Most of the operations examined in the following pages have never been credited to Sayeret Mat'kal, or even to a particular unit; most important, Israeli government officials have gone out of their way to deny any Israeli complicity in some of the awe-inspiring missions listed in the following pages. Through research of Israeli archives, interviews, and the analysis of foreign reports, it is, however, possible to form an elaborate and far-reaching résumé of the Chief of Staff's Boys' legacy. It is a listing of battles and operations that illustrates how one small, top-secret, and veiled military unit can alter the course of events in a most turbulent and cutthroat part of this world.

The story of this unit is an important one, but Israeli security concerns are of equal significance. This book, like many originating out of Israel and by Israeli authors, has undergone the scrutiny of the IDF Military Censor's Office, a unit of IDF Military Intelligence that prevents the leakage of classified material through open sources (newscasts, documentaries, journals, magazines, and books). To maintain security, and due to the life-and-death ramifications this practice entails, the narrative language includes an array of such phrases as "according to foreign reports," "it is believed," and "published reports indicate that . . ." To some, this practice may appear to be a bureaucracy-inspired nuisance. To those whose lives are on the line in the field, however, it is a well-founded necessity.

A book of this nature could never be completed without the assistance, generosity, and friendship of a great many people. Many, unfortunately, must remain anonymous, although they will know where and when I have relied on their expertise. I would like to thank my agent, Ethan Ellenberg, for his efforts; the historians at the IDF Archives in Giva'atayim; the photographers and soldiers at the IDF Spokesman Unit; Yossi Argaman, the editor of the IDF's weekly magazine, *Bamachane* (In the Camp); and the staff at the Israel Air Force Public Relations Unit, many of whom have offered me their friendship and kindness. I would also like to thank Lieutenant Colonel Shai Dolev and the staff of the IDF Military Censor's Office in Tel Aviv for their prompt and fair examination of my manuscript. Most important, I would like to thank my father-in-law, Nissim Elyakim, for his kind and unselfish dedication to the pursuit of my career. As was the case with my previous books, it would have been absolutely impossible to see this book materialize—*Me'aleph A'd Taf,* as is said in Hebrew—without his efforts as messenger, negotiator, and representative. I would also like to offer loving thanks to my wife, Sigalit, whose patience and ability to wade through chaos is not only commendable but most appreciated; she has truly been inspirational.

This book is dedicated to the memory of the victims of terrorism. May their sacrifices never be forgotten.

Samuel M. Katz
*January 1992*

# THE ELITE

# *Introduction*

———

The image is as haunting as it is inspiring. A darkened airport in the heart of Africa. Cold-blooded terrorists standing guard over an assembly of men, women, and children who are held hostage and threatened with murder only because they are Jews. The terrorists, too, are guarded, protected by a full battalion of soldiers. A very select group of Israeli commandos braves the physical and geographic obstacles and travels thousands of miles to execute one of the most daring, audacious, and breathtaking rescue operations in military history. The rescue is carried out with meticulous precision, terminating firepower, and unyielding speed. The operation commander, guiding his men from the forefront, is the lone fatality. The terrorists are humiliated in the brilliance of the operation and taught with the blasting impact of a bullet that there is no spot on this earth where they can evade Israel's military. The raid inspires a generation of Israeli military men to believe that the impossible can be done; the security of the State of Israel is limited only by the boundaries of the imagination and the steel of its courage.

Israel's July 3–4, 1976, raid on Entebbe is in essence the story of the Israel Defense Forces, the story of the Jewish state's war against terrorism and numerically superior ene-

1

mies, the story of bold strokes and unyielding heroism. It is the story of leadership and skill, military prowess and inconceivable imagination. Most of all, it is the story of Sayeret Mat'kal.

Ehud Barak is a man accustomed to answering late-night telephone calls. These interruptions have summoned him to supervise assault training in secluded bases throughout Israel and have brought him to the forefront of top-secret operations on the hostile shores of foreign lands. The midnight calls have also brought him to the hard benches of hospital emergency rooms, the chilling supervision of rabbinical rites at a morgue, and the unavoidable task of knocking on a door and informing a wife or parent that a soldier of Israel has been killed in action. *This* call, however, left Ehud Barak breathless. In a profession where emotion is a severe liability, Barak sat up, graciously thanked the caller, and closed his eyes in an all-too-brief moment of reflection and worry. Israel's defense minister, Moshe Arens, had been on the other end of the line. Major General Ehud Barak, the forty-eight-year-old baby-faced Israeli hero, had been informed that he would become the next chief of staff of the Israel Defense Forces (IDF).[1] For Israel, Ehud Barak was the obvious selection. He had been training for this position his entire life. He was the youngest general in Israeli history, and the IDF's most decorated soldier. He was a product of Israel's most enigmatic and important military unit, Sayeret Mat'kal. One of the Chief of Staff's Boys had, indeed, become chief of staff.

For the Jewish state as well as the rest of the region, the coming months would prove to be a critical political and military crossroads—a situation requiring the most capable and dynamic leadership available. Of course, Barak's rise to the top post in the IDF should have come as a surprise to nobody.

Ehud Barak, who at age thirty-nine became the IDF's youngest general, has at age forty-nine become its oldest chief of staff. He is, however, a man who could be considered a natural for the job. Moshe Dayan, Arik Sharon, and

Yitzhak Rabin all said, "He was born to be the IDF's commander."[2] An analytical thinker and a superb fighter, the stocky Barak is a man who inspires confidence and loyalty. Pinned to his uniform below the shiny metal parachutist wings and colored row of campaign ribbons for the 1967, 1973, and Lebanon wars is one royal blue I'tur Ha'Mofet (Exemplary Service Medal) and four Tza'la'shim Shel Ha'Ra'mat'kal (Chief of Staff citations), medals issued for unique acts of courage and daring. Usually the Tza'la'sh, as it is known in the IDF's intricate vernacular of acronyms and abbreviations, is a pair of small silver crossed daggers pinned to a colorful campaign ribbon. It is usually issued on the Independence Day following a conflict, in a nationally televised ceremony filled with honor and reverence. Barak's Tza'la'shim, however, are pinned to plain olive khaki ribbons, indicating that his multiple acts of rewarded bravery were performed during the deadly gray periods of peace that surrounded Israel's full-scale conflagrations. Barak's first Tza'la'sh was awarded after a sensitive mission in Syria in 1963.[3] The stories behind his other decorations are shrouded in mystery, speculation, and legend; they are state secrets of the highest order. The medals were all obtained while Barak was one of the Chief of Staff's Boys—either as a soldier or as the commanding officer.

Ehud Barak is undoubtedly a most remarkable soldier in an army that has produced a remarkable number of legendary figures in its forty-plus years of existence. Born in 1942 in Kibbutz Mishmar Hasharon in the Hefer Valley, young Ehud enjoyed the typical communal farm life-style of hard labor, comradeship, and unflinching patriotism that is typical of the *kibbutzniks* who have made it to the top rung of the IDF's ladder of command. Like many eighteen-year-old boys from the kibbutzim, young Ehud envisioned himself becoming a *tayas* (pilot) when he was conscripted into the IDF in 1959. The pilots of the Israel Air Force are truly an elite within the elite of Israeli society; young Ehud wanted to be a member of this exclusive club. Brave, cocky, and physically infrangible, pilots personified the true soul of the modern Israeli warrior. Behind the controls in their Mystere and Ouragon jets, it was their stamina and courage that would save Israel in event of full-scale war; confident, Ehud Barak knew his capabilities were enough to put him in the cockpit. But with a reported acceptance rate of only one per one hundred candidates, the IAF could not find a spot for Ehud Barak in pilot's training. "Serial No. 448200" was placed in a mechanized infantry unit: the 52nd Battalion.[4]

Disappointed though resilient, Barak quickly proved himself to be a superb infantryman. He was able to run through obstacle courses faster than his comrades; he was more accurate with well-placed bursts from his 9mm Uzi submachine gun than his instructors; and within his platoon he was a charismatic figure who inspired others to perform. Barak's athletic abilities, impressive intelligence, and disregard for the rules and trappings of rank did not go unnoticed in the close-knit command echelons of the IDF. The young corporal was soon monitored as a potential volunteer for a top-secret reconnaissance unit that had been created in 1957 in the aftermath of Unit 101, Arik Sharon's infamous band of retaliatory commandos. The commander of this about-to-be-created force, Avraham Arnan, had heard about the infantryman from the Fifty-second and went to Kibbutz Mishmar Hasharon to find out more about this mysterious young man. The kibbutz elders labeled Ehud Brog (his surname prior to it being Hebraized to Barak, the Hebrew word for lightning) as "a small, lock-picking bastard!"[5]

The unit, called Sayeret Mat'kal (General Staff Reconnaissance), was known to only a handful of officers on a need-to-know-basis. The IDF was searching for a handful of men who could execute the most impossible military tasks in distant lands without attracting too much public attention or fanfare. The commanders of the unit were not looking for cold-blooded killers, nor did they seek robots who would follow orders blindly. They sought innovative men who could, like spies, work alone behind enemy lines, and like guerrillas, improvise with skill, determination, and well-directed firepower when operating in hostile surroundings. To meet this incredible demand the unit's founding fathers looked for the best riflemen, explosives experts, and marksmen the IDF possessed. Ehud Barak was not only one of the unit's first choices, he became its soul; Sayeret Mat'kal was developed around his talents.[6]

In the years that followed his induction into the unit, Ehud Barak excelled in its spectacular surroundings; it was an environment of overachievers and skilled warriors. His rise through the stripes and bars of rank and leadership was swift: first squad leader's course, then officer's course, and then a return to the unit to command the covert operations he had performed so brilliantly as a conscript. Although he was known as a superb soldier, in the field he proved himself a courageous and cool-headed fighter. Following many combat missions there was a commando's course with the French army and, during the 1967 War, service with the elite Seventh Armored Brigade in the Sinai as part of a special intelligence squad that reconnoitered deep behind the Egyptian lines.[7]

The exploits of Ehud Barak and Sayeret Mat'kal, as will be seen in this book, have become the focus of much fanfare and fascination. They include the storming of a terrorist-held Sabena airliner on the tarmac of Lod Airport on May 8, 1972; the kidnapping of Syrian officers in Lebanon; Operation Spring of Youth in Beirut in April 1973; Entebbe; Abu Jihad; Sheikh Obeid; and many others. Barak's signature adorned them all. His talents for unconventional warfare made Sayeret Mat'kal the most potent, hard-hitting option Israel possessed against terrorism. Ehud Barak personified Sayeret Mat'kal in the same way the unit's unique and maverick esprit de corps and Hollywood-type exploits soon came to typify the entire Israeli military establishment.

Nothing about Ehud Barak can be considered ordinary. This is especially significant in an army that preaches the virtues of egalitarianism. Although he is not the first commando officer ever to hold the post of chief of staff—since 1974 the IDF's top job has been reserved for its elite unit veterans—he is the first commander of A'man (the Hebrew acronym for Intelligence Branch), or IDF Military Intelligence, ever to be selected for this honor and responsibility. Unlike other soldiers in his position of prestige and power, he has never fallen into the political mold of a particular party, such as Likud or Labor, nor did he develop as a favorite son of one defense minister or another. His achievements, much like those of the unit he commanded for so many years, came about through merit and not military nepotism.

For any operation, anywhere, and no matter how delicate and controversial the undertaking's results might be, Ehud Barak's presence was always required. In April 1984, when three Palestinian terrorists hijacked an intercity bus traveling between Tel Aviv and the southern city of Ashkelon, Military Intelligence Director Barak stood behind the barricades coordinating the rescue operation. As deputy chief-of-staff in March 1988, Barak supervised the delicate rescue operation of a bus carrying workers from their homes in Beersheba to the nuclear facility in Dimona, which had been hijacked by a suicide squad of el-Fatah Force 17 commandos, the praetorian guard of Yasir Arafat's PLO. That incident would, according to published reports, provoke Israel to respond with the assassination of the PLO's deputy commander, Abu Jihad (the nom de guerre of Khalil al-Wazir) in his Tunis lair in April 1988. It was a brilliantly planned and executed operation—one commanded and coordinated by Major General Ehud Barak from an Israel Air Force C-3 Boeing 707 hovering twenty thousand feet over the Mediterranean.[8]

From his first year as a raw infantryman to the hallways of the IDF general staff, Ehud Barak has made being different a staple of his military persona. While most IDF officers carry a 9mm or .22-caliber Beretta automatic tucked into the cracks of their back as personal sidearms, Barak carries the sleek and compact Czechoslovak Vz.61 Skorpion 7.65mm submachine gun—the favorite killing tool of Palestinian hit squads—strapped to his right thigh in a beaten khaki canvas holster; the weapon is a souvenir from a dead terrorist. Throughout his career Ehud Barak has also looked the part of master commando better than any other Israeli soldier. His mirrored pilot sunglasses, bright red beret, shiny olive battle dress jacket, and well-shined brown leather boots are tools of his appearance meant to display a feeling of confidence and daring and create an aura of respect and fear.

For Sayeret Mat'kal as well, being different and being the best was one and the same. The impossible became the probable, the dire became the almost routine, and the unexplainable became a pillar of its legend. The new weapons and technologies of war, the new strategies of attack, and the new techniques of counterterrorism the State of Israel would deploy were all perfected by the Chief of Staff's Boys. They became the cutting edge of the Israel Defense Forces; if the Israel Defense Force is considered the IDF's first line of defense, than Sayeret Mat'kal is its first line of special ops. The unit, like its longtime commander, followed its own set of rules and its own set of limitations.

On April 1, 1991, in a low-key ceremony in the Kirya—the sprawling four-square-block mini-city that serves as headquarters for the Israel Defense Forces, the Ministry of Defense, and various other spook agencies and offices—outgoing Chief of Staff Lieutenant General Dan Shomron, one of the heroes from the Entebbe rescue raid, placed an additional bronze metal leaf on each of General Barak's epaulets, formally inaugurating Barak as the IDF's fourteenth Ra'mat'kal (Chief of Staff) with the rank of lieutenant general. Being in the spotlight, however, will not remove the veil of secrecy that surrounds Lieutenant General Barak and Sayeret Mat'kal. With Barak's penchant for elite-unit operations deep in the enemy heartland, IDF covert operations are likely to grow more numerous, and the veil of secrecy will likely grow darker.

It is perhaps fitting that in one of the most dire times in Israel's embattled history, a man who has been called the Israeli James Bond and Israel's Rambo will command its defense forces. It is a period in which Israel finds itself at a military crossroads; a time that requires cool heads, intellectual insight, and skilled minds to dispatch Israel's shadow warriors into the abyss of spectacular operations that never make it to network news broadcasts or the pages of military journals. It is also a time, it can be assumed, that will require the well-honed talents of the Chief of Staff's Boys more than ever. As the commander of this special force in the field, as the man who must pull names out of the drawer and dispatch soldiers to points unknown in the Middle East, Ehud Barak is Sayeret Mat'kal; he is its past, and he is now its future. With Israel's most spectacular soldier now in full command of its most spectacular commandos, the boundaries of unconventional warfare are most certainly to be breached.

This is the story of Sayeret Mat'kal.

# NOTES

1. Net'a Shadmi, "Pitom Ani Roah Et Ehud Sheli Be'Sarbal Lavan," *Ma'ariv Shabat,* November 30, 1990, 3.

2. Rafi Ginat, "Koreh Yakar," *Olam Hazeh,* November 28, 1990, 5.

3. Emanuel Rosen, "Ha'ish She'Himtzi Et Ha'yechida Ha'Muvcheret," *Ma'ariv Sof Shavu'a,* September 19, 1990, 46.

4. Shadmi, "Pitom Ani Roah," 3.

5. Yosef Walter, "Mu'amad Le'Ra'mat'kal: Yesh Barak," *Ma'ariv Sof Shavu'a,* January 24, 1986, 6.

6. Rosen, "Ha'ish She'Himtzi," 44.

7. Walter, "Mu'amad Le'Ra'mat'kal," 8.

8. Yossi Melman and Dan Raviv, *The Imperfect Spies: The History of Israeli Intelligence* (London: Sidgwick and Jackson, 1989), 31.

# 1

## *The Legacy of Unit 101*

To the outsider, the installation looked more like a relic from the American Wild West than an army base in the Jerusalem hills. Surrounded by sun-ravaged mountains, sparse vegetation, and staggering heat, Camp Sataf sat atop a small hill, commanding all in its presence. The main gate was usually guarded by two heavily armed individuals—tommy guns or German MP-38 Schmeissers were standard issue—who carried razor-sharp commando knives for good measure. They were always unshaven and usually wore a mixture of civilian sweaters, captured enemy fatigues, and extravagant headgear—either Australian bush hats or Egyptian police red felt fezzes, tassels and all. Although their nonmilitary appearance would gain them several days in the stockade in any army—even in the Israel Defense Forces—the MPs stayed away from this base and even farther away from its soldiers. Permission to enter the base was issued on an arbitrary basis; it depended on the looks of any visitor and the intuition of the soldier on duty. And of course, entrance to Camp Sataf hinged on the decision of the unit's legendary commander.

The crackling of automatic gunfire was a permanent

fixture on the base. So, too, were the muffled blasts of explosions from grenades being tossed into steel drums, and the whining lurch of 52mm mortar shells being lobbed at targets close by or farther away in the surrounding hills. Beer bottles, bricks, tin cans, and unfortunate pigeons were all utilized for marksmanship competitions and individual target practice. There was no routine military discipline at the base; no marching drills, shined boots, or well-trimmed haircuts were seen. These soldiers were not meant to provide politicians and generals with awe-inspiring displays of marching skills, saber rattling, or standing at attention. They were, after all, Unit 101, the best of the best, answering to only two men: Arik Sharon, their divine influence, and the chief of staff. They were, after all, his boys. The Chief of Staff's Boys![1]

For the fledgling IDF in the 1950s, Unit 101 was a remarkable military element. Confident, cocky, and capable, the men embodied the strategic Israeli thought that only through qualitative superiority and brutal innovativeness could the Arabs be contained and controlled in battle. This David vs. Goliath ethic was, indeed, the justification for a commando force like Unit 101, but Major Sharon was by no means a revolutionary. He was an extension of traditional Israeli military thought, which had a proud and honored heritage forged in battle. In 1953 Unit 101 was the latest in a long line of small, elite units assigned to overcome the odds and make their few guns' bite much worse than their bark. It was, however, a unit that was significant for generations of fighters to come.

Even before the First World War Israel's pre-independence visionaries understood the precarious nature of their foothold in the land of Israel. Surrounded by hostile Arab neighbors, outnumbered and outgunned, Jews in the land of Israel depended on the implementation of three fundamental factors for their survival: the creation of a small, though potent, Jewish army capable of neutralizing the Arabs' numerical superiority with a man-for-man qualitative superiority; the execution of innovative and bold military tactics; and the ability to gather accurate and timely intelligence on their foes. Achieving these goals would not be an easy task. The Jewish population had extremely limited resources, both human and material, and the Jews had no martial heritage to speak of. The Zionist leaders understood that they needed to create one small, elite force of warriors to take care of all of their security needs, as well as to serve as a role model for the larger Israeli army that would follow the declaration of statehood.

There were many attempts to create that role model in the Haganah (Defense), the underground Jewish army in Palestine, from the Notrim (Guards) of 1936, a small unit of Jewish policemen that introduced the likes of Yigal Allon and Moshe Dayan to the Israeli military who's who, to the infamous Nodedot (Wanderers), settlement defenders commanded by Yitzhak Sadeh. Sadeh was a product of the Zionist vision and the early struggles to establish a Jewish homeland in a region engulfed by enemies and an inhospitable environment. Born in Odessa, in the Russian Crimea, Sadeh was a burly man known primarily for his military insight. Perhaps the most important element of Sadeh's vision was his understanding that the future State of Israel could never hope to defeat the Arabs on the battlefield unless the Jews could: (a) bring the battle onto enemy territory; (b) make the enemy's numbers insignificant through carefully directed firepower and hit-and-run operations; and, most importantly, (c) gather intelligence—know what the enemy was thinking, where he was moving, what he knew of you, what he carried, who were his friends and foes. In the days prior to advanced photo reconnaissance and satellite imagery, intelligence meant forays into enemy territory. That meant a select group of fighters, especially night fighters who could blend into any terrain or environment without provoking suspicion. That, of course, meant an elite unit of soldiers.

Sadeh later formed the Fo'sh (acronym for Plugot Sadeh, or Field Companies), a mobile unit of retaliatory commandos that combined firepower with the attribute of analytical intelligence. As Fo'sh commander, Yitzhak Sadeh chose each fighter personally. As the Fo'sh would be executing extremely sensitive missions, he chose only those whose loyalty was absolute (the British had compromised many underground operations by using well-paid or blackmailed Jewish informants); as they would live in the field and often pursue an enemy or be pursued by one, they had to be in perfect physical shape and able to kill without trepidation. Most important, they had to be suitably intellectual, so their minds would prove to be just as potent as their razor-sharp daggers and Lee Enfield .303 rifles. The Fo'sh, however, became too good for their own good. The Haganah high command feared the Fo'sh's elitism almost as much as the Palestinian Arabs feared their prowess on the battlefield, and the unit was ordered to disband.

Another elite Jewish military force of equal, if not greater, importance roamed through Palestine at the time. It was a force sanctioned by the British, commanded by a gentile, and it would serve as the first true laboratory of command for Israel's military leadership, as well as a testing ground for the strategies of elite-unit commando operations. In 1936 a young British captain was assigned to Palestine to help crush the Arab rebellion. He was an eccentric soul, a military revisionist, and a man who believed the unconventional to be mandatory—the unexpected and unimaginable a facet of pronounced military doctrine. He had proven his irregular warfare theories brilliantly in the Sudan and was brought to Palestine specifically to protect the Iraqi Petroleum Company's pipeline—a strategic piece of tubing that ran from the northern Iraqi oil fields to the port of Haifa—from Arab attack and sabotage. Unfortunately for the British high command, the captain they recruited for this most sensitive task was a devout, Bible-thumping Christian who believed passionately in the Jews' right to Zion. His name: Orde Charles Wingate.

Wingate had a profound impact on the molding of Israeli military doctrine. Defense, when fighting a numerically superior enemy, meant offense, and offense meant fighting deep inside enemy territory where the opposition was most vulnerable. Captain Wingate saw in the Jews a potential of biblical proportions—he felt that the Jews of Palestine had the courage, intelligence, and stamina to become world-renowned fighters; he would write to his cousin, Sir Reginald Wingate, "I have seen the young Jews in the *kibbutzim*. I tell you they will provide a soldiery better than ours. We have only to train it."[2] With the Haganah's okay, Wingate approached the commander-in-chief of British forces in Palestine, Sir Archibald Wavell, with a solid though highly controversial plan to stem Arab attacks against the pipeline: the establishment of a joint British-Jewish counterterrorist commando unit. Reluctantly Wavell agreed to his young captain's enthusiastic approach, and the Special Night Squads (SNS) were formed. To the Jews, Wingate became known as Ha'yedid (The Friend).

As Sadeh had chosen men for the Wanderers and Fo'sh, Wingate handpicked each member of the SNS. Volunteers were subjected to brutal questioning, grueling physical trials, and other intensively cruel examinations in which a potential recruit could prove his worthiness to serve in the unit. In one such test volunteers were blindfolded and taken to a desolate location in the unforgiving wilderness— usually a hillside surrounded by Arab villages. The hapless candidates were ordered to sit tight for an hour or so and then make it back to camp in an allotted time period. All those who succeeded were accepted for the next round of examinations; all those who failed made it back to the Haganah base camp and gladly fetched their gear. One Haganah veteran who passed the SNS test was the young Moshe Dayan, one of Israel's most famous soldiers and the man who, as Operations Branch commander, would eventually support the creation of Unit 101. Wingate taught these eager young men that courage bred confidence, and confidence afforded men the internal stature needed to execute deep-penetration forays into the heart of enemy territory.[3]

Wingate was never allowed to witness his grand vision of leading a large Jewish army in battle. His close-knit, intimate relationship with the Haganah caused concern in Britain, and in 1939 he was ordered out of Palestine as a security measure. His legacy, however, continues to this day.

The final elite force meant to lead the fight for the Jews' survival in Israel was the Pal'mach (Strike Companies), a joint British-Haganah venture meant to defend Palestine against the German juggernaut advancing from the desert wasteland of North Africa toward Palestine. To the British, the fall of Palestine meant an end to their colonial gains following World War I; for the Jews, however, a Nazi seizure of Palestine meant the termination of their religion and history.

With the Sadeh-Wingate doctrine serving as the cornerstone of Haganah military policy, ambitious operations were planned for the strike companies. Through harsh training the Pal'mach developed into a capable guerrilla force, and after the Haganah was allowed supervision of recruitment it covertly expanded to three times the British-allowed size. When the Allies invaded Lebanon and Syria on June 8, 1941 it was Pal'mach scouts who charted the advance routes and identified enemy positions through reconnaissance forays. They proved to be excellent intelligence gatherers and extremely quick on their feet, racing through impassable hills and wadis—dried river beds—in record time. When forced to engage Vichy French forces, the Pal'mach fighters also proved their worth in combat. They were deadly with the Lee Enfield rifle and 9mm Sten submachine gun, and they perfected the art of removing sentries with daggers and garrotes.*

The British prepared elaborate plans for sabotage and hit-and-run commando raids for Pal'mach units to mount against the invading Germans. Hundreds were ordered to train in the art of irregular warfare, while the Haganah secretly trained hundreds more. The Pal'mach was taught to fight with what manpower and materiel was available, rather than what was tactically advisable. These young and idealistic fighters were instructed in the most advanced forms of demolitions; as the Pal'mach lacked any type of artillery— very few mortars were even available—TNT was their

---

*During one battle with the French, near the village of Iskandrun, Moshe Dayan, a young lead scout, received a permanent injury to his eye, the best-known war wound since Nelson's.[4]

artillery. They refined small-unit assault techniques, learning how to overcome heavily fortified defenses with well-placed assaults by small shock units, and they perfected the art of sabotaging vital enemy installations. Although their British instructors preached the noble importance of a group effort, the Haganah representatives forged in their minds the notion that the ultimate Pal'mach unit was a fighter and his weapon.[5]

Courses were also given in long-range reconnaissance patrols, intelligence gathering (as well as material analysis and dissemination), communications, and weapons proficiency. The Pal'mach fighter learned to handle every weapon he or she might come into contact with, from French light machine guns to Italian grenades. They became particularly expert in Axis weapons—especially German—and were trained to field-strip a Schmeisser MP-38 with the same ease and expertise they would apply to their own Sten guns. *Krav maga* (contact fighting), an indigenous Israeli brand of practical-minded martial arts, was given high priority, and the art of cold-killing received critical attention. The Pal'mach fighters—men and women of the *kibbutzim* who had bodies hardened by agricultural toil and minds numbed by constant conflict with the Arabs—made excellent commando material. The British were impressed with their Jewish pupils and apprehensive about them. After the war, they realized, this knowledge would be used against them.

The Pal'mach was able to form unique and, in retrospect, remarkable subdivisions from the Jewish population of Palestine. A Syrian Platoon was created to operate in the Arab region of Syria and Lebanon as a fifth-column sabotage and intelligence-gathering force. Ha'Machlaka Ha'Germanit (the German Platoon), a force of fifth columnists tasked with infiltrating Nazi lines while masquerading as German military personnel, was also formed. They were to commit acts of sabotage, gather intelligence, and, when the orders were issued from the SOE (Special Operations Service), assassinate key German officials; it was one of the most important elements of the British government's P.P.O.S. (Palestine Post-occupation Scheme).[6] The force was made up entirely of Jewish refugees from Germany and Austria who knew the language and the mentality of the Nazis. It was a remarkable concept for Jews to learn to become Nazi soldiers; but as Israel would see many times in her brief history, the numerous and varied threats she faced sometimes dictated radical military moves. In 1943 a Pal'mach Balkan Platoon was also formed, and it consisted of Jewish refugees from Greece, Italy, Albania, and Yugoslavia. It fought with the SAS in the Aegean, as well as with SOE-assisted guerrillas in Yugoslavia.* The Pal'mach's Balkan Platoon, with the help of the ISLD (Inter-service Liaison Department), the espionage department of the British foreign office, eventually developed into the Jewish state's first true parachutist elements. Volunteers from the Balkan Platoon, including the infamous Hannah Szenesh, were parachuted into Eastern and Central Europe to assist downed Allied airmen, as well as to attempt to save what remained of the Jewish populations in the native lands.

When V–E Day finally arrived on May 8, 1945, the Pal'mach's two thousand-plus fully trained commandos readdressed the unit's objectives to the establishment of the State of Israel. This became a two-fold mission in which the forces of the Pal'mach would be in the vanguard of Haganah's efforts to bring survivors of the Holocaust through the British sea blockade of Palestine, as well as serving as shock troops in the conventional guerrilla campaign to remove the Union Jack from the land of Israel.

During the 1948 War of Independence the Pal'mach became less a special operations entity and more the professional military core of the newly created Tzahal (acronym for Tzava Haganah Le'Yisrael, or Israel Defense Forces), although one Pal'mach unit, which captured the "Mission: Impossible" daring and recklessness of the Special Night Squads and forces like the German Platoon, was its Seventh Reconnaissance Platoon.[7] It was a combat intelligence-

---

*A special Romanian Platoon was rumored to have existed. Its principal objective was to infiltrate Romania and destroy the ultra-strategic Ploesti oil fields.

gathering entity that left the safe domain of friendly territory to venture deep into the labyrinth of danger and uncharted paths of the enemy's domain. The lightly armed units—usually consisting of four to five soldiers led by an officer—were tasked with determining enemy strengths (and, hopefully, weaknesses) deep in his rear, as well as charting potential invasion routes. In many cases they wore khaki drill and *kefiyeh* headdress, so that from a distance, at least, they would blend in with the surroundings. If an Arab sentry or patrol came too close for comfort, however, their training and cold-killing skills were used with great effectiveness. In essence, the Seventh Platoon became *the* combat intelligence force of the Israel Defense Forces, a unit that knew few boundaries and operated freely in the most dangerous of enemy-held environments.

Oddly enough, the Pal'mach did not survive the 1948 War. Even though many in the IDF general staff wanted to refine its ranks and transform it into a special strike force capable of executing the most sensitive of commando operations, the left-wing politically active soldiers of the Pal'mach were seen as a political threat to Israeli democracy and, most importantly, to Prime Minister David Ben-Gurion's power. They were disbanded in 1949 and phased into the reserve infrastructure of Israel's citizen defense force.[8]

For several years, in fact, the fledgling Israel Defense Forces did not possess a cutting-edge commando unit. The Giva'ati Infantry Brigade possessed a LRDG-type force known as Shu'alei Shimshon (Samson's Foxes), which roamed the desert on heavily armed vehicles, but they were jeep-borne and trained and equipped solely for desert operations. The First Golani Infantry Brigade was considered top of the line, but following the war it became a national melting pot tasked with absorbing new immigrants. There was also a fledgling paratroop element born out of the Balkan Platoon, which was eventually expanded to include Pal'mach volunteers who trained secretly at a former SS base in the Carpathian Mountains of Czechoslovakia. When the 1948 War ended, however, so did the sense of urgency to incorporate them into the IDF's combat order of battle. The Tzanhanim (Paratroopers) were an adventurous and independent lot. Led by a few ex–SAS (Special Air Service), LRDG, and French Foreign Legion veterans, the majority of jumpers joined the airborne force primarily for promises of extra pay. Most of the time they mourned comrades killed in freak jump accidents, or sat half drunk playing cards between moonlighting stints at the Haifa shipyards or chasing the lovelies at a nearby Women's Corps training base.

The last hope, perhaps, for a truly unique fighting formation came in the form of the Na'ha'l (an acronym for No'ar Halutzei Lohem, or Fighting Pioneer Youth) Infantry Brigade, a force of farmer/soldiers who spent their military service protecting the boundaries of the Jewish state by establishing frontier *kibbutzim* at strategic and desolate points along the borders.

In fact, if the IDF in the 1950s projected any type of image to its foes, it appeared to shy away from such elite units, especially with its egalitarian mandate. It would take one man to reshape Israeli thinking: a young firebrand officer named Ariel "Arik" Sharon.

Ariel "Arik" Scheinerman (he had his name Hebraized to Sharon by Prime Minister Ben-Gurion in 1954, after receiving the command of the paratroop brigade) was born in Kfar Malal, fifteen miles northeast of Tel Aviv on the coastal Plain of Sharon, in 1928. A hard-to-handle youth known to hit his classmates over their heads with blunt objects for no reason at all, Sharon joined the Haganah at age seventeen, in 1945. By 1947 he had reached the rank of lieutenant and commanded a platoon in the Hi'sh (acronym for the Heyl Sadeh, or Field Corps), the ground army of the Haganah. He was known as a courageous commander and a well-liked officer who had quite defined views on Israel's Arab enemies. When full-scale fighting erupted his Hi'sh platoon became part of the Alexandroni Infantry Brigade's highly regarded 32nd Battalion; during the bloodletting at the police fortress at Latrun, overlooking the strategic Jerusalem–Tel Aviv road, the young IDF officer received his first bitter taste of combat, a bloody experience that would forever mold his concept of command, control, and military strategy. The battle for Latrun was an exercise in poor planning and inferior organization. It was a battle in which Israeli forces suffered horrific casualties; it was a fight in which wounded Israeli soldiers were left to die on the battlefield, and it was a tragic chapter of Israeli military history never to be repeated.

After recovering from wounds suffered at Latrun, Sharon returned to active duty against Egyptian forces in the Faluja Pocket. He had already earned a reputation as a fearless commander—a reputation that won him the command of Sayeret Golani, the reconnaissance company of the First Golani Infantry Brigade. Although it was a small force with limited potential, Sharon instilled his own view of aggressive, offensive, and preemptive military operations; some would say that the anger and sense of desperation forged in his soul by the Latrun debacle turned the young company commander into a visionary with revolutionary ideas. His success with Golani brought him notice in the upper echelons of the IDF chain of command, and in 1950 he was named chief intelligence officer of IDF Central Command. He was so capable in this task that a year later, in 1952, he was named chief intelligence officer of IDF Northern Command. While in Northern Command he was instrumental in the planning and preparation of a highly secretive operation in which five Arab Legion officers were kidnapped for interrogation and eventual exchange in a prisoner swap.[9] Ominously, this operation would serve as a precedent for several identical operations that Israel's most important special forces units would emulate in the following years.

Serving as chief intelligence officer of a territorial command would alter his conception of battlefield intelligence and of the means required to achieve mastery over a numerically superior enemy. Yet military service was mundane and, on the whole, unappealing. In the following years Sharon left the army temporarily to travel abroad and then studied Middle Eastern history at Jerusalem's Hebrew University. While he was in Jerusalem Sharon's life, as well as the course of Israeli history, would forever be altered. In mid-July, 1953, he was summoned to the headquarters of Colonel Mishael Shacham, commander of the 16th Jerusalem Brigade, to discuss the elimination of one Mustapha Samueli, a onetime Nazi agent who was one of the most notorious murderers operating in the Israeli half of Jerusalem; he was also a well-paid agent for the Jordanian Muchabarat (Intelligence Service). To assassinate such a dangerous foe—living inside Jordanian territory, no less—required a special operations unit. No such unit existed in the IDF order of battle.

Since the creation of the Israel Defense Forces in May 1948, there had been senior commanders who felt Israel's vulnerable frontiers and outnumbered status warranted the creation of small, elite, and highly trained reconnaissance forces. Initially this thought centered on Israel's Arab minority—Druze Muslims, Bedouins, and Circassians—who could patrol sensitive areas and at the same time infiltrate enemy territory as a result of their shepherdlike skills, intimate knowledge of the desert, and Arab appearance. Once inside enemy terrain these indigenous Israeli Arabs could blend into the hostile surroundings without too much difficulty. Not being Jews, however, these loyal citizens of Israel were viewed with suspicion and apprehension. They could not be trusted with top-secret information or to execute top-secret special operations. Although a unit made up entirely of Israel's minorities would eventually be established—it was known as Unit 300—minorities were kept out of Israeli special operations for many years.

In 1951 IDF Southern Command made a noble attempt to incorporate Bedouins and Israelis into a counterinsurgency force to secure Israel's indefensible frontier with Egypt. Palestinian infiltrators and Egyptian military intelligence agents had been crossing the border virtually at will, initiating a year full of terror and chaos in southern Israel. This new force first centered around an entity known as Yechidat Shaked (Almond Unit), a force of Bedouin and Circassian scouts and trackers supported by heavily armed jeep-borne infantrymen. Eventually, however, a specialized retaliatory, preemptive, and patrol force was formed; it was known as

Unit 30, the title given to it not for mysterious designation reasons, but as a result of the number of men it initially possessed. Unit 30 was a valiant attempt by Colonel Moshe Dayan, a senior operations officer working out of Southern Command, to emulate the brilliance of Wingate's SNS with the abilities—and limitations—of the Israel Defense Forces. For a year the unit worked, but the rigid-minded traditionalists who held power had little patience for a force that feigned military discipline, carried any weapons it found, and operated according to its own guidelines. It was disbanded in 1952.

When Mustapha Samueli's reign of murder, rape, and—most importantly for the IDF—hostile espionage activities increased to epidemic proportions in the summer of 1953, the IDF could not field a trained force of commandos capable of crossing the border and eliminating the boisterous felon with the low profile such a deed demanded; the IDF general staff feared that sanctioning a large infantry assault in search of a single man was overkill and might spark full-scale war with the Jordanians. Realizing an unconventional approach was needed in the Samueli matter, Colonel Shacham summoned Sharon to his office. Rumors about the twenty-five-year-old major with a gigantic appetite and a boisterous, overbearing personality who was something of a maverick sparked great curiosity and interest.

Their meeting was short and to the point. Shacham explained the importance of the target, the primary and national objective of the mission, and, of course, the need for absolute secrecy—this was not an operation the State of Israel wanted to take credit for. Most of all, Shacham requested—ordered—that Sharon bring him success; failure would be politically embarrassing for Israel. Sharon would be allowed to select a force of his own choosing, but the mission would have to be executed in the very near future. As the two concluded their discussions Shacham patted the large major on the back and said to him in a slow and revealing whisper, "There are those who study the feats of others, and there are those who will study yours."[10]

For the raid against Mustapha Samueli's home in Nebi Samuel, a village just across the Israeli frontier in Jordanian territory, Sharon chose seven men, all friends from the 1948 War or from more peaceful days at the university. These were men he trusted and knew to possess the combat skills and courage that would get them through the mission. The most prominent among this group were Shlomo Baum, an NCO who had served under Sharon in Sayeret Golani, and Yosef Sa'adieh, one of the most capable sappers ever to serve the Pal'mach. The eight fighters, dressed in civilian garb and armed with American .45-caliber Thompson sub-machine guns, daggers, Molotov cocktails, and grenades, prepared to cross the border into Jordan.

After avoiding several Arab Legion posts along the heavily defended frontier the force slipped through the unforgiving hills, thick woodland, and deep ravines. They reached Nebi Samuel undetected, careful to retain their cover and remain invisible—they remembered how, in 1948, the village had become a deathtrap to the Pal'mach's Harel Brigade. After slinking through the unmanned streets looking for the proper door they located Samueli's home. They quickly prepared TNT charges by fixing them to the entrance area, and they lit the detonating fuse. Excited, sweating, and hoping to burst into the house with tommy guns ablaze, Sharon's men were horrified to see the device's fuse fizzle, burp, and then start a small fire in the door. Sharon ordered his group into action anyway, lobbing several British Mills grenades—leftovers from the Mandate—into the house. No one responded because Samueli was not at home. Immediately the town was ablaze with activity; residents fired wildly into the air, not knowing what had happened, while Sharon's men overheard the fatal news that the legion was on its way. They disappeared into the mountains and returned safely to Israel.

Eventually the mission to terminate the threat from Nebi Samuel went to a combined intelligence and military force that trapped the elusive criminal in a snare operation and then decimated him in an ambush of well-directed gunfire. Yet Israel's pursuit of Samueli led Shacham to push the IDF general staff to establish a special, covert antiterrorist commando force. The importance of this force to Israeli security would be acute. Any time a foreign power threatened the Jewish state through unconventional means, a select group of individuals would be summoned to attack specific, highly sensitive targets in brilliant, daring, and spectacular operations. The aftermath of their actions would have to be, in many cases, completely deniable, but it had to leave the enemy with the clear message that the perpetrator had, indeed, been Israel. The creation of fear and awe was an essential objective of any such force. Yet it would have to be a small and covert entity; the commandos would operate in unobtrusive uniforms and carry a wide assortment of weapons not registered to any particular armed force in the region. They would not have the trappings of conventional armies. They would be deniable. When dirty tasks had to be executed, this was a most important factor.

The IDF chief of staff, Lieutenant General Mordechai Makleff (who himself was a victim of Arab terror at an early age), looked favorably on Shacham's request. He agreed Israel was slowly sinking into a sorry state where the citizenry would be at the mercy of Arab infiltrators. Makleff also realized that the IDF was, in many cases, desperately in need of a role model, a dedicated star all other units could look up to and hope to emulate. Most importantly, Makleff realized that Arik Sharon was the only man Israel had at the time who was both confident and charismatic enough to lead this new force. He was a natural-born leader and a man the Arabs could soon learn to fear.

Although very few Israelis would actually hear of it in the media, Unit 101—its name a direct and highly respectful reference to the American 101st Airborne Division—would forever change the way the Jewish state waged war and defended itself from terrorist attack. Although it would eventually become one of the most important military formations ever incorporated into the Israel Defense Forces, it existed for a little less than half a year.

Fearing the abilities of such a military wild card—heavily

armed and expertly trained, no less—the IDF general staff ordered that Unit 101 was never to consist of more than fifty commandos. This was an easy order to carry out, considering that the force began with only a commander, his deputy, and two officers. Like Sadeh and Wingate before him, Sharon went to great pains to handpick each Unit 101 fighter; the unit accepted only volunteers. Within weeks of its formation, however, news of a special antiterrorist force began to filter through the IDF rumor mill. Infantrymen, tank soldiers, and gunners—all bored with day-to-day service in a less-than-glamorous military environment— flocked to Camp Sataf, the unit's base headquarters, to volunteer their services. Unit 101's first conscript volunteer, however, was also its most famous. He was perhaps the most spectacular, capable, and enigmatic soldier ever to serve the Israeli army. When a young scout from the Na'ha'l Brigade named Meir Har-Zion presented himself to Sharon and simply said, "I'm here," history was set on its course.

Meir Har-Zion was a truly incredible individual, a man who was possessed by the need to court danger.[11] Prior to being conscripted into the IDF in 1952 he was known to cut through Transjordanian territory regularly on nature outings to the Dead Sea oasis at Ein Gedi; at the age of sixteen he trekked alone on a pilgrimage to the ancient Nabataean city of Petra, traditionally the site where Moses struck the rock. Although any traveler caught by Jordanian police or Bedouin tribesmen would consider death a reprieve, the young Har-Zion scoffed at the inherent dangers. "Who'll catch me?" was his popular comment. He had a natural feel for the terrain and direction that was simply uncanny. He could race through the mazelike hills around Jerusalem in record time, finding the quickest path to take by merely reconnoitering the area with a glance. He was confident and arrogant, with a very chauvinistic view of the Arabs. It appeared to everyone at Camp Sataf that Unit 101 was designed for Har-Zion.

News of this new and exciting unit brought volunteers, mainly paratroopers who were sick and tired of the rigid forms of discipline they were forced to endure while masquerading as Israel's best soldiers. They in turn brought friends, acquaintances, and anyone else found along the way, allowing the unit to expand. Only the best were accepted. The combination of these paratroopers, foot soldiers, and tankers created a cohesive and diverse blend in the unit, as well as a healthy dose of competition; to balance things out, Sharon brought a few ex–Pal'mach fighters into this most amazing grab bag of military formations.

In the very beginning of Unit 101 Sharon's rogue commando force consisted of less than twenty fighters; but intensive training was attended to with great seriousness, as if it was of battalion strength. Every morning Sharon woke his men for the customary one-dozen-plus-kilometer run, followed by grueling physical exercises and martial arts; drills and precision marching were never mentioned, and the sight of a soldier saluting any officer—even Sharon himself—was rare. Morning inspection resembled a meeting in a prison courtyard rather than a daily function at a military installation—unkempt men with ten-day beards and ragged black market–bought military gear gathered together to hear the schedule for yet another eighteen-hour day of training.

Camp Sataf was a truly unique base, built to resemble an Arab village. The soldiers of Unit 101 were taught only one element of military life: how to attack. Sharon would train his fighters as they crawled through fields peppered with skin-pricking thorns that tore through their fatigues and mercilessly sliced across their flesh; he would teach them to crawl stealthily and speedily alongside a stone fence while poised for assault, and to throw a fragmentation grenade into a tin drum meant to stand in for the living room of a terrorist leader. After each grenade toss the fighter was forced to examine the fragmentation damage and learn how to achieve a higher death count with a single grenade.

Most importantly for the fighters, they were taught to understand and respect their weapons and never to fear using them. Ammunition was in short supply, and unit attacks were meant to pour accurate fire into a concentrated target, destroying it in brutal haste. As a result, Unit 101 commandos had to become expert shots—if a fighter ran out of ammo, he had to use his dagger or hands to kill an enemy soldier and then steal *his* gun and ammo. Bottles were thrown into the air to simulate moving targets; hapless birds flying overhead simulated escaping enemy soldiers or guerrillas; and cigarettes attached to the corners of buildings were used to create sharpshooting exercises. The fighters were taught how to fire from the hip in accurate bursts, learning the art of spraying an area with fire while assaulting a heavily defended position. At night, just after they would sit through exhaustive lectures on strategy, camouflage, and infiltration techniques, experts taught the tired fighters how to inflict quick, silent, and fatal knife wounds; close-quarter killing would be required, and it would be good to learn this skill before sleep. The men of Unit 101 would learn that war is not for the fainthearted.

Training was enhanced by the indoctrination and psychological studies of the commander. Arik was a master manipulator of speech, a charismatic orator who instilled in each of his men the feeling that the security of the state depended on their actions and rested upon their shoulders. They were the elite of the nation, the guardians of Zion, and Arab acts of terror would be reacted to with a tenfold Jewish response. There had to be a unit within the army that received the special top-secret missions and executed them in a decisive fashion with surgical precision. Such a unit would become a national role model and would eventually raise the quality of the entire army; conventional units such as the Golani and Na'ha'l brigades would struggle and compete in order to reach Unit 101 standards of courage, guts, insolence, and proficiency. To keep their edge up Arik would usually split the force into small groups and then have them compete against one another. They might have been the best in the IDF, but who would be the best within the unit was the overriding concern.

Sharon also taught his men insolence. He often lambasted his superiors on the telephone, usually while his men sat gleefully outside his office. He often referred to them as "dumb shits" or "assholes," and in tirades against them on the phone he would season his anger at these bureaucratic imbeciles with vivid descriptions of their sex lives with a whole host of partners and farm creatures![12] Many have argued that Ariel Sharon became Israel's true defense minister in 1953!

Above all, Sharon was a soldier's soldier. Loyalty to one's commander and the leader's commitment to his soldiers were absolute and sacrosanct. He instilled in his men a fanatic sense of duty and loyalty; he brainwashed them into telling the truth following a mission, even if they failed. He respected his men and treated them as equals. They in turn adored Sharon, viewing him as the master of a special family rather than as a commander who led them for the three years they served as conscripts in the IDF. It was an esprit de corps that would come to typify similar IDF elite units in the years to come.

Although Sharon sent urgent cables to Operations HQ in Tel Aviv pleading for work, the IDF brass seemed apprehensive about unleashing this new force. "We're ready," he kept telling them; to reinforce this point, he conducted forced marches inside enemy territory. Finally the "Y'allah" ("Let's get on with it") was received at Camp Sataf. They were operational.

Their first job came on August 30, 1953, when twenty-five Unit 101 fighters crossed the border into Egypt to assassinate Major Mustafa Hafaz, the commander of Egyptian Military Intelligence in Gaza and director of all Palestinian terrorist activity. They were also to terminate a guerrilla squad living in the El-Bourj refugee camp in the Gaza Strip, a sprawling and squalid facility housing over six thousand Palestinians and protected by heavily armed Egyptian troops. Twenty-five Gazans were killed in the attack, many of whom were innocents. Colonel Hafaz's home was destroyed, but the Egyptian spymaster was in the field with agents at the time. When the 101 fighters returned to base, the disillusionment in their eyes was apparent. Even Meir Har-Zion was quoted as saying, "Ha'zehu Ha'oyev?" ("This is the enemy?").[13]

Operations Commander Moshe Dayan, however, was

more practical. At last revenge and fear had been inflicted on the Arabs who for years had killed and mutilated Jews with impunity. In 1952 alone there were over three thousand cross-border fedayeen raids or criminal forays into Israeli territory; hundreds of Israelis were killed in these attacks. For years the paratroopers and the Na'ha'l infantrymen, the elite of the IDF, had attempted cross-border retaliatory strikes, but they usually failed, often in embarrassing fashion. Sharon's force of fearless raiders was a new phenomenon. In Dayan's opinion, the burly major proved his talents as a rising military star, an officer who had displayed brilliant combat skills and courageous traits. Of Har-Zion, Dayan commented, "He is the greatest Jewish fighter since Bar-Kochba fought the Romans."[14]

For the next three months Unit 101 mounted nightly raids against Jordanian, Egyptian, Lebanese, and Syrian positions. The soldiers, usually led by Har-Zion, traveled deep into the heart of enemy territory on reconnaissance forays. When a band of guerrillas was located, or a Jordanian policeman or a group of enemy soldiers was spotted, the results would be quick and bloody. Within a short period of time—and through Unit 101—the Arabs learned to fear the Israeli soldier. Unit 101 developed a Superman image in the Arab mind; nowhere was one safe from its wrath. It could do the impossible.

The impossible, however, became the bloody and unacceptable. On the night of October 13, 1953, Palestinian fedayeen crossed the Jordanian border and reached the town of Yahud. After evading police patrols they located the house of the Kenias family and tossed a grenade through their window. Suzanne Kenias and her two children—Shoshana, three, and Reuven, one and a half—were killed in their sleep. The Israeli public was outraged. Unit 101 was ordered to retaliate.

IDF planners received intelligence that the Arab raiders came from the Jordanian town of Kibya—a town with two thousand residents, defended by a sizable Jordanian military contingent. Operations commander Dayan envisioned a large-scale operation with diversionary action taken against two nearby positions. It would be the largest retaliatory operation against an Arab town since 1948 and would involve conventional elements of the 890th Paratroop Battalion. Hundreds of fighters participated in the raid, and their supplies included nearly a ton of explosives. On the night of October 14, 1953, they struck.

Operation Shoshana, as the Kibya operation became known, ended in absolute disaster. After successfully crossing the frontier, the joint paratroop/Unit 101 task force silenced enemy opposition and then, in a traditional Byzantine response of retribution, planned to demolish the town's homes—mainly those belonging to the rich and influential —as a warning to prevent further support for fedayeen activities. Arik Sharon, looking on at the transpiring events through tattered field glasses, saw a constant stream of civilians fleeing the battle area to take shelter in the olive groves in the overlooking hills. Assuming the town to be empty, Sharon gave the order for the homes to be razed. Thunderous explosions rocked the foundations of the ancient hills as forty-five buildings folded in muffled clouds of smoke and debris. Victorious, the Israeli task force made the two-kilometer trek back to the border in haste. Celebration was in the air.

The next morning the State of Israel awoke to the news that sixty-nine Kibya residents had been killed in Operation Shoshana; horror and outrage were the reactions of the man and woman in the street. The Israeli prime minister, David Ben-Gurion, would attempt to sweep the matter under a political rug by proclaiming to the media that the murders were committed by outraged settlers in response to the fedayeen attack in Yahud. Privately, however, Ben-Gurion feared political repercussions from the tragic incident at home, but on the whole he considered the operation a success. He summoned Sharon and senior Unit 101 officers to his Jerusalem office for a meeting to offer praise for their success at making the Arabs fear a Jewish military response. With the doughty founding father of the Jewish state patting

Sharon gently on the back, the force was now placed above the law.

In the months to follow, Unit 101 participated in dozens of operations against guerrilla bases, as well as, in November 1953, an IDF military police station in Tiberias. The incident—a response to one of their own being maltreated for not carrying the proper documentation—resulted in several military policemen being hospitalized, some in critical condition. The raid, carried out with the precision needed to attack an enemy capital, was executed with the blessing of Moshe Dayan. Oddly enough, as every newly conscripted soldier can attest while listening to stories in the IDF's Conscription and Absorption Base, this story remains a vibrant element of IDF legend, although it is now Sayeret Mat'kal that is impervious to MP inspection.

Other Unit 101 raids in locations as deep into enemy territory as Hebron and Nablus were also common.

In January 1954 the newly appointed chief of staff, Lieutenant General Moshe Dayan, ordered Unit 101 incorporated into the 890th Paratroop Battalion, hoping to expand the scope of Israel's most spectacular unit tenfold. The paratroopers did not want their ranks filled with bloodthirsty killers, while Unit 101 fighters resented the loss of their unique status. Internal differences aside, the move was a necessary one designed to conventionalize spectacular operations to meet conventional enemy targets. War with Egypt seemed imminent.

The 890th Battalion would eventually expand into the 202nd Paratroop Brigade. The retaliatory raids of the unit's newly established reconnaissance force, Sayeret Tzanhanim (Paratroop Recon)—commanded, naturally, by Lieutenant Meir Har-Zion*—dwarfed the exploits of Unit 101. The paratroopers made a name for themselves by parachuting into the Mitla Pass on October 31, 1956, to initiate the 1956 Suez Campaign, and the course of Israeli elite forces was set.

---

*Lieutenant (Res.) Har-Zion is the first and last officer ever to receive a battlefield commission and reach officer's rank without attending the IDF's officer school, Ba'had (Training School) 1.

Nevertheless, the mystique and legend of Sharon's short-lived force remains intact to this day, even though it was a ragtag outfit that wasn't airborne or marine qualified.

Although Sayeret Tzanhanim distinguished itself in the Mitla Pass, it was a conventional force learning to operate on an increasingly complicated battlefield. When truly special operations were required, or missions deep inside enemy territory were needed to support the work of Military Intelligence, no such need-to-know-basis unit existed. Israel's reconnaissance units did not possess a unique intelligence force, and A'man (acronym for Agaf Mode'in, or Intelligence Branch) did not possess its own specially trained force of commandos. Somehow a marriage of both military objectives would have to be consummated.

# NOTES

1. The term "Chief of Staff's Boys" has become a slang catchphrase of sorts to describe the most elite, toughest, and most secretive of all Israeli special forces. While in many published accounts it has become the calling card for Sayeret Mat'kal, it was first known as a reference to Arik Sharon's Unit 101.

2. Yigal Allon, *Shield of David* (London: Weidenfield and Nicolson, 1970), 101.

3. Yosef Finkelshtein, "Kommando Ein Harod," *Ma'ariv Shabbat,* April 20, 1988, 7.

4. Nicholas Bethell, *The Palestine Triangle* (London: Steimatsky Publishing, 1979), 105.

5. Yigal Allon, *The Making of Israel's Army* (New York: Bantam Books, 1970), 18.

6. Ya'akov Markovitzki, *Ha'Yechidot Ha'Yabashtiot Ha'Meyuchadot Shel Ha'Pal'mach* (Tel Aviv: Ministry of Defense Publications, 1989), 58.

7. *Ibid.,* 95.

8. Yoav Glover, *Lama Pirku Ha'Pal'mach* (Tel Aviv: Schocken Publishing House Ltd., 1986).

9. Eilan Kfir, *Tzahal Be'Heilo Entzyklopedia Le'Tzava Ule'Bitachon: Tzanhanim, Heyl Raglim Mutznach* (Tel Aviv: Revivim, 1981), 33.

10. Uri Milshtein, *Ha'Historia Shel Ha'Tzanhanim: Kerech Aleph* (Tel Aviv: Schalgi Ltd. Publishing House, 1985), 210.

11. Ariel Sharon and David Chanoff, *Warrior: The Autobiography of Ariel Sharon* (New York: Simon and Schuster, 1989), 84.

12. Uzi Benziman, *Sharon: An Israeli Caesar,* 47.

13. Hanoch Shinman, "Sharon Zocher," *Bamachane,* November 4, 1987, 20.

14. Ariel Sharon, "Hoo Haya Lochem Amiti," *Yediot Sheva Yamim,* April 29, 1988, 47.

# 2

## The Unit That Never Was, Is Not, and Probably Never Will Be

The effect of Unit 101's short-lived existence and its role in revitalizing Israel's innovative fighting spirit was marked and extensive. Under confident leadership and with the daring exploits of a few select units, such as Unit 101, the IDF managed to transform itself into a modern and mighty fighting force. Following the 1956 War, the Israel Air Force (IAF) proved to be the master of the Middle Eastern skies—the "best of the best pilots," as the IAF flyers were called, were simply unbeatable in their French-built Ouragon and Mystere jets. The IDF's Armored Corps proved its worth as well, slicing through heavily defended territory in rapid outflanking movements with Sherman and AMX-13 main battle tanks, reaching the Suez Canal in record time. The IDF's paratroopers and infantry formations also reaped well-deserved praise and attention: The 1st Golani Brigade successfully seized Rafah, while the paratroopers forever endeared themselves to Israel by parachuting into the Mitla Pass gauntlet.

Militarily, only the IDF/Navy and its intelligence corps were neglected. One incident of neglect precluded hermetic protection of the nation's sea lanes; another case of negligence invited military disaster.

The early 1950s was a dark period for Israeli military intelligence. In 1953 an elaborate Israeli spy ring belonging to A'man's ultrasecretive Unit 131, its special operations force, was captured in both Alexandria and Cairo, Egypt. In the ensuing trial of the Susannah Spies, as they became known, two members were executed and the remainder imprisoned for over ten years. Their capture, clouded by numerous conspiracy and failed-effort theories, signaled the inherent dangers of espionage activities in nations where diplomatic cover was not available. In more conventional terms, Israel's intelligence-gathering methods were haphazard, volatile, and extremely dangerous; with a small fleet of photo-reconnaissance aircraft and limited technical means, its ability to constantly monitor enemy troop movements was limited. One tragic incident in 1954 underscored this urgent shortcoming.

In early 1954 Mod 2 of Israeli military intelligence, entrusted with SIGINT (Signals Intelligence), produced a small eavesdropping device it hoped to plant along Syrian wired-communication lines connecting their Golan Heights fortifications to one another.[1] The device, known in Hebrew as ha'mitkan, had to be connected to Syrian telephone lines manually, meaning a force of soldiers had to cross the heavily fortified frontier, reach the target, maintain the device, and then return back to friendly lines, all without being noticed, apprehended, or killed. Needless to say, it was an aggressive task meant for specially trained Intelligence Corps commandos. Israel had no such force.

As a result, A'man commanders had to seek talent elsewhere. In this case, that meant Lieutenant Meir Har-Zion's Sayeret Tzanhanim. Faithfully, the independent-minded reconnaissance leader offered military intelligence five of his best commandos for the proposed operation. The group was "volunteered" for the mission—when Har-Zion told them that they were about to offer themselves for a most honored task, refusal might have warranted a wicked slap to the head!—and the troops were immediately rushed to

Military Intelligence headquarters in Tel Aviv. Days later the squad crossed the dangerous border into Syria. They crossed the mine fields that followed the heavily fortified border's thick rows of concertina and then proceeded toward the designated telephone pole along the main fortification roadway near the fort of Tel Azzaziat, a position that would witness much bitter fighting in the 1967 War. They planted the eavesdropping device in the ground—it was equipped with a booby-trapped explosive mechanism meant to detonate if discovered—hooked the receiver line to the main telephone pole, and slinked back to the frontier. Mission accomplished. They returned to Israel cocky and cheated—it was not so dangerous after all.

For the next several months the five-man Sayeret Tzanhanim squad returned to the Golan Heights—site of the greatest concentration of Syrian forces anywhere—on a fairly regular basis to maintain the device and change its batteries. The crossings became so routine, in fact, that to prompt the Syrians into turning on their radio sets in order to let the Mod 2 radioman in northern Israel know whether or not the listening device was actually working, the Sayeret Tzanhanim squad would actually wake up Syrian units in the area with grenade attacks, or by firing wild bursts of machine-gun fire into the air. This obnoxious test of good luck earned them the nickname of the Wake-up Squad in A'man circles.[2]

Good luck ran out on December 8, 1954.

The squad, reinforced by two soldiers from the Golani Brigade, once again crossed into the Golan Heights, but this time the Syrians were lying in ambush. As the force continued on its routine path in enemy territory it was set upon by a large formation of Syrian troops. The officer in charge, Golani Lieutenant Meir Moses, thought it suicidal to attempt a firefight when so overwhelmingly outnumbered, so he surrendered. The squad was taken into custody and eventually brought to Damascus. They were brutally tortured and eventually coerced into taking the Syrians to the top-secret device; this occurred only after one member of the squad, Corporal Uri Eilan, committed suicide in his

Damascus prison cell rather than disclose secrets to the enemy. On March 29, 1956, the four survivors were exchanged for forty Syrian prisoners of war seized a few months earlier during a Meir Har-Zion–led Sayeret Tzanhanim operation. The exchange occurred under United Nations supervision at the Bnot Ya'akov Bridge, which separated Israel and Syria at the base of the Golan.[3]

The capture of live Israeli soldiers and the prisoner exchange were embarrassments for the IDF. To save face and in an attempt to guarantee better discipline in the future, Chief of Staff Moshe Dayan even court-martialed the four surviving members of the squad for not dying with honor in battle. For Israel, though, the incident was more than an embarrassment. It was an indication of the IDF's inability to combine combat intelligence and special operations.

In the aftermath of the 1956 Sinai Campaign A'man began to analyze the failure of the Golan Heights eavesdropping mission. Several acute problems and shortcomings needed to be addressed. First and foremost was A'man's inability to monitor enemy frontiers and troop movements, as well as to execute those special operations that helped make Israel's numeric inferiority less of a military liability. The case of the ill-fated eavesdropping device planted on the Golan Heights by the joint reconnaissance paratrooper/Golani task force in 1954, and Operation Yarkon, a deep-penetration intelligence-gathering foray mounted in the Sinai Desert prior to the 1956 War by soldiers from the Giva'ati Infantry Brigade in 1955, showed that conventional military intelligence-gathering operations behind enemy lines had to be executed by non-A'man, non–Intelligence Corps personnel. While these units were certainly combat-ready and highly capable, their training did not facilitate permanent intelligence work, nor did the security-conscious officers in the field security section of IDF Military Intelligence trust the average infantryman, paratrooper, or tank soldier enough to dispatch him on a top-secret operation inside enemy territory. Indeed, the worst-case scenario of the ill-fated squad captured by the Syrians atop the Golan Heights in 1954 proved beyond any doubt that such operations did, in fact, require a special type of fighter capable of special tasks in a most dangerous environment.

At the time the IDF/Navy did possess what it considered to be an elite force in its Ha'Kommando Ha'Yami (Naval Commandos). They specialized in seaborne operations and underwater sabotage but lacked sufficient experience in ground operations to be the sole commando/intelligence element capable of meeting A'man's requirements. There had been, however, serious talk in the IDF/Navy command structure about handing Ha'Kommando Ha'Yami over to the Ministry of Defense as a rogue force of underwater warriors and intelligence agents separate from the IDF command structure and subordinate only to A'man and Mossad operations[4] (Ha'Mossad Le 'Mode' in Ule'Tafkidim Meyuchadim, the Institute of Intelligence and Special Tasks, Israel's foreign espionage service and the equivalent in mandate to the American CIA). These plans were discussed in the general staff and in the hallways of the Kirya in 1954, until captured spies and soldiers in both Egypt and Syria turned the innovative minds of the Israeli defense community into conservative actors in a very volatile theater.

Following the 1956 Sinai Campaign the Israeli defense leadership was knocked out of a false sense of security. Prior to the war, peace with its Arab neighbors seemed at best a possibility. The activities of Unit 101 and Military Intelligence in defeating the *fedayeen* were seen as crucial to the boundaries and the lives of citizens in both Israel and the Arab states. But following the war, hopes turned to bloody anguish. The rebirth of the fedayeen convinced even the most faithful optimists that a period of peace would never follow a conventional conflict; the Israeli government was convinced by Egyptian and Syrian actions that the Arabs would initiate bloody and incessant wars of attrition against the Jewish state. There would be no peace treaties, no cross-border commerce or travel; a status quo of hostilities, casualties, and turmoil would, it appeared, forever haunt the State of Israel. Retaliatory strikes, such as the seemingly weekly attacks against Egypt and Jordan that preceded the 1956 War, were not, however, the solution; the Arabs had learned defensive measures against these rather primitive though courageously mounted operations and paratroop raids, and IDF casualties had gone from costly to unbearable. New tactics had to be formulated, with new weapons and a new intelligence-gathering focus.[5]

Prior to the 1956 War, Chief of Staff Lieutenant General Dayan gave Arik Sharon—commander of the 202nd Paratroop Brigade—and his reconnaissance mastermind, Lieutenant Meir Har-Zion, permission to form a top-secret unit from the brigade's best battalions for special commando and intelligence-gathering tasks inside Israel and at points beyond; it was to take on the most delicate of operations no other IDF unit could be trusted to execute. The prospect of such a force excited many in A'man headquarters who firmly believed that such an elite unit would enhance their day-to-day labors and add a most noteworthy dimension—it was the prospect of "real-time intelligence," reported to HQ in a matter of hours, that seemed so exciting and revolutionary. It also meant a unique unit that would be used for highly specific tasks—specific targets, specific attack force, and specific and successful results.

Dayan's ambitious plans were delayed, however, in September 1956, when Meir Har-Zion was critically wounded while commanding a raid against the Jordanian police fort at A-Rahawa in the south Hebron Hills. The loss of so shining a star as Har-Zion was a major blow to the IDF. In the raid, known in IDF jargon as Operation Jonathan, twenty-nine Jordanian soldiers were killed in fighting that was both close-quarter and brutally savage. Tracers illuminated the pitch-dark sky with brilliant bursts of red and green lines. Bayonets were used in the melee, as were the wooden stocks of Czech Mauser rifles. In typical Israeli fashion, the officer led from the front, and Har-Zion was the lone IDF casualty. He was shot in the neck, his life saved only following miraculous battlefield surgery by a paratrooper medic who had to dodge bullets and mortar fragments while stemming the massive blood loss from Har-Zion's arteries. Upon his return to Israel and following numerous medical procedures and a long period of rehabilitation, this once-unstoppable man's fighting abilities were greatly reduced. With his mighty physical prowess damaged by the shock of a lead projectile ripping through such a sensitive section of his anatomy, he was incapable of remaining in active service and resigned to the monotony of civilian life. The brilliant and epic military career of a man who had rewritten the book penned by men like Sadeh and Wingate had been cut short.

But there were other men in the IDF order of battle who were willing and able to meet the task ahead of them. They'd provide the innovativeness, cunning, and skill. They would become the best.

The loss of Har-Zion temporarily sidelined the formation of the top-secret intelligence-gathering unit Moshe Dayan had gloriously envisioned. It would not be a force like Unit 101, controversial and subordinate to brigade commanders and the Operations Branch (known in the IDF vernacular as Aga'm, the acronym of Agaf Mivtza'im). It would not be a force like Har-Zion's Sayeret Tzanhanim, which was but a cog in the conventional framework of a brigade's order of battle. It would be a special entity available to senior intelligence commanders and, most importantly, the chief of staff, ready at a moment's notice for operations with which no other unit could be entrusted. Dayan, a man whom detractors, as well as loyal admirers, have termed a megalomaniac, viewed this unit of Israel's best and most bombastic as his own creation, his force, his responsibility. Its success would be his glory. Its failure would be deniable and covered by strict military censorship.

In 1957 Dayan's unit would finally be sanctioned. Its combat doctrine would rely on the belief that "it is worthwhile to fight and die for accurate data and intelligence. Forewarned intelligence was not a bonus or a candied dessert, but a dire necessity for Israeli survival that had a dear price!"[6]

The true founding father of this ultrasecretive force, the man who would turn a tactical thought into reality for the chief of staff, was Major Avraham (Harling) Arnan; he was a man who, after his death from a prolonged illness in 1980, was called a "brigadier general and an anonymous force in the security and preservation of the State of Israel." The unit he helped see through was called, according to published reports and simple deduction, Sayeret Mat'kal (General Staff Reconnaissance).*

Avraham Arnan was born in 1931 in Jerusalem—a city that, in the late 1930s, was besieged by the violence and hatred of a nationwide Arab revolt. At the age of seventeen Arnan volunteered for service with the Pal'mach and fought with the elite Harel Brigade in the bitter close-quarter battles for Jerusalem in the 1948 War. A secretive man who kept his thoughts and actions to himself, he was considered a natural for the shadowy world of intelligence work. In 1949 he was recruited by Ma'man (acronym for Machleket Mode'in, or Intelligence Department). Arnan rose through the ranks of A'man's predecessor, the Intelligence Department, a close-knit network of full-time spies and soldiers that grew out of pre-independent Israel's secret warriors. Eventually he served as a commander of a unit that employed *shtinkerim* ("stinkers," the IDF term for informants). Working with informants—mainly Palestinian Arabs and Jordanians who sold state secrets and themselves for a hefty profit—was dirty work. Moving through breaches in the fortification that divided Jerusalem, informants met their handlers in filthy safe houses, conspicuously camouflaged in gritty neighborhoods. Those crossing the border were desperate profiteers who often bargained with the Intelligence Department liaison officers for more money or *tchupars* (a slang Hebrew/IDF term for freebie) of sex from local prostitutes willing to do the patriotic thing.[7] The world of the *shtinkerim* was as far from the glamorous espionage world that is the topic of spy fiction as could be imagined; it was also a slow, incomprehensive, and inaccurate system.

Such means of gathering intelligence convinced Arnan that waiting for intelligence material to arrive and relying on dishonest individuals was not an acceptable way for the State of Israel to formulate its defensive posture. It was in

*Several press accounts and books not required to undergo the scrutiny of the IDF Military Censor's Office have even gone so far as to give Sayeret Mat'kal the designation of Unit 269.

reality the most suspect form of intelligence gathered, as it relied on the word (or difficult-to-authenticate documentation) of unscrupulous people; it was the dirtiest type of intelligence gathered, since it involved, in many instances, blackmail or spiteful treason.

Yet in the mid-1950s the employment of *shtinkerim* was one of the IDF's principal means of keeping tabs on military and political developments in Arab lands. These primitive —though on the whole effective—methods led several innovative A'man officers to conceive new methods of active and aggressive intelligence gathering. Major Avraham Arnan was one such commander, and from his Jerusalem office he developed the means by which the nation's best and most capable soldiers would be dispatched into enemy territory to bring back the desired data under any circumstances, firsthand and reliably. His vision would eventually become a force of on-call spies who relied on speed, firepower, and cold-blooded courage. Like many officers who found revelations through experience and through the obvious—findings the top brass are usually too stubborn to see—Arnan might have had his notions go unnoticed and ignored were it not for the support he found in men of influence like Moshe Dayan.

Initially Avraham Arnan's quest to form his elite unit was seen as a nuisance by the rigid-minded conventional officers in the IDF general staff, who, after serving with the British army in World War II and in more conventional forces in 1948 and 1956, were unimpressed with promises of spectacular feats and decisive operations. Byzantine gestures were often viewed with great skepticism anyway. The IDF general staff\* nevertheless decided to humor the pesky Major Arnan, who made a nuisance of himself until his case was heard, and he was allowed the funding and authorization

---

\*The IDF general staff, known by its Hebrew acronym of Mat'kal, consists of the chief of staff, the commanders of the IAF, the IDF/Navy, the three territorial commands, the Operations Branch chief, the Intelligence Branch director, Manpower Branch director, Ground Forces Command chief, Chief Paratroop and Infantry officer, and several other representatives.

needed to bring about his force of commandos. Although to Arnan this decision appeared to be a victory, the general staff's main objective in acquiescing to his demands was to keep him in the desolate training environs of the Negev Desert and as far away from IDF HQ in Tel Aviv as possible.

To create something unique from the veiled promises of support he had received, Arnan turned to the most capable, insolent, and undisciplined men he knew—veterans of Unit 101. This was not the material with which commanders liked to work as the founding corps for a new unit, but they were the best. Veterans of Major Arik's retaliatory commandos were instrumental in bringing this unit of Arnan's—at the time only an idea and a few select scribbles on top-secret A'man memos—to fruition. They were adventurous souls who, although forced to assimilate back into the real IDF via service with the paratroopers and other chosen units, had never really found their niche in the large and suffocating confines of battalion-and brigade-size formations. They were, indeed, mavericks—men who thrived on being a cut above everyone else, men who performed above and beyond the call of duty as long as the duty was on their terms. Looking through old Unit 101 and Sayeret Tzanhanim files, long since sealed, Arnan sought out the names of those soldiers who had displayed bravery, earned consistent praise from their commanders, and shown decisive acts of individualism. Stints in the stockade were sometimes viewed positively, and escape from a stockade earned a soldier extra notice and a possible spot on the highly esteemed roster.

Slowly Arnan collected a list of the best veterans from Unit 101, as well as conscripts in conventional units who had greater promise. Instead of approaching them and immediately offering them spots in this new and small force, Arnan went to view them from the sidelines, observing these soldiers in combat maneuvers and seeing how they interacted within their units. He gained an insight that surpassed what could be found in any personnel file. The men he found included Menachem Digli, a wily and mischevous soldier (and eventual commander of the unit); Sami Nachmias, a veteran Intelligence Corps officer who became

the unit's *Ka'Man* (intelligence officer); and Dov "Dubik"
Tamari, one of the finest and most respected officers ever to
wear the IDF uniform (he became another commander of
the unit).[8] Other Sayeret Mat'kal founding fathers included
Amos Yaron, an eventual Major General, and Chief Paratroop and Infantry Officer during Israel's 1982 invasion of
Lebanon and, according to Ian Black and Benny Morris in
their book *Israel's Secret Wars,* former Mossad Director
Nachum Admoni. Another recruit, according to published
accounts, was Dani Yatom, an eventual OC Central Command and recipient of the blue ribbon I'tur Ha'Mofet
(Distinguished Service Bravery Medal), the IDF's third-
highest medal for courage in battle.[9]

The Unit 101 fighters proved crucial to this force-building
effort; with proper leadership and coddling these men were
capable of just about everything. The man who initially
brought the best out of them was, of course, Meir Har-Zion.
Recalled from a hospital bed and severe military disability
(he had been recuperating from a series of operations),
Har-Zion joined forces with Arnan to create one of the most
important military entities ever to serve the State of Israel.
Even with his soft speech and subdued physical presence,
Har-Zion was a supreme soldier; he still marched faster and
farther than the most physically fit soldier in the unit could
ever hope to, and he pushed himself far beyond the scope of
human endurance. While a fifty-kilometer forced march in
the desert sun without the luxury of water might be a harsh
training regimen, working one hundred kilometers inside
enemy territory was a realistic expectation to which the
soldier *had* to become accustomed without panic or surrender. The few fighters initially accepted into Arnan's unit
were, in fact, taught to operate within the guidelines of what
had not been done before. They were, after all, an experi-
ment, one that had to work. Arnan saw to it that his fighters
received the most modern—even nonissue—weapons
available on the market, and Har-Zion saw to it that they
knew how to use them with deadly accuracy. It was nevertheless a small unit; so intimate, in fact, that it was said that
the entire force could fit into the cargo area of a Land
Rover.[10]

As a result of the unit's small size and untested boasts of grandeur, there were very few senior officers in the IDF general staff who took it seriously. IDF Chief of Staff Lieutenant General Chaim Laskov, a unique IDF commander who at one time in his career was both an armored officer and former OC/IAF, had to be bullied into giving his final authorization for the unit's creation. In numerous instances Arnan received word that his program and reconnaissance force might be terminated within a matter of days by bureaucratic ruling. Outraged, he called senior officers to plead his case; slowly this visionary leader became a nuisance of great proportions. When he failed to secure even the most basic of guarantees he resorted to an obvious Middle Eastern response to guarantee the survival of his unit: bribery. Arnan sent Laskov a *shabariyah,* a gigantic curved Arabian scimitar emblazoned with gold and jewels, as a gift for Hanukkah, the Jewish Festival of Lights. When this childish gesture failed Arnan tried to convince the chief of staff once and for all that his was indeed a special force.

To achieve this most ambitious objective Arnan conceived a devious and masochistic plan. One of the unit's original soldiers, Eli Gil, who was also known by his nom de guerre of Da'ud* (David in Arabic), was dressed as an Arab by Arnan and dispatched on foot to the northern frontier with a bag full of IDF documents stamped *Sodi Be'yoter* (Top Secret). Only Arnan, Laskov, Da'ud, and the commander of the Israeli National Police knew of the undertaking. For days Da'ud roamed the heavily protected border area with Syria until he was finally arrested by a heavily armed border guard squad gleeful to have captured this "Arab" spy. They subsequently beat him mercilessly in impromptu interrogation sessions. Da'ud's ordeal contin-

---

*Viewing themselves as something of an irregular force, likening their behavior to that of a band of renegade Arab guerrillas rather than serving IDF soldiers, the soldiers all adopted secretive noms de guerre. Arnan, in fact, was known as Don Avraham, a reference to his Mafialike control and the Mafia-inspired loyalty he commanded.

ued for two weeks. He did not break. Arnan received his unit with an obnoxious "I told you so" to the chief of staff.[11] The unit's existence became official.

To expand his small force Arnan sought the best minds and bodies in the IDF. A soldier, however, could not simply fill out a request and volunteer himself into the unit—only a handful of Israelis even knew that the force existed. Arnan picked each potential candidate personally and then volunteered *him* into the force. He went to great lengths to question each one—his interrogation sessions soon became infamous throughout the IDF, even though, according to the official Israeli line, this unit did not really exist. According to published accounts, Arnan would arrange a "meet" between himself and a potential recruit in a true spy-movie setting; usually the recruit was not even told he was being considered for a spot in the unit. He would tell the candidate to wear a specific article of clothing, stand in a public place, and hold a folded newspaper tucked smartly underneath an arm. Any deviation from Arnan's original instructions resulted in a failing score, a terminated meeting, and, in most cases, a candidate standing hopelessly on a street corner for hours wondering what had transpired.

Arnan did not seek robots, nor did he pursue men eager to kill; overtly gung-ho individuals and men who wore their hatred for Arabs on their sleeves were also rejected. His recruitment process resembled that of an espionage service rather than a military unit; his people were to fit nicely into place inside the machinery of a cohesive and balanced unit. He was not looking for the perfect soldier, but for an individualist who was a bit intellect, a bit killer, and a bit bastard. The first soldiers, all Unit 101 veterans, included the advisor Har-Zion, the infamous Micha Kaphusta, and Jibli the Little, and they brought Arnan friends and comrades who were combat veterans and stalwarts seeking adventure and a challenge. The recommendation of a soldier already inside, a person forever considered an honorable individual, was sufficient to guarantee a preliminary interview with Arnan for possible service with the unit.

Arnan was also one of the first senior IDF officers to appreciate the value and integrity of new immigrants from the Arab diaspora. These newcomers to the State of Israel, mainly from Morocco, Yemen, and Iraq, were thrown into ghettos inside Israel by the elitist (European-born) establishment; these young men, upon age of conscription, were thrown into infantry formations, especially the First Golani Infantry Brigade, where they were to fight and learn citizenship in a khaki-colored national melting pot. Often disadvantaged, poor, and bitter, these men would, through design and self-pity, become an underclass. Arnan, however, realized that these Arabic-speaking soldiers were crucial to his unit and to Israel's intelligence needs; he also understood that they were proud and tough, and that when placed in a family environment they would excel beyond all expectation.

Arnan was also persuaded to recruit the "blonds"—a derogatory term for the European Ashkenazi Jews especially used for the elite socialists from the *kibbutzim.* Yet to make them "Arab," in the unit's sense of the word, he would send them to friendly Bedouin tribes in the Negev Desert for intensive and unforgiving Arabic orientation. It was clear to all involved that once Arnan okayed a soldier for service in the reconnaissance formation, that soldier had been released from the IDF proper and had enlisted in a very private army.[12] The soldiers Arnan eventually obtained for the force were taught from the get-go that they were no longer true elements of the IDF; they ceased being average soldiers in an army that preached the egalitarian ideal the moment they survived Arnan's preliminary interview. The unit maintained a series of unique acceptance ceremonies and traditions; its soldiers were taught to do what they wanted to, where they wanted, and how they wanted. Stories of items missing from other IDF bases soon led the authorities to Arnan's unit, and the stories of Arnan's men perfecting their martial arts skills on the noses of military policemen became unwritten history.

Arnan was a true believer in the sacrosanct relationship a nation has with its military and security forces. No sacrifice was to be too great to achieve the upper hand. Arnan's spiritual mentor was the infamous Captain David Sterling, the founder of the British Special Air Service (SAS), and indeed, Arnan's Bible was Sterling's book, *Who Dares Wins*. According to Emanuel Rosen, a respected Israeli military journalist, a "Who Dares Wins" sign decorates the unit's mess to this very day.

Slowly the secretive reconnaissance force achieved some respect and even assistance. Supporters included the director of A'man, Major General Chaim Herzog, OC Central Command Major General Meir Amit (who eventually replaced Herzog as A'man director and would become the director of the Mossad), and Colonel David "Dado" Elazar, the commander of the IDF's Armored Corps. Arnan and Elazar, a future chief of staff, had been comrades and close friends in the Pal'mach; Dado supplied him with covert shipments of petrol, rations, vehicles, and—most important—one Ehud Barak, the unit's most enigmatic and important soldier.

Through an extremely close-knit esprit de corps established around Arnan's personality the unit began to mold itself into a capable fighting formation. They became the Intelligence Corps's technical, operational, and professional branch. Major Arnan became the godfather of the Intelligence Corps, a figure who, like the rulers in the underworld, could be approached to solve a problem that was too delicate for a conventional approach. Like his special-unit predecessor, Arik Sharon, Arnan owned a charismatic charm he used on his men. He instilled in them a sense that they were a special reconnaissance force sanctioned to face death on a daily basis; he wanted them to understand that dire reality and thrive on it. On Fridays, before the traditional Sabbath weekend leave, Arnan was known to gather all of the fighters and read them passages from Meir Har-Zion's memoirs on irregular warfare and scouting techniques.

While training, he wanted them to behave like dastardly bandits; when in the field, to fight liked wounded animals. He honed their skills through a brutal regimen of arms proficiency, pyrotechnics, reconnaissance, and cold-killing.

According to foreign reports, other courses included high-speed evasive driving skills, scuba, and cycling.[15]

To teach them courage, several assignments inside Israel were ordered. These included "liberating" animals, fruits, and supplies from nearby *kibbutzim;* the unit's first memorial was built from cinder blocks liberated from a construction site, and Ehud Barak once stole a jerrican full of fuel from the jeep of the OC Southern Command, Major General Avraham Yoffe. It was an act that became part of IDF folklore, as did Barak's liberation of a billboard at a bustling junction—an act that took the lone commando three days to complete. There were raids against military police stations and wild parties complete with bathtubs full of whiskey. Years before these exploits were copied in many movies about Israeli commandos, the unit had already gone Hollywood.

By 1960, even before Sayeret Mat'kal had performed a mission against an enemy, it was already legendary within the IDF. Through Sayeret Mat'kal's work with Uri Yarom, the commander of the IAF's first helicopter squadron, the force developed its own techniques for infiltrating and extracting forces, gathering intelligence, and executing hard-hitting commando strikes. The unit had IMI (Israel Military Industries) produce special hardware just for its needs: a folding variant of the indigenous 9mm Uzi submachine gun; a nylon watch cover to reduce glare during nighttime operations; and a winter parka hood with earphone slots to fit communications gear. The unit perfected its performance by borrowing extensive debriefing techniques from Arik Sharon's Unit 101. After each assignment all points—both exemplary action and embarrassing mistakes—were discussed over and over again. To this day, according to Emanuel Rosen, such debriefings and the ability to learn from mistakes still separate the elite of the IDF: the elite reconnaissance units, squadrons, and tank formations.[16]

By 1960 Sayeret Mat'kal was ready for its first assignment. Not surprisingly, it was the close ties to the helicopter squadron and its proactive intelligence-gathering techniques that initiated the unit's being brought into the IDF's operational order. The induction came after a severe breakdown in A'man's ability to recognize or even locate the enemy's preparation for a surprise attack.[17]

On the night of January 31, 1960, the IDF conducted its first large-scale retaliatory raid following the 1956 War. This time, however, the target was not the Gaza Strip or the Hebron Hills, but the Golan Heights and the Syrian position at Tewfiq; the target was a deserted town towering above the Sea of Galilee and Kibbutz Tel Katzir. In January Syrian soldiers and artillerymen disguised as peasants infiltrated the demilitarized zone and initiated a day-long bombardment of the surrounding Israeli agricultural settlements. An Israeli military response was expected, and the raid, codenamed Operation Locust, was carried out by a Golani Brigade task force. Dozens of Syrians were killed, and tension in the area was elevated to a war frenzy. It appeared that full-scale war would once again grip the Middle East.

In a show of Arab solidarity meant to prevent Israel from preemptively attacking Syria and possibly diverting the Jordan River's waters, the Egyptians secretly sent a huge military force into the demilitarized Sinai Desert; the moves began on February 18, 1960. Under cover of darkness and in total radio silence the Egyptians moved their Second, Fifth, and Seventh Infantry brigades and elements of the elite Fourth Armored Division toward the Israeli frontier. Nasser's gambit was a complete success. Not only had the UNEF (United Nations Emergency Force) observers not been aware of the Egyptian moves, but neither had the Israelis. Only on February 23, after a series of intelligence reports reached A'man HQ, did Major General Chaim Herzog order a newly acquired Sud.Aviasion SO.4050 Vatour IIB aircraft to conduct a photo-reconnaissance sortie over the desert peninsula. It was almost too late.

The findings, meant to alleviate concerns about war, shocked and outraged the Israeli defense community. Not only had the IDF lost track of the Fourth Armored Division for several days, but in the end over five hundred Egyptian T-54/55 MBTs were counted spread out along the Israeli frontier; two additional infantry divisions were discovered spread out along the Um Katef–El Arish–Rafiah line. IDF

Southern Command had only twenty frontline tanks in position to meet an Egyptian attack.

Immediately the general staff ordered the IAF placed on full alert. Combat units, including the Golani Infantry Brigade and the elite Seventh Armored Brigade, were rushed from the north to assume defensive positions; a partial mobilization of the reserves was also ordered. A wider conflagration seemed imminent. Two huge armies had gathered in the desert sands to do battle, but common sense prevailed, and war was averted. President Nasser once again reaffirmed his position as leader of the Arab world, while a deafening sigh of relief was sounded in IDF HQ in Tel Aviv.

For A'man, Operation Broom, the code name of the mobilization, was a traumatic experience. Intelligence material gathered on Egypt from various reliable sources was ignored; expensive intelligence-gathering activities such as photo-reconnaissance flights were compromised for budgetary reasons; bureaucratic differences between the Intelligence and Operations branches complicated a coordinated effort; and, it has been argued, a lack of A'man experience in dealing with a surprise attack bred overconfidence.[18] A'man's inability to deal with the threat of surprise attack would eventually haunt IDF Military Intelligence in a manner that would make Operation Broom seem inconsequential.

To insure that enemy movements were never concealed for long from A'man eyes, Sayeret Mat'kal was finally brought into the IDF's operational order of battle. Such close calls with intelligence-failure-inspired disasters justified the existence of the unit, and Arnan was quoted as proclaiming, "There will be no more Operation Brooms."[19] On August 1, 1963 the unit was dispatched on its first operational assignment deep in Syrian territory. The mission, commanded by Second Lieutenant Ehud Barak—who was fresh out of the officer's course—was assisted by Uri Yarom's helicopter fleet; it was the first time an IAF whirlybird was used in an intelligence operation. The mission was a complete success, using Major Arnan's unit as

A'man's cutting edge. For his courage and command Second Lieutenant Barak received the first of his four Tza'la'shim Shel Ha'Ra'mat'kal (Chief of Staff Citations), medals issued for unique acts of courage.[20]

Although the full details of the heliborne foray into Syria remain state secrets to this day, it has been revealed that the operation was carried out in the unit's typically independent manner. According to the reports, the raid into Syria was of the most sensitive nature. Success insured Arnan's force would flourish; failure would insure its sudden chief-of-staff-ordered demise. The operation, however, met with several difficulties and hitches, problems that prompted the nervous generals in Tel Aviv to order the mission aborted. Undaunted, Lieutenant Barak simply shut off his radio and continued with the operation without the top brass "busting his balls."[21]

A'man-sanctioned intelligence operations against Syria, Egypt, Jordan, and points beyond intensified in dramatic fashion. The unit, however, returned to its veil of absolute secrecy with few of its activities between 1963 and 1968 ever being mentioned in either the foreign or the Israeli press. Accordingly, the unit continued its ways, from conducting intelligence-gathering forays into the enemy heartland to mounting wild raids against Women's Corps installations.[22] It is known that Dov Tamari replaced Arnan as unit commander in 1963; that Ehud Barak underwent a commando's training course in France; during the 1967 Six-Day War he participated in a top-secret reconnaissance formation that raced through the Sinai and, it is believed, to points beyond in the southern theater of operations.

Sayeret Mat'kal's role in the 1967 War remains an enigmatic point of speculation and rumor to this day.

In the years prior to and after 1967 War several IDF reconnaissance units, or *sayerot,* flourished. These included the three territorial command reconnaissance forces, Southern Command's Sayeret Shaked (Almond Recon), Central Command's Sayeret Haruv (Carob Recon), and Northern Command's Sayeret Egoz (Walnut Recon); the conventional paratroop and Golani Brigade reconnaissance formations;

and, in 1968, a Druze Muslim reconnaissance force known as Sayeret Ha'Druzim (Druze Recon), which was established to pave the way for an Israeli assault on Damascus.[23]

The postwar realities would force Sayeret Mat'kal out of its much-coveted prewar veil of absolute secrecy. Intelligence warfare talents would soon be overshadowed by spectacular actions throughout the Middle East in an undeclared war against a most cunning, elusive, and deadly enemy.

# NOTES

1. Oded Granot, *Heyl Ha'Mode'in: Tzahal Be'Heilo Entzyklopedia Le'Tzava Ule'Bitachon* (Tel Aviv: Revivim Publishers, 1981), 54.

2. *Ibid.*, p. 55.

3. *Ibid.*, p. 56.

4. Uri Milshtein, *Ha'Historia Shel Ha'Tzanhanim: Kerech Daled* (Tel Aviv: Schalgi Ltd. Publishing House, 1987), 1426.

5. Eilan Kfir, *Tzanhanim-Ch'ir Mutznach: Tzahal Be'heilo Entzyklopedia Le'Tzava Ule'Bitachon* (Tel Aviv: Revivim Publishers, 1981), 31.

6. Emanuel Rosen, "Ha'Ish She'Himtzi Et Ha'Yechida Ha'Muvcheret," *Ma'ariv Sof Shavu'a,* September 19, 1990, 42.

7. Rafi Sutton and Yitzhak Shoshan, *Anshei Ha'Sod Ve'Ha'star* (Tel Aviv: Edanim Publishers Ltd., 1990), 111; Yossi Melman and Dan Raviv, *The Imperfect Spies* (London: Sidgwick and Jackson, 1989), 155.

8. Emanuel Rosen, "Ha'Ish She'Himtzi," 44.

9. Michal Kedem, "Profil: Aluf Dani Yatom," *Hadashot,* December 12, 1990, 3.

10. Emanuel Rosen, "Ha'Ish She'Himtzi," 44.

11. *Ibid.*

12. *Ibid.*

13. There have been differences in several accounts as to whether or not Ehud Barak was a veteran of the 82nd Battalion or the 52nd Battalion. The IDF is traditionally close-mouthed concerning its force's numeric designations.

14. Yosef Walter, "Mu'amad Le'Ra'mat'kal: Yesh Barak," *Ma'ariv Sof Shavu'a,* January 24, 1986, 6.

15. Christopher Dobson and Ronald Payne, *Counterattack* (New York: Facts On File, Inc., 1982), 82.

16. Emanuel Rosen, "Ha'Ish She'Himtzi," 44.

17. See Oded Granot, *Heyl Ha'Mode'in,* 65.

18. *Ibid.*

19. Emanuel Rosen, "Ha'Ish She'Himtzi," 44.

20. Uri Milshtein, *Ha'Historia Shel Ha'Tzanhanim,* 1550.

21. *Ibid.*

22. Naomi Levitski, "Aluf Teflon," *Mosaf Hadashot,* July 21, 1987, 6.

23. Salim Kadur, "Sayeret Ha'Druzim: Ha'Yachsanim Shel Ha'Yach'Sar," *Bamachane H'ul,* July 1987, 42.

# 3

## Operation Gift

*Beirut International Airport*
*December 27, 1968*

There was a time when international air travel was exciting principally for the adventure of crossing boundaries, continents, and oceans in a matter of hours. The only fear involved was that of a crash or collision, but the odds for such tragedies were generally one in ten million, and most passengers remembered hearing statistics that one was more likely to slip in the shower than crash into the side of a mountain. Air travel was an escape, a peaceful and time-saving luxury that was only beginning to be enjoyed on a massive scale. That would all change on July 22, 1968.

The hustle and bustle at Rome's Fiumicino Airport was particularly chaotic that July night. The hot Mediterranean sun had taxed the airport's air-conditioning system beyond all reasonable limits, and it had yet to recover in order to handle the evening's crowds, passengers laden down with luggage and souvenirs. In the departure terminal passengers heading for Tel Aviv sought out the blue and white sign of Israel's national airline, El Al, and stood on the short line to present their passports and tickets to the young service agents manning the counter.

After obtaining a seat each passenger was directed to a

gate; but most, especially the Israelis, raced to the duty-free shops for a last-minute binge of cigarette and liquor purchases. The call for Flight 426 to Tel Aviv was made in Italian and English, followed by a brusque mention of the gate in Hebrew for Israeli passengers. Through the passageways encased by thick, soundproof glass the eager travelers proudly glanced at the illuminated El Al Israel Airlines blue and white Boeing 707 that was to ferry them home. "In a few hours we'll be back in Tel Aviv" was the prevalent phrase spoken in the crowd. Little could anyone realize how wrong that was.

El Al (the Hebrew term for "to the skies") in 1968 was in the throes of a lucrative and uniquely proud rebirth. Formed on November 11, 1948, El Al, like the entire nation, was rejoicing in the glory of Israel's sweeping military victory over Egypt, Jordan, and Syria in the June 1967 Six-Day War. David had once again felled Goliath—only this time the Mach 2 Mirage fighter had replaced the slingshot. In six days of blood and fire the State of Israel had been transformed from a beleaguered nation important only to world Jewry into a regional superpower whose tenacious and courageous people had earned the world's respect. Jews the world over who remembered Israel only during after-meal prayers at Passover or through pushing coins into *pushke* charity coin boxes now felt militant, resolute, and powerful. Gentiles, too, identified with the Israeli victory, and they flocked to see the land where Joshua had made the walls come tumbling down, where Christ had taught, and where the desert had been made to bloom. Travel to the Jewish state reached record levels, and El Al was the airline to get them to Israel from locations as diverse as New York and Nairobi.

One group, however, was not enamored of Israel's victory in the 1967 War: the Arab world. President Nasser's Egypt was humiliated in battle, losing the Sinai in record time to a numerically inferior army. King Hussein's Jordan lost the prize of the Middle East, the Old City of Jerusalem and the West Bank, as well as his entire air force and much of his army. Ba'athist Syria lost its ultrastrategic perch over northern Israel, the volcanic plateau known as the Golan Heights, and with it the ability to shell the agricultural settlements surrounding the Sea of Galilee at will.

The big losers were, of course, the Palestinians. Since 1948, when the State of Israel achieved its born-in-battle independence, the Palestinians had lived in squalor, misery, and anger. They suffered a humiliating military defeat at the hands of the Israel Defense Forces—a setback the Palestinians have yet to recover from. Through their pain and anger the one unifying hope to which they clung in diaspora and in desperation was the creation of their own state. The formerly Palestinian territory Egypt occupied following the 1948 war—the Gaza Strip—and the large chunk Jordan assumed for her own—what is now known as the West Bank—were not turned over to the Palestinians. Instead, in Arab propaganda broadcasts transmitted from Beirut to Baghdad, the Palestinians were urged to accept their status as refugees until the "glory of the Arabs will recover Palestine and push the Jews into the sea."[1] And so they waited, but liberation never came. In June 1967 they lost the opportunity to watch the Arab armies push the Jewish state into the Mediterranean when Israel turned the tables and struck first and hard. Bitter and nurtured by their state sponsors, many in the Palestinian ranks opted to declare war against the country that had placed them in this predicament—Israel—and against the nations of the West, the former colonial powers, bourgeois antirevolutionaries, and states whose trade and contacts legitimized the Jews' ownership of their Falastin. The terrorist war had begun.

The Palestinian terrorist option wasn't born as a result of the 1967 Arab defeat; the war's outcome simply served as its rite of passage from the regional arena to the international stage. In the tumultuous days that preceded the 1956 Sinai Campaign the Palestinians had been armed, trained, and guided by the Jordanian and Egyptian military intelligence services to perpetrate acts of violence against Israel. These guerrilla warriors became known as the *fedayeen* (men of sacrifice), and they proved an evasive and deadly foe. Their hatred for the Jewish state, cultured in the refugee camps, was expressed in their terrorist attacks against civilian targets, mainly in southern Israel. Israel tried through retaliatory strikes performed by Arik Sharon's Unit 101 and, later, his 202nd Paratroop Brigade to crush the *fedayeen* and their host-nation sponsors once and for all. It couldn't. Terrorism and guerrilla warfare could not be destroyed through conventional means or solely by conventional military might.

The Israelis responded with a logical and terminating strategy: to cut off the head of the beast and therefore make its claws harmless. On July 11, 1956, A'man assassinated the two Egyptian intelligence officers who were responsible for running the *fedayeen:* Lieutenant Colonel Mustafa Hafaz, the commander of the Palestine desk, who was killed at his headquarters in Gaza, and Colonel Salah a-Din Mustafa, the Egyptian military attaché to Jordan, killed in his Amman office.[2] Following the coordinated and brilliantly executed killings, *fedayeen* operations against Israel ceased for ten years.

On January 1, 1965* a lone Palestinian guerrilla carried out a minor and failed bombing mission against the Israeli National Water Carrier. The raid marked the emergence of a new military group in the Arab-Israeli conflict: Yasir Arafat's el-Fatah. Arafat, an ex-engineer who had become embroiled in militant Palestinian politics at Cairo University and, later, in Kuwait, formed the Palestine National Liberation Movement in the summer of 1957, along with several colleagues. These included Saleh Khalaf, known also by his nom de guerre of Abu I'yad,** and a man who would figure quite prominently in the history of the Chief of Staff's Boys, Khalil al-Wazir, better known by the nom de guerre of Abu Jihad.

The name Fatah was based on a loose acronym of Harakat Tahrir Falastin (The Struggle for the Liberation of Palestine) and was modeled after the Algerian

---

*It is considered the birth date of the Palestinian revolution; it is known as Fatah Day. Celebrations usually include a terrorist attack along Israel's frontier with Lebanon, on the West Bank, or even inside Israel proper.

**Abu I'yad was assassinated in Tunis on January 15, 1991, by a bodyguard apparently loyal to renegade terrorist leader Abu Nidal.

Front de Libération Nationale (FLN); it quickly established secretive cells throughout the Middle East and in much of Western Europe.[3] It would not rely on the political propaganda of the Arab leadership and would trust nobody but the men of the camps, the men tasked with liberating the homeland through indiscriminate terror. Their military strategy was based on poor man's logic: Since the Palestinians were too weak to defeat Israel conventionally on the battlefield, they would provoke harsh Israeli retaliation through acts of terrorism and sabotage. This, of course, would lead to a full-scale war between the Jewish state and the Arab world—one the Arab would clearly win.[4]

On September 17, 1967, Fatah carried out its first post–1967 War operation with the bombing of an irrigation pipe at Kibbutz Yad Hannah.[5] Through various acts of sabotage and intensive clandestine operations in the West Bank and Gaza Strip, Yasir Arafat's Fatah was making a name for itself as the most prominent military arm of the Palestine Liberation Organization, a blanket group that represented and attempted to unite all the Palestinian guerrilla forces that had developed over the years. Fatah was the most conventional of these groups, attempting to imitate the guerrilla successes of the postwar era seen in China and Vietnam. Yasir Arafat embraced the operational tactics of Mao and Vietnamese General Vo Nguyen Giap. He was a firm believer in Mao's strategies of popular support and sporadic, constant military attacks. Yet the geography of the Middle East did not facilitate a Southeast Asian–style war of liberation, and Fatah's initial campaign met with failure in the harsh and unforgiving desert wilderness of the Jordan Valley. The IDF was able, through elite-unit reconnaissance squads and excellent intelligence work, to keep Fatah out of the cities and vulnerable in the fields—the desolate hills and deserts of the West Bank—where they were easy prey for highly mobile IDF units, which terminated these squads with brutal firepower. Other methods for a war against Israel had to be found—other groups were waiting in the wings for their opportunity to strike and strike hard.

While Yasir Arafat's Fatah preached the liberation of

Palestine, several other PLO groups used the destruction of the Jewish state as a battle cry for a much larger goal—a worldwide socialist revolution that would begin in the Middle East. The most prominent of these groups was the PFLP (Popular Front for the Liberation of Palestine), led spiritually and militarily by Dr. George Habash, and commanded operationally by a terrorist genius, Dr. Wadi Haddad. Habash, a Christian from the town of Lydda (or Lod), joined forces with Haddad in their Amman, Jordan, practice where, legend has it, they wrote prescriptions on the backs of propaganda leaflets.

In the mid-1960s the two moved to Lebanon, formed the Arab Nationalist Movement, and, following the humiliation of the 1967 War, created the PFLP as the military arm of their radical political organization. Although Arab governments such as Syria and Iraq were wary of the PFLP— especially their pan-Arabism preaching—they were allowed to take up positions in Jordanian refugee camps where they sought out only the most politically sound individuals who presented certain signs of intellect and abstract thought. Agents recruited from Western Europe's blossoming community of revolutionaries also had educated backgrounds and intellectual attributes. Arafat's Fatah, on the other hand, sought out the illiterate and unintelligent —men who blindly followed orders and who were willing to pull a trigger and kill without contemplating the risk.

Following the battle of Karameh on March 21, 1968 (known in the IDF vernacular as Operation Hell), in which the Palestinians, along with Jordanian armor support, gave as good as they got to the attacking IDF forces, the Soviet Union began to display active interest in the movement. The Marxist PFLP, its views amenable to Moscow's (and the KGB's line), got most of the military aid. The fire for immense bloodshed was being fueled.

In the summer of 1968, as Arafat's Fatah was battling IDF units in the mountainous hell of Fatahland in the Lebanese-Syrian hills and the desert wasteland of the Jordan Valley— and losing—Dr. Habash was preparing to place the Palestinian war on a world stage. Rome would be the site of his opening salvo.

Among the thirty-five passengers preparing to board El Al Flight 426 were three men with definitive Byzantine features who clutched duty-free shopping bags and had smoldering Marlboro cigarettes fastened to their drying lips. The men were clearly Arabs, but they aroused little suspicion. There were, after all, Arab citizens living in Israel, as well as nearly a million new refugees following 1967. Hijacking was as yet virtually unheard of. There was no need to feel frightened, especially in an Italian airport.

The three were, in fact, members of Dr. Habash's PFLP, and their leader, Captain Rifat (the nom de guerre of Ali Shafik Ahmed), was, according to published accounts, a well-trained pilot. According to other accounts, one member of the terrorist group using the nom de guerre of Abu Nidal (not to be confused with the later terrorist genius, Sabri Khalil al-Banna) navigated the flight and said he was a former pilot with Gulf Air.[6] In any event, it was clear that Dr. Habash and his operations chief, Dr. Haddad, had chosen their soldiers well for this ground-breaking mission.

As the midnight flight taxied on the dark tarmac and lifted off for the three-hour flight to Israel the passengers withdrew to their comfortable reclining seats and lowered their trays, expecting a quick hot snack. The chief steward, Jacques Merav, opted to get the obligatory dinner out of the way as soon as possible, so that both the tired passengers and the crew could relax during the short flight. As the trays of kosher food were prepared a stewardess—a pretty young sabra with golden locks—ran toward him, screaming in hysterics. "They've hijacked the aircraft," she stuttered, "they've hijacked the flight." As Jacques Merav anxiously raced toward the front cabin of the 707 he saw the flight's first officer, Maoz Poraz, bleeding and staggering; he mumbled, "I've been shot!" El Al Flight 426 was no more. Its new name was the Liberation of Palestine, and its course was southwest—toward Dar el-Beida Airport near Algiers, Algeria.[7]

Over the course of the next three weeks the hijacked El Al flight remained a painful reminder to the Israeli leadership of how vulnerable its citizens were to acts of Palestinian terrorism. At first the twenty-three non-Israeli passengers were released, followed by free passage for Israeli women and children. The remaining Israeli males, however, were detained in an Algerian Muchabarat (Intelligence Service) barracks until Israel agreed to release sixteen Palestinian prisoners from its jails. The Palestinian "air war" against the State of Israel had begun.

The hijacking of Flight 426 was a watershed in the military history of the Middle East; the situation's unfolding events were full of precedents and never-to-be-repeated scenarios that have come to typify Israel's international campaign against terrorism. Israel's acquiescence to the terrorist demands and prolonged negotiations to secure the release of the remaining hostages and of the aircraft were a national humiliation. Yet almost immediately following the hijacking of Flight 426 the Israeli government prepared the groundwork to protect its aircraft against terrorist skyjackings. This primarily came in the form of active input from Israel's counterintelligence and internal security entity, the Sherut Ha'Bitachon Ha'Klali, better known by its initials as simply the Shin Bet. Shin Bet skymarshals armed with Uzi 9mm submachine guns and Beretta .22 low-velocity automatics were placed aboard each and every El Al flight; it was an ominous statement that the Israelis would fight it out in the skies rather than acquiesce to terror. Complementing this effort were El Al security officials who interrogated passengers, searched each bit of carry-on and hand luggage, and made El Al infamous for stringent and near-hermetic security. This distinction also brought on a negative reputation for delays, best illustrated by the fact that many used to say that El Al stood for "every landing always late."

The PFLP was not through with its attacks on El Al.

Next time, however, the El Al passengers were called to their gate in Greek, not Italian—the target was chaotic

Athens International Airport. On October 26, 1968 the Athens terminal had yet to install the beefed-up security that the new wave of aerial assault demanded; some would say, with justification, that Athens would never make its airport safe. An El Al Boeing 707, fully loaded and awaiting permission to taxi toward takeoff position, suddenly found itself the target of wild bursts of automatic fire and incendiary grenade blasts. Two young Palestinians armed with submachine guns and grenades tucked neatly in their bags had reached the Greek capital via an Air France flight from Beirut. Although acting nervous, chain-smoking, and constantly picking at their unkempt Afros, the two sparked little scrutiny or suspicion from the Greek authorities. They were, of course, untouched in Beirut, the new mecca for Palestinian terrorism. Their uninterrupted barrage crippled and ignited the airliner; one Israeli engineer was killed, and a stewardess was critically wounded. Dozens of other passengers received lesser wounds. The terrorists, valiant in Greek custody, would soon be released following a PFLP hijacking of an Olympic Airways flight and Greek submission to Palestinian threats of additional acts of terrorism.

As the body of the victim was returned to Israel, Prime Minister Levi Eshkol convened an urgent cabinet meeting to deal with this latest act of terror. A response would come thirty-six hours later. This time retribution would be swift and potent. It would come from a very special force.[8]

From the moment that El Al Flight 426 was hijacked in July 1968, the "minds of the IDF," secretive men in the Kirya (the Tel Aviv district that houses IDF, the Defense Ministry, and, it is believed, Mossad HQ) began contemplating contingency plans that would free the Israeli captives from their Algerian detention; it was known as Mivtza Tshura (Operation Gift). Eight years before the name Entebbe became public knowledge, there was thought that Israel could pull off a remarkable and, some have said, suicidal rescue, bringing her captives out of Algeria. Although the details of the operational planning remain classified to this day, the scheme is believed to have addressed Arab aviation as the means of securing the release of the El Al passengers. This meant either an IDF hijacking of an Arab—Air Algerie—aircraft, or perhaps the destruction of several Arab aircraft as retribution and deterrent. The Palestinian terrorists who had attacked the two El Al craft had, after all, originated in a sovereign Arab state, one with its own national airline and civilian transportation interests. Although an attack against Algeria, over three thousand kilometers from Israel, would be a most difficult undertaking, the controllers of Israel's special forces were cocky and confident. The plan, however, never came to fruition. The first Operation Gift was shelved on behalf of diplomatic and bloodless efforts to obtain the release of the hostages.[9]

Yet the most talked-about plan for Operation Gift was an IDF raid against Beirut International Airport—the Arab aviation target closest to Israel and the safest militarily to assault. The plan called for an IDF elite unit to land in Beirut and steal several airliners, which would be flown to Israel. The million-dollar jetliners would be released in a prisoner exchange for the hostages of the El Al hijacking.[10]

Attacking Beirut, only ninety kilometers from the Israeli frontier, was much easier and safer than exposing the IDF's small air and naval elements to risk, detection, and possible attack during the long trek to the Algerian coast. Lebanon circa 1968 was a peaceful nation trying to ignore its immediate neighborhood and continue to serve as the Middle East's sin and financial center—a city where sex and smuggling overshadowed the plight of the Palestinians (who populated dozens of teeming refugee camps). Beirut International Airport was the Byzantine hub of Arab air traffic, a cog that allowed the illicit Lebanese machine to maintain its commerce and neutrality intact. From European airliners bringing in investors' fortunes to the private Learjets ferrying in sheikhs and their appetites for fun and excitement, Beirut International Airport was one of Lebanon's most important resources. If the damage of any entity could influence the Lebanese to cease and desist the PFLP from using its territory as a base of operation, this would be the target.

The revised thought behind the Israeli action was simple, and its message unavoidable: Airliners would not be seized and bartered in acquiescence but destroyed in fiery retribution. The destruction of an Arab airliner would be an explosive message to Arab governments that embraced Palestinian terrorism with their national resources. The political message would be unavoidable. Israeli commandos could make Arab air travel as precarious as Palestinian terrorists had attempted to accomplish with El Al. It was an eye for an eye, or an airliner for another.

The prevailing factor behind Israel's response to the PFLP attacks in Rome and Athens was the nation's unwillingness to accept terrorism on her frontiers. In the north, Palestinian guerrillas operating in Lebanon and Syria shelled the Galilee settlements with mortar and rocket fire and also conducted armed incursions. The aftermaths were often bloody massacres; the Jordan Valley desert had become known as the Land of the Pursuit, a desolate land where the IDF mounted ruthless search-and-destroy operations against heavily armed Palestinian terrorists infiltrating from Jordan. And in the Gaza Strip the chaotic and blood-chilling seeds for a full-scale guerrilla campaign against Israel were being sown. Jerusalem, the Israeli capital, was ravaged by bombings of university lunchrooms, supermarkets, and department stores. Israelis were not safe in their own country, let alone when traveling abroad. Enough was enough.

While the blueprints for Operation Gift were neatly filed under the Contingencies section at IDF HQ, the debate among Israel's leaders as to how to react to the attack in Athens varied. In a meeting that included Prime Minister Eshkol, Defense Minister Moshe Dayan, Transportation Minister Moshe Carmel, IDF Chief of Staff Haim Bar-Lev, Mossad Director Major General (Res.) Tzvi Zamir, Shin Bet Director Yosef Harmelin, and several other foreign ministry, El Al, and military representatives, the matter was discussed in an open forum. The debate among those gathered was not over whether or not to strike out, but where to do so. Options discussed included the destruction of Palestinian training facilities in southern Lebanon; a mini-invasion of southern Lebanon with a prolonged Israeli presence until Lebanon put its house in order; the aerial bombing of PLO training facilities and staging points in Syria; and finally, a combined paratroop-armor assault into Fatahland, near Mt. Hermon in Syria and Lebanon. In the end, according to Prime Minister Eshkol's military secretary, Brigadier General Yisrael Lior, the decision was decisive and unanimous. In the smoke-filled room embroiled in colorful discussion, Eshkol, a dowdy Eastern European who was dwarfed by the proud sabras in IDF uniforms, stood up and said, "They came from Lebanon, they trained in Lebanon, their bosses are in Lebanon. We will attack Beirut."[11]

From the onset it was clear which unit would be tasked with the raid: Sayeret Mat'kal.[12] The unit had participated in countless special intelligence-gathering forays in the years between 1963 and 1968. They were considered the most professional of the Sayeret or commando forces in the IDF's order of battle and were well-suited for the lone-wolf combat a raid into Beirut entailed. These fighters were most comfortable when operating alone in a truly unconventional role; their intelligence background would also come in handy should they be forced to infiltrate the Lebanese labyrinth due to opposition at the airport overwhelming their small numbers and forcing them to scurry. While both Chief of Staff Bar-Lev and Operations Chief Weizman reveled in the capabilities of the Chief of Staff's Boys, there was genuine concern that such a high-profile mission would attract unwanted publicity to the activities and identities of the troops. The fact that other units would be required to help bring the force to Beirut turned out to be a convenient veil for security considerations.

Initially Colonel (Res.) Haim Nadel, the head of the operations department in Aga'm, volunteered to command the operation, but Chief of Staff Bar-Lev refused his plea, arguing that it was foolhardy to send a man who knew all of the IDF's secrets into Beirut.* Although Nadel would eventually bully his way into the mission, the overall commander would be the OC Paratroopers and Infantry Forces Brigadier General Rafael "Raful" Eitan, one of the most charismatic and courageous officers ever to wear the uniform of the Israel Defense Forces.

Born in 1929 in the Jezreel Valley Moshav Tel Adashim, Rafael Eitan, it was rumored, knew how to clean and fire a pistol by the age of seven. At seventeen Eitan volunteered into the Pal'mach; he served in Harel Brigade, a formation known as a breeding ground for several future IDF Chiefs of Staff and for its epic and bloody close-quarter battles for Jerusalem against the heavily armed Transjordan Arab Legion. Raful, as he became known, was critically wounded in the battle for control of the city's Katamon section; it would be the first of his many war wounds. Awarded the command of the elite 890th Paratroop Battalion in 1955, Captain Raful first distinguished himself in Operation Olive Branch, a 1955 retaliatory strike against Syrian positions around the Sea of Galilee, and in Operation Bundle, October 27, 1955, after which he was awarded the red-ribboned Distinguished Service Medal for leading a charge against determined Jordanian machine-gun fire. On October 31, 1956 it was Raful's 890th Battalion that parachuted into the ultrastrategic gauntlet of the Mitla Pass in Israel's airborne opening salvo of the 1956 Sinai Campaign. In 1967 Raful was the commander of the conscript paratroop brigade that

---

*Security considerations, always an IDF obsession, would keep several officers with extremely intimate knowledge of IDF secrets out of Operation Gift. According to Yosef Argaman, in his book *It Was Once Secret,* one such officer was an intelligence warfare genius, Colonel (Res.) Zalman "J'imka" Gendler. Although instrumental in the planning of the raid, he knew too much, and it required a chief of staff directive to keep him from boarding one of the helicopters to Beirut. Undaunted, he agreed to the order on the condition that another officer bring him back a bottle of arac (a Levantine anise liquor) and a branch from a willow tree—foliage that grew near the airport, and which he planned to plant in his garden!

led the IDF's assault into the Gaza Strip and Sinai. During his push toward the Suez Canal Raful was struck in the head by an Egyptian bullet. A quick heliborne flight to the hospital and a resilient nature propped Raful not only back into IDF service, but into a job as head of the Paratroop and Infantry Command, a task that would place him in charge of most elite-unit operations during the war of attrition.

In retrospect, Raful was the perfect choice to lead Operation Gift.* Proven to be coolheaded under fire, and a commander not likely to let adversity and changing military situations alter his common sense. Raful's task force would include:

• Force Yairi—the vanguard element of the raiding party that according to published reports was commanded by the Sayeret Mat'kal commander, Lieutenant Colonel Uzi Yairi. It consisted of twenty-two commandos who would be ferried to Beirut International Airport via a Sud.Aviasion Super Frelon SA-341K heavy transport chopper and land at the airport's northern end. They were to sabotage (destroy) the Arab aircraft in the immediate area; other airliners were not to be touched. After successfully completing this part of the assignment Yairi's force of fighters would proceed to the London rendezvous position (a point where the airport's two runways merged) for the helicopter ride back home.

• Force Digli—the secondary element, also consisting of twenty-two commandos. Force Digli was commanded by Sayeret Mat'kal Deputy Commander Major Menachem Digli. It, too, would land via Super Frelon helicopter, and its fighters would roam through the southern tier of the airport, an area bordering one of the poor and militant Muslim slums near the El-Ouzai section and the teeming Palestinian refugee camps. After sabotaging all the Arab aircraft located in their section, Force Digli would proceed toward London and coordinate the evacuation with Force Yairi. Should

---

*According to Brigadier General Yisrael Lior, when Chief of Staff Bar-Lev informed the cabinet that his choice for operation commander was Raful, Defense Minister Moshe Dayan, a paper tiger in Israeli history, quipped, "Good. . . . We really haven't heard much from him lately."

anything go wrong—should the Lebanese army or heavily armed Palestinian units from the nearby refugee camps intercede and make a heliborne exfiltration impossible—Force Digli would be responsible for securing a beachhead to facilitate a seaborne evacuation. This made Force Digli the most important element of the attack, and as a result, according to accounts, they were equipped with heavier weapons than the other units involved, including Belgian-made bazookas and rifle-launched antitank grenades.

• Force Negbi—the non–Sayeret Mat'kal entity consisting of twenty-two commandos from the conscript paratroop brigade's reconnaissance force, Sayeret Tzanhanim, commanded by Company Commander Captain Gadi Negbi. Negbi's force would be heli-lifted via a Super Frelon and would be responsible for sabotaging Arab aircraft from the central part of the airport all the way to the boundaries of the main passenger terminal. Negbi, a career reconnaissance officer who was known for his abrupt personality and courageous battlefield exploits, was considered one of the most prestigious non–Sayeret Mat'kal junior commando officers in the ranks of the Israel Defense Forces.

The entire force would be flown to Beirut through the services of Lieutenant Colonel Eliezer "Cheetah" Cohen, one of the trailblazers behind the Israel Air Force's deployment of helicopters. The fleet of Bell 205 helicopters and Super Frelons would also provide an airborne ambush component all around Beirut, preventing Lebanese reinforcements from reaching the airport.[13] One Bell 205 would be Raful's hovering CP. Raful was known to have personally commanded many pursuits of Palestinian terrorists in the Jordan Valley from the air. When terrorists were found the brigadier general would cock the helicopter's door gun, a 7.62mm FN MAG, and shoot several quieting bursts of tracer fire himself.

The importance of Operation Gift and the lives of the Chief of Staff's Boys was perhaps best illustrated by the massive interservice support systems built into the mission's planning. The IAF was donating the services of six Super Frelons (virtually its entire fleet of the aircraft) with two held in airborne reserve; in addition, seven Bell 205s would hover above the chaotic scene and serve as medevac and evacuation craft should combat be involved. A flight of four Nord Noratlas N-2501-IS transports would fly around Beirut in the event that a large-scale emergency rescue was required to save the Mat'kal and Tzanhanim force from potential disaster. A squadron of Dassault Mirage IIIC air-superiority fighters would be flown over the Mediterranean, just in case they had to provide 30mm cannon fire ground support to the operation; more squadrons were placed on full battle alert in case they'd be called upon to do battle with the Mirages and Hawker Hunters of the Lebanese air force. Just off the coast of Beirut a mini-fleet of six IDF/Navy torpedo boats positioned itself in a stealthy fashion, just in case evacuation by sea was deemed a last resort. According to published reports, the flotilla maintained a complement of naval commandos to assist in case of any eventuality. For an attack against a civilian target, the IDF was taking nothing for granted.

In Jerusalem, inside the secure walls of the prime minister's office, IDF Chief of Staff Lieutenant General Bar-Lev made the final presentation of Operation Gift to Levi Eshkol. He brought with him a wall-size aerial reconnaissance photograph of Beirut International Airport and used a silver metal pointer to guide Eshkol through all the stages the three task forces were to undergo. It was an impressive and confident presentation, and an effective one as well. The usually mundane Eshkol was visibly impressed, especially by the assurances that only four to five Arab aircraft—a significant number, in his estimation—would be hit on the tarmac, and that both Israeli and Lebanese casualties would be kept at the absolute minimum. The green light was issued.

Even before Operation Gift was finally authorized by Prime Minister Eshkol, its file in the IDF Operations Branch had grown with a wealth of intelligence material. Slowly and with assurances of accuracy, A'man and Mossad sources were tapped for any possible tidbit that might make the operation in the Lebanese capital a success. Information was obtained on the Lebanese army forces stationed near the area. This was most important, since a Lebanese army commando platoon was based only a few kilometers away; an armed Lebanese gendarme unit was positioned only minutes away; and significant forces from the Lebanese military were based throughout the city, capable of reacting in a matter of minutes to the Israeli attack. In-depth information on Lebanese civilian air traffic was gathered, and the schedules of all airlines passing through Beirut were monitored and recorded, their timetables tabulated and placed in the charts for the "computers" (planners) in Operations Branch HQ. Smaller details—no less important —were also taken into consideration. These included the number of Lebanese gendarmes who would be on duty that evening; what type of sidearms they carried; and how many loaded magazines they carried on their utility belts. Clearly, nothing would be left to chance.

The last-minute intelligence work that went into the operation had to remain low-key. In order to keep a minimum profile and keep security high, Chief of Staff Bar-Lev refused an IAF Operations Section request to allow IAF photo-reconnaissance flights over Beirut International Airport. This might have sparked suspicion and prompted preventive defensive measures to be incorporated around the airport. The preoperation intelligence data would have to come from the files of A'man, Mossad, and Shin Bet archives. Since only Arab airliners were to be targeted, the Mat'kal and Sayeret Tzanhanim commandos were given plastic cutouts with illustrations of all the Arab airliners' emblems. From Syrianair to Middle Eastern Airlines, the carrier of Lebanon, the commandos memorized symbols and aircraft types and were frequently quizzed as to which symbol belonged to which airline by unit commanders Lieutenant Colonel Yairi and Major Digli. Even though these rough and tough fighters were more adept at throwing grenades in maneuvers, this memorization process was crucial to the operation's success; small index cards with illustrations were also distributed among the soldiers.[14] Given the chaos of a timetable (the commandos would only

70

be allowed thirty minutes on the tarmac) and the possibility of fire fights, the dangerous chances of mistakenly bombing an Air France or Swissair aircraft were very real. If such a scenario were to transpire, the diplomatic eruption against Israel would be more damaging than anything the Jewish state had yet encountered in the international community.

D-Day: Saturday, December 28, 1968. Raful decided to spend the entire day with his forces and train them at Lod Airport, Israel's air terminal to the rest of world. While this decision not to train at a covert facility away from prying eyes was met with robust objections by A'man field security officers, it was practical, and in such operations, practicality saved lives. While passengers leaving and entering the Holy Land took off and landed, men dressed in civilian clothing ran across the rain-soaked tarmac with rucksacks full of imaginary explosives. El Al mechanics and airport personnel were told nothing and were expected to say nothing. Training lasted for nearly eight hours. Aircraft were "borrowed" and parked in the manner in which it was believed the Arab aircraft would be set up at Beirut. Simulating helicopter landings, the men used jeeps as staging points while Brigadier General Raful, proud and stoic in his uniform, stood in observation on a rooftop, his stopwatch glued to his left hand.

The method for achieving the desired result was simple. A lead unit from each of the three forces would race from its helicopter and identify and secure its target. Once everything seemed peaceful, the commandos would signal in the sabotage crews equipped with explosive devices. After several dry runs during which curses in Arabic, brusquely shouted orders in Hebrew, and frustration filled the air, the aircraft were finally sabotaged in time. A rare smile ran across his lips, and finally Raful relayed the two magic words to Chief of Staff Bar-Lev: "They're ready!" Troops under Raful's command were usually ready—he was a commander who inspired obedience and going the extra mile.

Just after 20:00 hours, following a day of incessant maneuvers and last-minute preparations, Raful stood in front of his men and their helicopters for the predeparture inspection. The commandos, divided into their groups, stood at ease and appeared relaxed. The khaki canvas rucksacks laden with explosives and ammunition were a burden, but the line of soldiers managed to stay neat and orderly. Although this was a combat mission, Raful ordered his men to wear class A red berets and class A uniforms; the silver metal parachutist wings, insignia, and heraldry were all to be proudly displayed. This violation of combat fashion was ordered for two simple reasons. First, it would identify the force as being Israeli, leaving a lasting impression on Lebanese and Arab civilians looking on at the transpiring events from the terminal and tarmac. Second, it was a matter of tradition and military protocol of having the soldiers wear their dress uniforms when traveling beyond the boundaries of their home base. Raful, also a showman in such matters, realized that the sight of red berets scurrying around a tarmac engulfed with destroyed airliners would be most dramatic.

This was, however, a combat mission. Over their class A tunics the commandos carried a full battle kit with extra supplies of ammunition, hand grenades, and explosives. Below the red beret and brass metal Heyl Ha'Raglim (Infantry Corps) badge, the faces once shaven smooth before such out-of-base trips were covered by concealing layers of black grease. Before lining up for the inspection each soldier had to display his dog tags and Geneva Convention card. Casualties were expected to be considerable.

Most of the commandos carried the K'latch (AK-47) 7.62mm assault rifle. These Soviet-produced assault rifles were captured in such abundant numbers from the Egyptians and Syrians during the 1967 War that they, along with other such infantry weapons, became standard-issue items for all IDF elite units. They were favored by the Ha'Kommando Ha'Yami and Sayeret Golani (the reconnaissance commando element of the First Golani Infantry Brigade, and one of the finest units in the IDF's order of battle) and were considered indestructible and highly reliable. For this raid, however, they would be more than a status symbol. Since it did not appear as if the combined Sayeret Mat'kal and Sayeret Tzanhanim force would be engaging an enemy at close range (a scenario where the compact, rapid-firing Uzi 9mm submachine gun would come in very handy), the accurate, reliable, and—with its maximum range of three hundred meters—practical K'latch was employed.

Raful's address was short and to the point. He was not known as a man generous with words or quotes. He reassured his men and made sure they all knew what the military and political purpose of the operation was, as well as the message it relayed to the Israeli public. He also wished them the best of luck. As Haim Nadel looked on silently he recalled Operation Chief Weizman's last-minute advice to him: "Think with your head and take care of your ass!"[15]

Last drags were aggressively pulled on stublike cigarettes, and last trips to the latrine were attended to quickly. As Lieutenant Colonel Cheetah Cohen ordered his fleet of aircraft to switch on engines the commandos made one final check of their weaponry, gear, and comrades; they employed a buddy system in which one soldier took care of another. The egg-beater rotor blades of the helicopters produced a hypnotic percussion of approaching danger as the commandos sitting inside realized that training was over. It was time for *tachlis* (the real thing). The next stop would be Beirut.

At 20:37 hours eight Super Frelon and eight Bell 205 helicopters took off from the northern Israel Ramat David Air Base. They cut across the Jezreel and Zevulun valleys, flying at a high altitude to minimize unwanted public attention to their activities in the darkened Middle East skies.[16] The flight from central Israel to the Lebanese capital took nearly an hour. The helicopters flew in a direct path toward Beirut in an eastward approach from the sea, opting to risk Lebanese air force radar detection in order to conserve their precious supplies of fuel. As the neon lights of cosmopolitan Beirut materialized the helicopters reduced their altitude to two hundred meters; it was a chilly winter's evening, and the heavy sea mist engulfed much of the airport. Visibility at the airport would indeed be poor; this would hamper both the Israeli helicopter fleet and Lebanese attempts to respond militarily. Winter was a most volatile time to enter into combat in the Levant.

The lead Super Frelon—with Force Digli—touched down on the tarmac unnoticed by the Lebanese. As the landing boards touched the ground the lead squad raced to its designated sector and began to identify aircraft for destruction while the sapper squad and the covering force assumed defensive firing positions. Moments later Raful's airborne CP, a Bell 205, landed, as did the remaining choppers. They quickly disgorged their forces of commandos and sped back into the Levantine skies. Operation Gift was now fully under way.

Force Digli proceeded toward its targets in a well-choreographed ballet of agility and speed. A squad commander, always an officer, would race twenty to thirty yards toward the target; his movements were covered by nearly a dozen men whose AK-47 gun sights monitored every possible sniper position, prepared to silence any opposition with well-placed automatic fire bursts. The Mat'kal commandos were legendary shots; they were warriors proficient with virtually every firearm known to be used in the Middle East. They wasted very few rounds; most of their shots found their way into the center of the target. Their procession dance of intermittent advance was repeated until almost the entire force was advancing in stalled spurts of apprehension and precision.

Force Digli, which landed first, was the only section of the operation to encounter organized military resistance. It was subjected to sporadic bursts of rifle and sidearm fire coming from a multitude of angles; the Lebanese efforts were uncoordinated and highly inaccurate. Force Digli responded with determined, full-automatic bursts of 7.62mm fire aimed toward the muzzle blasts blinking in the distance; this deterred attempts to interfere with their main work— the destruction of the three airliners found in their area. Five kilograms of high explosives were allotted per aircraft, the devices to be placed under the fuselage and near the bases of the wings—this, it was felt, would result in absolute destruction. For the hundreds of airline passengers attempting to leave Beirut that night, many looking on from the terminal, it was a remarkable sight. It would develop into a frustrating sight when their airliners were targeted for destruction. Seeing heavily armed men in red berets running like track-and-field stars underneath aircraft was beguiling. It was almost comical, but the results certainly were not. Force Digli succeeded in obliterating three Arab airliners. The blasts illuminated the runways and much of the airport in an eerie yellowish glow.

Force Yairi, the second to land, touched down in the central section of the tarmac and encountered the largest group of aircraft—three groups of parked jetliners spread out near the military section of the airfield. Although this force, too, encountered minor resistance (a police car venturing to the chaotic scene to see what the hell was happening), the problem was removed with a volley of warning shots fired into the air. In the end, Sayeret Mat'kal Commander Yairi's group destroyed eight Arab passenger jets.

Force Negbi, which operated on the eastern section of the main runway, encountered four aircraft; one of them, identified as belonging to an Arab airline, was found in a hangar. One sapper from Force Nagbi had mistakenly positioned his five-kilogram packs on that aircraft even though a group of Arab workers was still laboring in the building, despite warnings shouted at them in English and Arabic to get the hell out. Luckily, the device failed to detonate. Had it gone off, it would certainly have killed the workers, and possibly hundreds more. The aircraft had just been replenished with thirty tons of jet fuel, and its detonation would have resulted in a hellish fireball that would have engulfed much of the airport—and the IDF commando force as well.

Protecting the activities of the red beret saboteurs were several low-flying Bell 205s equipped with FN MAG 7.62mm light machine guns, .50-caliber heavy machine guns, and smoke-grenade launchers; they hovered above the roadway connecting the airport to the rest of the city. It would be a coordinated airborne ballet of road-blocking power. The helicopters fired ninety-five smoke grenades onto the narrow roadway, which was inundated by irate motorists and police vehicles attempting to reach the scene.[17] To exacerbate the confusion, the helicopters dropped hundreds of large industrial nails onto the main roadway to puncture the tires of any vehicle getting too close for comfort to the main terminal area. Road lights were taken out as well, plunging the smoke- and nail-filled thoroughfare into pitch-black darkness. The chaos inflicted on the Lebanese motorists lasted well into the night.

Several gallant elements of the Red Crescent (the Lebanese Red Cross) and Beirut fire brigade attempted to reach the destroyed airliners, fearing, perhaps, that there were wounded civilians burning in the wreckage. Israeli officers using bullhorns warned them not to come close, and anti-tank rifle grenades were fired in bursts to persuade them forcefully. Another difficulty occured when the crew of a Middle East Airlines Caravelle jetliner refused to leave its aircraft. The crew members finally departed their doomed craft when the menacing business end of the AK-47 replaced diplomatic language and courteous pleas.

With much of the IAF's minuscule helicopter fleet in Beirut that evening, Operation Gift was a monumental military gamble. It was, however, an operation that went virtually unopposed. Chief of Staff Bar-Lev had ordered Raful not to remain on the ground over thirty minutes, a most difficult and frugal timetable. In true IDF fashion, the operation lasted exactly twenty-nine minutes. At the London rendezvous point the joint Sayeret force lifted off for the ride back to Israel. As the helicopters veered into a sharp and evasive angle the sight of fourteen flaming skeletons of what had once been high-flying airliners littered the tarmac; according to one commando, "the airport was illuminated with what looked like torchbearers."[18] The destruction of aircraft was well beyond anyone's expectations—well beyond the thoughts of officers in IDF HQ, the prime minister, and the commandos on the field.

The mission was a brilliant success. Israel had made an

irrefutable statement against Arab support for Palestinian air piracy, and not a single civilian or Israeli soldier was wounded or killed.

When the force returned to Israel Raful offered all the commandos his praise and a wink; it was obvious they would meet again in the near future under more difficult circumstances. The mission, in fact, captured the world's attention and admiration; Israel's warriors had once again proven that they were capable of the impossible. Much legend would also emerge from Operation Gift, the most famous being that Raful left the CP to enter the terminal, headed toward the bar, presented the bartender with an Israeli ten-pound note, and demanded a cup of coffee. Such reports filtered throughout the Lebanese press, and eventually into the world's media; some reports even had Raful befriending the Lebanese barman and hoping that he'd one day have the opportunity to use his newly acquired note of Israeli currency in the Holy Land. One thing was sure, however: Raful would return to Beirut.

At 23:00 hours on December 28 the IDF spokesman released a statement on Israeli Army Radio regarding a commando action conducted at Beirut International Airport. "The raid," the report said, "was meant to teach a harsh lesson to the allies and sponsors of international terrorism. Several Arab airliners were destroyed in the operation, and there were no losses reported to our force."[19]

Throughout Israel, news of the operation sparked quiet expressions of pride and anxious thoughts of increased hostilities; Israelis realized that this was only a harbinger of worse to come. Internationally, however, Operation Gift produced much less praise and, in many unexpected circles, more outward anger. The most outraged non-Arab response came from France. Once Israel's principal arms supplier, France had been at odds with the Jewish state ever since Israel went against President de Gaulle's demand that Israel not strike first in what would eventually become known as the Six-Day War. When the news of Operation Gift reached his office he decided once and for all to teach his "subservient" ally an unforgettable lesson. Since the success of the raid was facilitated by the use of French-produced helicopters, de Gaulle ordered an all-encompassing arms embargo against Israel.* It would not be the last time one of Israel's moves against terrorism would meet with international scorn.

The Israeli press has never officially attributed Operation Gift to the anonymous commandos of Sayeret Mat'kal. In fact, they are still referred to in official accounts as either "a special paratroop force" or "an elite unit." Anonymity intact, Sayeret Mat'kal's role in the war of attrition would continue. Its leading role in Israel's war against terrorism continues to this day.

# NOTES

1. The popular line in Arab capitals from Beirut to Baghdad was that the next war would result in the Jewish state being pushed into the sea. These boisterous claim were supported by numerous more horrible illustrations of massacre, pillaging, and even rape against the Israeli populace; the graphics were clearly anti-Semitic in cartoons reminiscent of the days of *Der Sturmer*. Although the Israelis took the propaganda effort with a grain of salt, it did rally the Arabs into a war frenzy, and the emotions were multiplied and nurtured in the Palestinian camp.

---

*Israel would circumvent the embargo by having a Mossad/A'man/ IDF/Navy operation "liberate" already-paid-for missile boats from their Cherbourg port; the chapter became known as the Boats of Cherbourg. In the case of fifty already-paid-for Mirage V fighter bombers the French refused to turn over to the IAF, an A'man and Mossad operation simply saw to it that the original blueprints for the Mirage were obtained from a Swiss aeronautics engineer, and that Israel built its own copy; the aircraft became known as the Nesher (Eagle) and would eventually develop into the successful Kfir series of indigenously produced fighter bombers.

2. Ya'akov Caroz, *The Arab Secret Services* (London: Transworld Publishers Ltd., 1978), 68.

3. Edgar O'Ballance, *Language of Violence: The Politics of Terrorism* (San Rafael: Presidio Press, 1979), 51–52.

4. *Ibid.,* 53.

5. Ze'ev Schiff and Raphael Rothstein, *Fedayeen: Guerrillas Against Israel* (New York: David McKay Company Inc., 1972), 74.

6. Neil C. Livingstone and David Halevy, *Inside the PLO* (New York: William Morrow and Company, 1990), 264.

7. Sharon Segev, "Ha'Hatifa Ha'Rishona," *Biton Heyl Ha'Avir,* July 1988, 100.

8. Eitan Haber, *Ha'Yom Tifrotz Milhama* (Tel Aviv: Edanim Publishers, 1987), 328.

9. Eilan Kfir, *Tzanhanim Ch'ir Mutznach: Tzahal Be'Heilo—Entzyklopedia Le'Tzava Ule'Bitachon* (Tel Aviv: Revivim, 1981), 121.

10. Uri Milshtein, *Historia Shel Ha'Tzanhanim: Kerech Daled* (Tel Aviv: Schalgi Ltd., Publishing House, 1987), 1582.

11. Yosef Argaman, "Raful Lo Shata Kafeh Be'Terminal," *Bamachane,* February 1, 1989, 23.

12. Christopher Dobson and Ronald Payne, *Counterattack: The West's Battle Against the Terrorists* (New York: Facts On File, Inc., 1982), 85.

13. Yosef Argaman, *Ze Haya Sodi Be'Yoter* (Tel Aviv: Ministry of Defense Publications, 1990), 286.

14. *Ibid.,* 288.

15. Yosef Argaman, "Raful Lo Shata," 24.

16. Eilan Kfir, *Tzanhanim H'ir Mutznah,* 122.

17. Uri Milshtein, *Historia Shel Ha'Tzanhanim,* 1583.

18. Interview, Galei Tzahal,* December 12, 1984.

19. Yosef Argaman, "Raful Lo Shata," 24.

---

*Galei Tzahal is the name of the IDF radio station, meaning "IDF Air Waves."

# 4

---

# *Angels in White and the Death of Captain Rifat*

---

*Operation Isotope 1*
*Lod International Airport*
*May 8–9, 1972*

Israel, May 1972. The National Police border guards who manned the principal checkpoint just outside Israel's bustling Lod International Airport, a few miles east of Tel Aviv, appeared tense and serious. Belgian-made FN FAL 7.62mm assault rifles were held with firmer grips than usual, and piercing eyes scanned all oncoming vehicles with skepticism, apprehension, and a sense of impending danger. A terrorist alert had been sounded, and the likely target was Israel's airport. The "green berets," as the border guards were known, were determined to ensure that no terrorist attack would make it through their barricades. Unfortunately, when it came, the attack arrived from a most unexpected location.

Jordan, September 1970. At a spartan military facility located in Jordan's desert hills, King Hussein's routine inspection of his troops sparked little fanfare or attention. Dressed in neatly pressed dark olive fatigues, the king had a chestful of shiny medals, and Royal Jordanian Air Force pilot's wings added a minor bit of dazzle to a serene and mundane setting. The few dozen men stationed at the base—all tank soldiers from one of the Jordanian military's finest units, the 40th Armored Brigade—stood stoically in line, presented arms, and waited for the much-vaunted royal visitor to inspect their ranks and perhaps offer some words of inspiration to see the unit through difficult times. Their vehicles, British-made Centurion main battle tanks, were adorned in a green and mustard camouflage scheme and had their 105mm main armament guns uncharacteristically facing east, toward Amman, the capital.

The troops in this "elite of elite" formation were all Bedouins, nomads of the desert whose allegiance to the Hashemite crown was infrangible and sworn on their blood. They were a proud people whose resilience was as lasting as the tales of the desert. Recent events in their sacred land, however, had caused them great pain and anxiety. Their displeasure with King Hussein's restraint in light of a supreme challenge to Jordanian independence was expressed in a most remarkable and poignant message. Alongside an antenna positioned to the rear of one of the mighty Centurion tanks, next to the flag of Jordan and the battalion's proud markers, was a white lace brassiere.[1] It was a statement of embarrassment and of pleading. How much longer would King Hussein force his loyal Bedouin soldiers to behave like women? The time for action was now!

Tensions in Jordan were high. Since Israel's conquest of the West Bank during the 1967 War, the Hashemite Kingdom of Jordan had played host to hundreds of thousands of refugees as well as hundreds of small, heavily armed Palestinian liberation groups that set up camp in the hills opposite the River Jordan. Initially the new fedayeen were welcomed by the Jordanians, who viewed their terrorist forays into Israel as a method of retribution. Welcome soon turned into dread. Undisciplined and motivated only through hate, the Palestinian guerrillas loyal to Arafat, Habash, Jibril, and Hawatmeh soon became a Jordanian liability. Their operations against Israel always resulted in harsh Israeli retaliation. As the Palestinians usually set up

# Samuel M. Katz

their camps in areas populated by Jordanian and Palestinian civilians, the majority of victims tended to be the innocents. Armed and dangerous men soon became part of the landscape of Jordanian cities and villages. Palestinian guerrillas ignored Jordanian laws, sensibilities, and sovereignty; extreme friction existed between the two camps.

War in Jordan was imminent, as the indiscriminate and chaotic spasms of bloodshed were simply unstoppable. The fuse was lit on September 6, 1970—a day better known to the world as Skyjack Sunday. Jordan became the focal point of the world's spotlight as three airliners were seized by Palestinian terrorists working on behalf of Dr. George Habash's Popular Front for the Liberation of Palestine (PFLP) and flown to the kingdom without prior authorization or even notification. A Trans World Airlines (TWA) flight from Frankfurt to New York was hijacked in midair. A Swissair flight was hijacked during a flight from Zurich to New York and flown to the RAF's deserted Dawson's Field in the Jordanian desert near Zarqa. A third aircraft, a Pan Am flight from Amsterdam to New York, was hijacked and flown to Cairo.[2] The world's press was summoned to the closely guarded perimeter, and cameras recorded the heavily armed men and women, their heads draped in red and white *kefiyeh* headdresses, milling about in victory dances. It was a theater of tragedy and bloodshed.

Supposed to complete this massive collection of hijacked aircraft was an El Al flight from Amsterdam to New York. One of the terrorists, however, missed the flight; one was killed in a midair gun battle with Shin Bet skymarshals; and the most famous terrorist, Leila Khaled, was overpowered and captured. Coincidentally, one of the passengers on that El Al flight, unbeknownst to the terrorists, was Major General Aharon Yariv, the IDF's director of Military Intelligence and the architect of Israel's developing war against Palestinian terrorism.

The El Al flight was diverted to London, provoking what nearly became a firefight between British police, Aharon Yariv, and the Shin Bet guards for custody of the captured terrorists. After much haggling and yelling Leila Khaled was finally awarded to Scotland Yard. The British might have won the battle, but they surely lost the war. On September 9, just three days later, a British Overseas Airways Company (BOAC) aircraft was hijacked during a routine flight from Bombay, India, to London. It, too, was directed to Dawson's Field, where it joined the two other airliners.

The terrorists' demand was simple: release Miss Khaled at once, or the hostages would be executed one by one. Whitehall acquiesced immediately. After torturing the passengers on Dawson's Field by confining them in an ovenlike aircraft sitting on a desert tarmac without air conditioning, fresh water, or sanitary toilet facilities, the Palestinians allowed the hostages to leave the aircraft once Leila Khaled, the femme fatale of the Palestinian revolution, was secure in their embrace. Although Israel had not released the dozens of captured terrorists and guerrillas it was holding in its jails—the principal demand to be met before any of the hostages would be released—the terrorists opted to end the ordeal. Amid much coverage by the international press the jubilant Palestinian terrorists detonated explosive devices planted aboard the airliners in a dazzling display of destructive ability. Nearly $36 million worth of state-of-the-art aircraft was turned into flaming and twisted steel on a strip of desolate desert. Victory for Palestine had been achieved.

It would be extremely short-lived.

On September 16 King Hussein dissolved the parliament, and one day later he unleashed his vengeful Bedouin brigades into the refugee camps around Amman, Ramtha, and Irbid. According to King Hussein, "The hijacking of the airliners is the shame of the Arab world."[3] He was determined to right that wrong.

The fighting in what became the Jordanian Civil War was particularly vicious, even by Middle Eastern standards of brutality. Jordanian gunners pummeled the densely populated camps with glee, lobbing hundreds of shells into shantytown bunkers holding gallant flag bearers of the Palestinian nation. Jordanian soldiers—even the Palestinians in King Hussein's army—utilized their tanks' 105mm main guns against buildings, huts, and loosely constructed hutches in refugee camp shantytowns, often at point-blank range. Devastation and carnage were absolute. Bedouin snipers from the Jordanian army's elite Special Services Group, utilizing World War II–vintage U.S.–made M-1 carbines fitted with high-power scopes, displayed their impressive marksmanship abilities by picking off anyone and everyone who showed signs of belonging to the *fedayeen*.

According to reports that emanated from both sides, atrocities were commonplace. Palestinian fighters were known to have butchered Jordanian civilians and captured soldiers in cold blood, while Jordanian troopers were said to have raped countless women of all ages in the refugee camps, as well as dragging prisoners chained to the backs of tanks along unpaved roadways for all to witness in absolute horror. Thousands of wounded died helplessly in the streets as Jordanian military authorities forbade medical teams from the Red Crescent to treat the casualties. Prisoners on both sides were sadistically mistreated, brutally tortured, and summarily executed. The fighting was so fierce that Palestinian guerrillas swam across the Jordan River to surrender to Israeli soldiers rather than incur the unforgiving, sadistic wrath of the Jordanian soldiers.[4] Most of the Palestinian terrorists who had once found salvation in Jordan were forced into a second diaspora in the unforgiving political landscape of Lebanon, where the PLO soon set up shop. The civil war, in fact, became a protacted struggle of attrition that lasted until July 19, 1971, when Jordanian Premier Wasfi Tal declared that there were no more *fedayeen* bases in Jordan.

The final death count in the two weeks of fighting—which included a Syrian mini-invasion of northern Jordan in a "Damascus show of impudent solidarity with the Palestinians," as well as diplomatic efforts that eventually brought on Egyptian President Nasser's fatal heart attack—is believed to exceed ten thousand. Although Yasir Arafat has claimed that twenty-five thousand Palestinians were murdered in the conflict, the Israelis estimate that only three thousand were killed in the fighting. The result, no matter what the final grisly body count came to, was a dark tragedy for the Palestinians; it was a devastating event akin to the loss of their homeland in 1948. It was known in Arabic as Ailul al-Aswad (Black September), and it would be avenged in a manner that would leave the world reeling in horror and awe. The PLO responded to its defeat by creating its own special force of terrorists that would perpetrate destruction for its own sake. In statements originating from Lebanon and Syria the world was warned of what was to come.

To accomplish its feat of placing the crimes perpetrated against the Palestinian people on the world stage, the Black September Organization would rely on the best minds and guns of the Jihaz al-Rasd (War Intelligence Section), the PLO's security and intelligence entity; it was commanded by Saleh Khalaf (Abu I'yad), Khalil al-Wazir (Abu Jihad), and one of the organization's most ambitious and capable officers, Ali Hassan Salameh (Abu Hassan), the terrorist mastermind who would eventually be known as the Red Prince. The foot soldiers of this new and most dangerous entity would come from all points of the Palestinian political spectrum. Pan-Arabist socialists from the PFLP joined ranks with the Nasserites in the DFLP (Democratic Front for the Liberation of Palestine), who in turn joined ranks and flocked to known Rasd officers for the chance to volunteer for this unique force of avengers. Unlike el-Fatah, the Black September Organization was to be a sacrosanct entity into which only the most loyal and capable souls were recruited. Intensive, sometimes brutal interrogations were conducted to ensure that new fodder for the cause were not American, Israeli, or worse, Jordanian intelligence operatives attempting to infiltrate the organization.

Initially the Black September Organization's ability to mount operations of importance was limited. Targets, after all, had to be chosen very carefully. Abu I'yad, the spiritual leader of the group, urged that the violence and bloodshed continue to expand, but actions would have to be covert due to the obvious political considerations—Arafat and the PLO needed the ability to disclaim any act too bloody. Black September developed into the first of the PLO's many deniable covert forces. The group's primary objective, ostensibly, was the overthrow of King Hussein and vengeance against the enemies of Palestine, although attacks against Israel would, of course, flourish.[5]

Black September's first true act of vengeance was a bold statement of its aims and its capabilities. On November 28, 1971, in an operation masterminded by Mohammed Yusef Najjir (better known by his nom de guerre, Abu Yusef), the commander of Black September's notorious Killer Section, four Black September gunmen* ambushed Wasfi Tal, the Jordanian premier, in a hotel lobby entrance in Cairo and fatally wounded him. Although initial reports indicating that the Black September gunmen actually lapped the blood of the dying Jordanian premier were exaggerated, the emergence of this new and extremely violent force worried many Western intelligence officials, especially in Israel. Their fears, however, were temporarily relieved when a failed Black September assassination of Tal's successor was attempted on December 15, 1971, in London; and on February 6, 1972, Black September assassins murdered five Jordanians accused of spying for Israel. Jordan, it appeared, was the sole target of Black September. In the spring of 1972, though, Black September widened its net, and Israel's worst fears concerning Abu I'yad and his mysterious force were realized.

In the early months of 1972 intelligence reports filtering into A'man headquarters in Tel Aviv had warned of a potential large-scale Palestinian terrorist attack targeting Lod Airport. Although the sources of these reports remain classified to this day, they were based on the testimony of deep-cover agents who had infiltrated the Palestinian terrorist infrastructure, as well as from counterintelligence surveillance of suspicious individuals who reconnoitered aerial activity stemming from the Israeli air terminal. Brigadier General Emanuel "Manno" Shaked, the head of the Operations Department in the general staff, had even prepared contingency plans to meet any possible threat.[6]

---

*The four gunmen were eventually released by Egyptian authorities following a show trial that served more as a propaganda show than as a process of criminal justice.

Taking threats by Palestinian terrorists to crash-land a hijacked civilian airliner into the heart of downtown Tel Aviv very seriously, the general staff had antiaircraft batteries moved to the metropolis from their stationary frontier positions; these included, according to published accounts, Hawk surface-to-air missile batteries. There was also sincere concern that Palestinian terrorists would attempt to seize control of the Lod Airport arrival lounge, possibly by producing a vast arsenal of automatic weapons and grenades from unexamined baggage.* To counter this possibility, additional units of border guard policemen were stationed at the airport, sharpshooters were positioned at strategic vantage points, and armored cars—Soviet-produced BTR-152s captured from the Egyptians in Sinai —were sent to patrol the tarmac.

Nobody on the IDF General Staff knew exactly how the Palestinians would mount their attack, or from where. As a result, they viewed this threat with misgiving and did not take it too seriously. One very special IDF unit, however, did take the threat extremely seriously, according to published accounts. There was a list of concerns: Which type of plane would be seized? From which airline? What tactics, doctrines, or strategies would the terrorists employ? Which weapons would they use? Would they be suicidal, destroying themselves and their hostages? These questions needed to be answered if the rescue force had any hope of successfully executing an assault. But so, too, did others. If a midair battle was to be waged, which type of small arms and munitions could be fired without harming the precious air-pressure balance? How could one break through sealed aircraft doors from the outside? How could the attackers ensure that the aircraft's fuel tanks would not ignite in a

*Tragically, this scenario came to pass on June 30, 1972, when three Japanese Red Army terrorists working on behalf of the PFLP produced Czech-built assault rifles and grenades from their travel bags and murdered twenty-nine passengers—mainly Catholic pilgrims from Puerto Rico—in what became known as the Lod Airport Massacre.

firefight? There were dozens of unanswered questions and possibilities to be considered. Unfortunately, time was clearly running out.

The elite unit requested a spare airliner from El Al—a small and modest solicitation!—so that its fighters could train under as realistic conditions as possible, but the national airline refused. Bullet holes and boot marks in the first class cabin were, after all, bad for business. Undaunted, and in keeping with a reputation for doing whatever the hell they wanted to do anyway, the force, led by unit commander Lieutenant Colonel Ehud Barak, opted to override the official rejection. They broke into the defensive perimeter at Lod Airport, entered the hangar housing a foreign-carrier aircraft, and they proceeded to make believe that it was being held by fanatic terrorists. The aircraft was a target of the commandos as the men began kicking in its doors, playing with its hydraulics, and examining the exterior design of emergency exits and cockpit cabins.[7] When El Al learned of this they panicked in the fear that TWA, British Airways, or Air France might retaliate in an airliner air war of sorts. As a result El Al management immediately acquiesced, and the commandos were allowed to practice on equipment that would otherwise ferry Israeli tourists to Europe.

Unlike a conventional military objective, storming an airliner loaded to capacity with frightened hostages and determined captors was a relatively new undertaking. Training routines were discovered, refined, and then, of course, rediscovered. Success or failure of such an operation did not depend on the abilities of the fighters; in this regard, Sayeret Mat'kal was second to none. But success or failure rested on the intangible elements of psychological portraits, screaming hostages, and timetables, which provided odds no sane military commander could feel comfortable with. The art and craft of storming a Boeing 707 was attended to with great care—climbing aboard the wings, moving stealthily along the fuselage toward the emergency exits, cocking .22 and 9mm Berettas a millisecond before kicking in the door, and eliminating a terrorist presence from the aircraft. The commandos had no way of knowing if the hijacked aircraft would be a 747 jumbo or, perhaps, an aging British Caravelle. Uncertainty bred doubt and concern.

According to the general staff's Operations Department commander, Major General Shaked, who was kept abreast of the developments of the general staff's reconnaissance commandos, "There was a real and gut-wrenching feeling that if an aircraft was, in fact, hijacked to Israel—we are lost!"[8]

The questions of the IDF planners and doubters were answered on May 8, 1972.

Security at major airports throughout Europe had been vigilant in the spring of 1972, but it was by no means hermetic. The increased preventive measures seemed to concentrate on El Al—after all, Israel's flag carrier was a natural target for Palestinian terrorists. On airport tarmacs in London, Rome, and Vienna El Al flights were protected by armored cars carrying heavy machine guns and a complement of battle-ready troops. Other international carriers, however, refused to accept the threat, and business went on as usual—even for those airlines serving Israel. In Brussels, in the early afternoon hours of May 8, 1972, the call for Sabena Belgian Airlines Flight 751 created a long line of passengers eager to pass through the obligatory security examination. In all, ninety-nine passengers boarded the flight, including four individuals—two men and two women—who held forged Israeli passports; they were Black September terrorists embarking on a most daring undertaking straight into the heart of Israeli civilization.

The four were commanded by none other than Captain Rifat, known for the El Al hijacking to Algeria, who had left the PFLP for more lucrative tasks in the Ailul al-Aswad. This followed his participation in another successful airliner seizure—a Lufthansa West German Airlines flight from New Delhi to Athens forced to land in Aden, South Yemen. Captain Rifat's second-in-command was Abdel Aziz al-Atrash, a Jordanian-born el-Fatah gunman who was one of the first to join Black September from the el-Fatah rank and file. The other two terrorists, Ruma Isa Tanus and Tirza

Ish'ak Halasah Samirah, were women recruited, according to terrorist talent-seeking doctrines, for their "simplicity."

Although Belgian gendarmes carrying submachine guns patrolled the Brussels Airport terminal, the four terrorists were able to slip past the gauntlet of security unhindered. In their specially adapted travel bags the four carried 9mm handguns and fragmentation grenades; the two women carried potent supplies of plastic explosives hidden in their bras, in the cleverly positioned inner linings of their panties, and even inside their vaginal cavities. They had departed from Beirut a week earlier in two separate pairs, making stops in Frankfurt and Rome before meeting in the Belgian capital. Several passengers were suspicious of the four "Arab-looking" individuals who gazed aimlessly outside the terminal window, searching for something beyond the realm of understanding of the other passengers. Some people— especially the Israelis in the line of ninety-seven passengers —wanted to contact the Belgian security personnel but thought it not a prudent thing to do. After all, nobody really expected *it* to happen.

At 17:35 hours, as Sabena Flight 751 made its way over the snow-capped mountains of Yugoslavia following a brief stopover in Vienna, Captain Rifat slowly stood from his window seat and proceeded toward the unprotected cockpit, his movements sparking his three comrades into action. Abdel Aziz al-Atrash slowly stood up as well, while both females headed to the restroom to produce their instruments of terror from their undergarments and body cavities. Clutching newly acquired packages, they returned to their seats. A few minutes later, according to Yitzhak Mizrahi, a jeweler on the flight, "the quiet on board was shattered by screams, cries, and shouts in Arabic, English, and French. Hijack!"[9] Flight 751 had, indeed, been seized. It was renamed Victorious Jeddah, and while the pilot, Reginald Levy, feared that the gun pointed at his head meant that the aircraft was heading to Beirut, Amman, or Damascus, Captain Rifat ordered the RAF–World War II veteran to remain on course and continue to Palestine.

News of Flight 751's seizure reached Israel at 18:05 on the

evening of May 8. A control tower in Nicosia, Cyprus, informed Israel that a hijacked aircraft was heading toward its airspace. This, to many in the IDF general staff, was the worst-case scenario materializing right before their eyes. Immediately Defense Minister Moshe Dayan, IDF Chief of Staff Lieutenant General David "Dado" Elazar, Operations Branch OC Major General Yisrael "Talik" Tal, Intelligence Branch OC Major General Aharon Yariv, Central Command OC Major General Rechavem "Gandhi" Zeevi, IAF commander Major General Mordechai "Motti" Hod, and OC Paratroop and Infantry Branch Brigadier General Raful Eitan were summoned and ordered to the control tower at Lod Airport; they were joined by Transportation Minister Shimon Peres and other anonymous and assorted members of the intelligence community. Chief of Staff Elazar ordered Brigadier General Shaked to summon the unit. Immediately a call was placed to Lieutenant Colonel Ehud Barak, who was at home. Manno told him, "A plane has been hijacked, bring whoever is hanging around the base to Lod at once and start calling the others.* You're needed!"[10]

Flight 751 landed at Lod at 19:05 hours and was escorted to a remote air strip where either a massacre or a brilliant display of commando proficiency would transpire. Although the principal fear among the Israeli who's who assembled at the control tower was the systematic execution of hostages should the terrorists' demands not be met, a nagging worry was that the Boeing 707 would be used as a giant kamikaze bomb, one that would destroy much of the airport and hundreds of passengers. As a result, instantaneous and frantic security procedures were implemented at Lod. Passengers and awaiting family members were evacuated, aircraft was removed from main runway positions, and the facility was sealed from all incoming traffic. In fact, even as Flight 751 was making its final approach over the Tel Aviv skyline and due east toward the barren plains at Lod, border guard policemen were busy loading belts of 7.62mm ammo

---

*According to published reports, Sayeret Mat'kal had been operating at the time in the Gaza Strip, engaged in an extremely bloody and irregular counterterrorist campaign.[11]

into their FN MAG light machine guns mounted on armored cars that ringed the facility's perimeter. The only vehicles the border guard green berets allowed to enter the terminal were those of Ehud Barak's men, who came in military vehicles, in private cars, and on motorcycles; of course, convoys of ambulances and fire-fighting vehicles were rushed to the airport.

Many of the commandos arrived in uniform, while others came in track suits and shorts. Understandably concerned that a large-scale terrorist operation was under way, the Border Guard sentries gave many of the commandos in civilian attire a hard time getting permission to enter the airport, although arguments and threats of fatal karate blows proved convincing enough; Border Guard policemen, in keeping with the need-to-know aura of Sayeret Mat'kal, were not told that members of a special unit were going to pass through their positions. In retrospect, the commandos didn't even require authorization to enter the airport. Had permission been denied, they would have simply climbed over the fence and assembled as ordered. After all, they had done it before.

Upon pulling his aircraft to a full halt on the darkened runway, Captain Reginald Levy established radio contact with the control tower and the Israeli authorities; a direct line was arranged to patch Prime Minister Golda Meir's office into the transpiring events. With a 9mm automatic pointed to his temple, Levy read off the names of 317 Palestinian terrorists in Israeli jails; the terrorists demanded they be released and flown to Cairo before the Sabena hostages were released. Concerned about an international incident that might have repercussions the State of Israel could not bear, Prime Minister Meir ordered that "whatever needs to be done *should* be done." There would be no surrender or acquiescence to terror; the military option was likely to be used.[12]

As the Israeli leadership—both in Jerusalem and at the airport—began to coordinate its forces to deal with the crisis, Lieutenant Colonel Barak was organizing *his* means to deal with the unfolding events. As the fighters filtered into the airport a cohesive force began to gather. Although he did not know exactly what their role would be in the situation, Barak ordered several of his fighters into the thorny under-brush surrounding the runway. Slowly and silently the commandos crept on their stomachs, inching their way to within safe eyeshot of the seized airliner. Lying in wait on the thorny foliage was not a pleasant experience at all. Laden down with a full battle load of ammunition, gre-nades, and filled-to-capacity canteens, the commandos knew that if the shit hit the fan, they'd be hitting the mess first. With their AK-47 assault rifles locked and loaded the commandos peered through their gunsights for any pos-sible target. This was not a scenario, however, in which a weapon with a cyclic rate of fire of six hundred rounds per minute could be realistically employed. Nerves were becoming frayed. If ever there was a time for a cigarette, this was it! Of course, lighting up was forbidden, and the only contact that dark night was the near-silent chatter of radio traffic and hand signals. Nobody knew what to expect.

To the paratrooper officers in the gathered group of politicians and generals tasked with solving this chaotic situation, it was clear that there was only one solution: a military response. It would have to be one on Israeli terms and without risk to the lives of the hostages. The most pressing objective was the immobilization of the airliner. That would keep the terrorists and hostages within reach and contain the crisis within the boundaries of Israel. Should the plane take off and land in an Arab capital, a repeat of the July 1968 hijacking to Algiers was possible. Or perhaps a terrorist, in a desperate and mad political gesture insuring martyrdom, would detonate the aircraft and kill everyone on board.

Grounding a fully loaded airliner is no easy task under normal civilian aviation conditions, let alone when tired and desperate individuals are holding over one hundred hostages. After consulting with El Al technicians, it was determined that the safest means for turning the Boeing 707 into a bus with wings was to drain the oil lines powering the hydraulic fluid system in the aircraft. Such drainage would ensure that the plane would not fly, but the leak would not set off emergency lights inside the cockpit.

Lieutenant Colonel Barak led the combined force of commandos and El Al mechanics toward the aircraft. They were dressed in dirty white coveralls and were ferried by jeep to within fifty meters of the aircraft's rear, and then they proceeded slowly on foot to the plane's undercarriage. As Barak curiously gazed up at the aircraft and the commandos aimed their AK-47s in defensive postures, a mechanic summoned only an hour earlier from his bed opened the hydraulic valve and tinkered until a drip and then a gushing flow of black liquid engulfed the assembled squad.[13] Mission accomplished. The terrorists paid little attention to the activities of men milling about in white coveralls. The group members retraced their footsteps and made it back to the hastily established CP.

The man who entered into negotiations with the terrorists was the A'man director, Major General Yariv. An old pro at dealing with terrorists, Yariv began a slow and deliberate discussion with the group's leader, a man who identified himself only as Captain Rifat. Yariv's tactics were meant to buy time for A'man psychologists to prepare a mental portrait of Captain Rifat, as well as to allow the hydraulic oil to drain completely from the aircraft. Yariv had begun to explain—in full and monotonous detail—the intricate bureaucratic difficulty involved in releasing so many prisoners from custody when Captain Rifat cut him off brusquely to make an ominous demand. He ordered that the Israelis refuel the aircraft at once or prepare to see dead hostages. The fear was that the terrorists had second thoughts about landing in Israel and were preparing to take off for Cairo or Amman.

Once again Lieutenant Colonel Barak had to remove his olive fatigues and loaded-to-capacity web gear and slip into the grease-covered El Al mechanic's uniform he had been given. Once again he led a combined group of commandos and mechanics toward the beleaguered aircraft. This time the group was allowed to approach the aircraft in the open under the guise of refueling the plane, but of course they didn't pump any fuel. A new crew of mechanics examined the aircraft and determined that draining the hydraulic fluid was not sufficient to neutralize the aircraft; further tinkering was required. This presented the negotiating staff sitting in a cloud of cigarette smoke in the control tower with a quandary. Refusing the terrorist demands might result in the token execution of innocent hostages. Truly immobilizing the aircraft, so that the terrorists would be able to determine what was going on, risked a bloodbath. After phoning El Al mechanics—both on active employment and long since retired—and examining aircraft manuals, it was decided to drain the oil from the hydraulics throughout the aircraft, as well as to cut off the navigation controls and steering mechanisms; it was also decided to slice through the wires that controlled the warning lights. This way the terrorists would have no way of knowing that their Victorious Jeddah had been sabotaged.

Besides the obvious military importance of the immobilization of the aircraft, it was hoped that if the terrorists ordered the pilot to take off at once, there was little danger that the plane would crash and kill a great number of hostage passengers. Nothing, however, was left to chance. Cleverly hidden behind a row of eucalyptus trees was a fleet of ambulances and fire engines.[14]

While Major General Yariv continued his negotiations, attempting in vain to convince Captain Rifat that the logistics involved in releasing over three hundred prisoners were complex and would take time, the team of generals and politicians noticed a monkey wrench being thrown into their elaborate plans. At 22:02 hours the Sabena flight's main engineer opened the front cabin door and slid to the tarmac—ostensibly to fix several problems with the electrical power and hydraulics that had come to his attention. "Ma le'azazel hoo ose?" ("What the hell is he doing?") was heard at the forward Israeli CP; not knowing if the individual was an innocent or a terrorist, the commandos lying in the darkened field gingerly placed the pressure of their trigger fingers on their AK trigger housings. The leaders tried to figure out a way to inform the Belgian crew that the mechanical difficulties were deliberate, but communications were impossible, and the unknowing Belgian crewman was the focus of over a dozen gunsights.

At 23:00 hours Lieutenant Colonel Barak once again returned to the aircraft with his team of commandos and mechanics. This time they let the air out of the 707's tires and removed the metal pins that connected the wheels to the main landing gear. Only when the aircraft began listing to one side did Captain Reginald Levy realize his aircraft was being intentionally grounded. Not wishing to alarm the terrorists, Levy gave a silent hand signal in the cockpit, and a sigh of relief went through the Belgian crew. One way or another, their ordeal would end soon, and it would end in Israel.

While Ehud Barak was shuttling between the Sabena aircraft and his perplexed commanders, the remainder of the Sayeret Mat'kal commandos summoned to Lod had managed to reach the airport. Although the unit, according to foreign reports, was believed to be a conscript force, reservists were called as well. One of those Milu'imniks was an NCO named Itzik who had completed his mandatory military service with the unit a year earlier. Although out of the game, he was one of the unit's legendary marksmen with an automatic, and his services were urgently needed. In fact, he was one among several reservists—all especially proficient with handguns—who were called up.[15] It was obvious that explosive action would be taken.

As the negotiations continued into the early morning hours and Major General Yariv and an intelligence officer known only as Haim continued the process of stalling for time, Ehud Barak assembled his commandos at the nearby headquarters of Israel Aircraft Industries in a hangar that housed a Boeing 707. Two teams of commandos armed with 9mm Berettas and Uzi 9mm submachine guns were positioned at the sides of the aircraft. Should the terrorists act in a violent fashion, these commandos would be tasked with engaging the terrorists alone. The force, led by Sergeant Sh.*, remained in position—four hundred meters away—

---

*Identities are protected for security reasons.

throughout the crisis.[16] The training lasted through the night. Although the commando force had practiced for such a scenario, this was it—show time! Under direction of Lieutenant B., a cocky and brilliant young officer, the force honed its movements: up the Boeing's wings, across the fuselage to the emergency exits, and finally the explosive entry into the aircraft.

The noise of boots stomping on the fragile wing frame filled the echoing hangar, as did shouts of *"Yoter maher"* ("Faster!") and *"Ze a'adain lo beseder"* ("It's still not right"). In Israel, where there are twenty viewpoints for every ten citizens, the debate among the commando officers as how to coordinate the rescue mission was heated and emotional. Such debate in the Israel Defense Forces is common and, in fact, welcomed. It is a unique attribute of the IDF's egalitarian ethic that senior commanders and junior officers (as well as NCOs and "mere" conscripts) can openly discuss and debate military strategies, planning, and conditions. This *ozen kashevet* (sympathetic ear) contributes greatly to Israel's traditional military success; rank is rarely pulled, and dissenting views are never held against a soldier. The debates inside the hangar continued, as did the maneuvering and calibrating of tactics and assault techniques. Throughout these exercises, in which a stopwatch dictated success or failure, Barak was in contact with the Chief of Staff and the Defense Minister. Every development in the negotiations was relayed to the commandos—after all, that dictated when or if the unit would be required to act.

After several hours of absolutely exhausting assault practice a rare smile appeared on Lieutenant Colonel Barak's face. Finally the method for attack had been established and perfected. The commandos would disguise themselves as El Al mechanics, wearing white coveralls, and would approach the aircraft as if to conduct preflight maintenance. As they milled about the aircraft—under the watchful gaze of an armed terrorist, it was believed—they would slowly and discreetly position themselves close to the aircraft's four emergency exits. When unit commander Barak sounded the signal—a loud, elongated whistle—the commandos, divided in groups of two or three, would, if necessary, eliminate the watchful terrorist and then proceed to enter the aircraft. They would race along the passageways of the 707 in established teams and eliminate the terrorists with .22 Beretta automatics. The specially adapted .22-caliber rounds were less powerful than the 9mm, for example, but this was not a situation where massive firepower was needed. The terrorists had to be immobilized and the hostages secured. Justice—either biblical or judicial—would take care of the rest.

Ambulances were left with their engines running, just in case they would be needed in a hurry, and passenger buses were positioned to evacuate the hostages as quickly as possible from the aircraft. To make their descent from the exits comfortable, dozens of military mattresses were readied.[17]

The return of the commandos to the forward CP signaled to all that they were ready. They were given a quick "IDF breakfast" of cottage cheese, olives, black coffee, and as much nicotine as could be absorbed into the lungs of a human being; they were then told to sit tight and wait. Negotiations, however, were still under way; in fact, they were expanding. Haim, speaking in flawless Arabic, was ordered to enter into a psychological discussion with the hijackers; he was trying to establish their mood, status of alertness, and any other bits of invaluable intelligence that might aid the rescue attempt. It was a most difficult task—especially considering that the terrorists were resigned to their own deaths and that the assembled who's who of the top brass expected the intelligence officer to solve the problem for them. Haim's efforts were assisted and complicated by visits from a Belgian government contingent that wanted to offer the hijackers $2 million to forget the whole mess (they refused), as well as a visit by representatives of the International Red Cross who offered their assistance. The IRC contingent proceeded toward the aircraft but was not allowed to enter; Captain Rifat addressed them with a bullhorn and reiterated his demands. To buy time, Israeli

Defense Minister Dayan dispatched the IRC representatives once again—a clear effort to buy more time and hopefully wait the terrorists out.

At 13:00 hours on May 9 the terrorists sent Captain Levy on a last-minute mission to the Israelis to prove once and for all that they meant business. They warned the Israelis that they'd be sending them the Sabena pilot with a small gift: a potent sample of the explosives with which they'd blow up the aircraft should their demands not be met. Levy's mission, a brief discussion with the Israeli political and military leadership, proved crucial to the execution of the rescue assault. First, he provided accurate information on the weapons the terrorists brandished as well as on their mental outlook. Second, he told an inquisitive Lieutenant Colonel Barak that there were in fact four terrorists—two men and two women. The Israelis had prepared their attack under the assumption that there were only three terrorists (and that there were only gunmen, not gunwomen) on board the aircraft. Last-minute adjustments had to be made to the commandos' plan. The IAI hangar was cleared of all civilian employees once again, and the commandos resumed work to refine their assault plan.

The thinking at the forward CP was that once the terrorists were convinced that the Israelis had acquiesced to their demands, they would be lulled into a premature sense of security and jubilation—and then they would be ripe for termination. To accomplish this objective, an elaborate masquerade was orchestrated at Lod. It involved agreeing to the terrorists' demands. A TWA airliner, parked at Lod after bringing a planeload of tourists in from New York, was drafted to ferry the 317 released Palestinians to Cairo. The "released" individuals would be, in fact, IDF personnel, who exchanged their olive fatigues for track suits—the favored attire among prisoners released from Israeli incarceration. They were brought to Lod on special-looking buses; according to several reports, the soldiers had their heads shaven and were Sephardic Jews chosen for their Byzantine features.[18] Captain Rifat was even allowed to speak to the released terrorists on a telephone link-up the

Israelis, mysteriously enough, were only too happy to provide.

By midafternoon the time for action was nearing. Emergency contingencies were readied while Barak's force shed its olive fatigues and put on the El Al coveralls. Each man's .22, fully loaded, cocked, and with one round in the chamber, was placed inside an inner pocket. As they completed their final briefing and made their way to the El Al luggage carrier that would ferry them toward the hijacked aircraft, Brigadier General Manno Shaked shouted *a'tzor* (stop) at the top of his lungs. In the haste to end the ordeal in the only way they knew how, Lieutenant Colonel Barak had forgotten one small detail: the commandos were still wearing their brown leather parachutist jump boots—a tragic giveaway. The El Al depot was immediately raided and proper work boots found. Taking nothing for granted this time, Barak inspected his troops, making sure they looked like civilian mechanics and not commandos. After a brief smile Barak ordered his men to take their planned positions.

Through the short ride to the tarmac on El Al luggage pulleys the group (some reports say there were twelve commandos involved in the raid, while other eyewitness versions placed seventeen coverall-clad commandos at the scene) attempted to act and appear as natural as possible, but the men had to be physically poised for action should a nervous terrorist open fire. As they slowly approached the aircraft they received instructions from the IRC representative who was obeying the terrorists' demand that he remain at the foot of the plane. According to Captain Rifat's careful orders, each mechanic approached the cockpit area and presented himself, opening up his outfit to prove that he was unarmed. Immediately Lieutenant Colonel Barak—the man who, in true Israeli fashion, would lead the assault—issued a quick order to his men to conceal their weapons as best they could. Should their true identities be discovered, they were to deal with the terrorist looking on and then break into the aircraft as planned. A mere security check would not hinder their plans.

As Captain Rifat looked on from the cockpit window each

commando/mechanic presented himself, showed "documentation," and then slowly opened up the front zipper of the coverall, dropping the white nylon jumpsuit to his lower chest area. As the procession continued a member of the Sabena crew was lowered to the tarmac and ordered to frisk each individual. The stewards, still smartly dressed in their blue and white Sabena uniforms, naturally discovered that the men entrusted with refueling the aircraft were carrying weapons. At first the commandos simply relied on body language and a blink, but then Lieutenant Colonel Barak explained that the weapons were merely for self-defense. Whether or not the Belgians knew what was transpiring, they kept quiet about it. According to one of the commandos, in an anonymous interview with the Israeli press, "This was the most anxious segment of the operation."

Barak's men quickly assembled at their strategic points of entry, appearing as if they were attending to the aircraft while waiting for the right moment to begin the assault. In an almost comic interruption one of the commandos asked Barak if the mission could be delayed a few moments while he raced to the nearby bushes to empty his bowels. The commando was a young reservist named Tzur who had arrived at Lod only hours earlier, after serving as a skymarshal on an El Al flight. As the dozen or so commandos milled about looking busy and Tzur attended to his needs, the generals, politicians, and intelligence agents looking on from the main building stood in silence and in utter disbelief. "Over a hundred lives are on the line, and this guy is taking a dump!" A few moments later, however, Tzur resumed his position and awaited his commander's whistle.[19]

At 16:29 hours on May 9 Lieutenant Colonel Barak shouted the magic word *"hikon"* (stand by). The force produced shiny black Berettas from their outfits, placed them in their left hands, and pointed the weapons skyward as they prepared to jump into firing position. Slowly three teams of three climbed aboard the wings while a fourth group managed to free a hatch underneath the cockpit. Seconds later, when the roar of jet traffic taking off and landing nearby seemed muted, Barak's long-awaited whistle was heard. The rescue of Flight 751 was under way.

Itzik, an NCO in the unit personally selected to participate in the operation by Barak, led the assault through the left side door. He immediately encountered a terrorist—Abdel Aziz al-Atrash—and blew him away with an unforgiving point-blank burst of .22 fire. One down. Another squad, which had entered through a rear door, was alerted by screaming passengers that a terrorist was hiding nearby, lying on the floor in fetal position. The terrorist was Ruma Isa Tanus. She was rushed outside without being harmed. Two down.

Sergeant Uri, another veteran commando NCO, managed to enter the aircraft without any difficulty but encountered Captain Rifat, who shot half a magazineful of 9mm fire in his general direction. Uri, realizing that he had been hit in the hand by a bullet, rolled to the floor inside a galley. He rose to his feet in a Ninja-like burst of leg muscle and inner balance and immediately aimed his weapon at the terrorist leader. Rifat, however, sought refuge in the forward lavatories. It was a fatal mistake. Three commandos lunged into the crouched firing position and pumped magazineloads of lead into the lightly armored lavatories; the low-velocity cartridges tore through the fiberglass walls and into the desperate captain. The restroom door was kicked in, and Captain Rifat's termination was confirmed. Three down.

The last terrorist was Tirza, known to the hostages by her nom de guerre, Samira. Although no weapons were discovered on her body, she was carrying an electronic transmitter that, it was believed, could activate a booby-trapped explosive device positioned in the front of the aircraft. In immediate and no-nonsense fashion the commandos proceeded to interrogate her, attempting to determine if there could be a fifth terrorist on board. During the questioning she was slapped around and manhandled. The questioning was carried out by Marko, one of the burliest fighters among the commandos, who shook Samira frantically, fearing that seconds were ticking down before the explosives she had planted turned the 707 into a fiery coffin for all those on board. During the struggle Marko's gun went off, wounding Samira and Lieutenant B., a man who, according to legend, was Benjamin "Bibi" Netanyahu.[20] Bibi, a man who would become known to millions of Americans as Israel's ambassador to the United Nations and as Israel's deputy foreign minister during the Iraqi SCUD attacks and the 1991 Madrid Middle East peace talks, would also become his nation's most eloquent and impassioned spokesman against terrorism. As will be seen later in this book, his brother Yoni was also a member of Sayeret Mat'kal and was killed while leading the rescue raid on Entebbe, Uganda, nearly four years later.

After the needed information concerning the explosives was obtained from a badly bleeding Samira, she was led down the wing and into custody; the commando force was now reinforced by the remainder of the summoned unit, wearing regular olive fatigues and AK-47s that made them appear overdressed for the occasion. It was four down— side retired.

The rescue of Flight 751 became known as Operation Isotope 1. It lasted all of ninety seconds, in which over sixty .22-caliber bullets were fired in deliberate bursts aimed at anyone that moved. Tragically, that included passenger Miri Holtzberg, twenty-two, who stood up during the assault. She was killed, and a few other passengers were wounded.

The top brass emerged from their command post, embracing the white-clad Barak, greeting released hostages, and addressing the press. Politicians are, after all, politicians. The ambulances were returned to hospitals and emergency clinics throughout Israel, while the 317 about-to-be-released "Palestinian terrorists" were denied their short plane trip to Cairo and returned to their day-to-day jobs in the IDF. Passengers preparing to board flights out of the country, and family and friends who came to greet newly arrived travelers, went about as if nothing had happened. Lod was back to normal, although the respite from bloodshed would be all too temporary.

The commandos were immediately removed from the

scene and allowed a few moments of celebration among themselves and, later, with the grateful former hostages they had freed.

Terrorism, which appeared to be the scourge and currency of the early 1970s, was dealt a humiliating defeat at Lod—one still held in high regard in the history books.

Operation Isotope 1 was a precedent of enormous proportions. It proved that military forces could defeat terrorist attacks head-on if a nation and its leaders were willing to take the risk of promulgating an unflinching policy against acquiescence. The operation proved once again that the soldiers of the IDF—especially the Chief of Staff's Boys—were capable of just about anything. The brilliant operation proved again that Israel, more than any other nation, was at the cutting edge of developing and perfecting battlefield innovations. The operation and the reputation of the Chief of Staff's Boys was not lost on police, intelligence, and security forces throughout the world, such as the British SAS, nor was it lost on other IDF units. One such force, Sayeret Haruv, the IDF Central Command's reconnaissance battalion, demanded a role in any future airline rescue operation. Since Lod Airport, in the absolute center of Central Command, was within their jurisdiction, they trained intensively in storming an enemy-held airliner, utilizing the Sayeret Mat'kal–developed tactics as a role model.[21]

In a much-covered-up event, Sayeret Haruv would finally have its chance to storm such an aircraft. In 1973 an Italian airliner was hijacked to Lod's Ben-Gurion International Airport. Immediately Sayeret Haruv was summoned from an operational assignment in the Jordan Valley to Lod, where equipment was readied for an assault. Unfortunately for the fighters preparing their AK-47 weapons, rappelling hooks, and stun explosives, a fierce debate was under way between the OC Central Command, Major General Zeevi, and A'man boss Major General Eli Zeira as to which unit—Haruv or, it is believed, Sayeret Mat'kal—would execute the rescue bid. Zeevi and Haruv won; unfortunately, the hijacker turned out to be a mental patient armed with a plastic gun.* The unit's chance for glory was seriously undermined.[22]

Operation Isotope 1, in fact, became Sayeret Mat'kal's calling card even though the unit was never officially credited with the undertaking. In their 1977 film on the Entebbe raid titled *Operation Yonatan,* Israeli producers Menachem Golan and Yoram Globus even began their movie with a rousing ad hoc Mat'kal training assault on a terrorist-held airliner.

Hollywood aside, neither the Israeli press or the government ever admitted to the fact that Sayeret Mat'kal executed Operation Isotope 1. In various accounts they are referred to as an elite unit, a chosen unit, or a special force of commandos. In fact, following the operation they were referred to in the Israeli media as "Israel's Angels in White." No matter who was given public credit for the brilliant raid, Sayeret Mat'kal's war against terrorism, and Black September in particular, had only just begun.

# NOTES

1. Although this famous incident was quoted in numerous books and journals—most notably David Hirst's *The Gun and the Olive Branch* (London: Futura Publications Ltd., 1978), 307—this was reaffirmed by a senior Jordanian military analyst who, for obvious reasons, wishes to remain anonymous.

2. Ariel Merari and Shlomoh Elad, *The International*

---

*Coincidentally, one of the Sayeret Haruv commandos who stormed the Italian airliner was Major Yair Klein, a man who would be implicated in exporting arms and providing training to Colombian drug dealers in the 1980s.

Dimension of Palestinian Terrorism (Tel Aviv: Jaffe Center for Strategic Studies, Tel Aviv University Press, 1986), 131.

3. John Laffin, *Fedayeen* (New York: The Free Press, 1973), 60–61.

4. Abd'allah Franji, *The PLO and Palestine* (London: Zed Books, 1982), 118.

5. Edgar O'Ballance, *The Language of Violence: The Blood Politics of Terrorism* (San Rafael: Presidio Press, 1979), 109.

6. Roni Elroy, "Ha'Pritza Be'Lavan," *Biton Heyl Ha'Avir,* March 1987, 8.

7. *Ibid.,* 10. Although Ehud Barak isn't mentioned by name as the commander of the unit in this IAF magazine article, it is known and accepted as absolute fact that the wily lieutenant colonel was the unit commander mentioned.

8. *Ibid.,* 8.

9. Merav Arlozorov, "Ha'Termit Pa'alah," *Bamachane Hutz Le'Aretz,* September 1987, 12.

10. Uri Milshtein, *Ha'Historia Shel Ha'Tzanhanim: Kerech Daled* (Tel Aviv: Schalgi Ltd. Publishing House, 1987), 1596.

11. Roni Daniel, "Model 1971," *El-Ha'Matarah,* Vol. 13, 1990, 26.

12. Roni Elroy, "Ha'Pritza Be'Lavan," 10.

13. *Ibid.,* 10.

14. Interview with El Al employee working at the airport on the night of May 8–9, 1972.

15. Merav Arlozorov, "Ha'Termit Pa'alah," 12.

16. Uri Milshtein, *Ha'Historia Shel Ha'Tzanhanim,* 1597.

17. *Ibid.,* 1597.

18. Edgar O'Ballance, *Language of Violence,* 113.

19. Merav Arlozorov, "Ha'Termit Pa'alah," 12.

20. *Ibid.,* 12.

21. Ron Edist and Ya'akov Erez, *Sayerot U'Mi'utim: Tzahal Be'Heilo Entzyklopedia Le'Tzava Ule'Bitachon* (Tel Aviv: Revivim, 1983), 100.

22. *Ibid.,* 100.

# 5

## An Even Swap in the North

*Operation Crate 3*
*June 21, 1972*

April 2, 1970. The atmosphere at the anonymous air base in
northern Israel was calm and confident. The control tower
was bustling with activity—radio chatter engulfed the enclosed glass space as officers and NCOs gazed through radar
screens and field glasses in a mad dash to control the dense
air traffic surrounding the sprawling facility. The tarmac
was chaotic, but orderly in a mad military sense. Ground
crewmen hurried about pulling hoses, driving fuel trucks,
and loading five-hundred-pound bombs onto jets painted in
a dazzling three-color camouflage scheme. The miragelike
vapor of burning jet fuel immersed the landscape in a
shimmering portrait of destructive power. Planes took off
with external fuel tanks, bombs, and missiles—and they
returned empty. The roar of engines was deafening.

One of the aircraft taking off that afternoon was a
McDonnell-Douglas F-4E Phantom—the sledgehammer of
the Israel Air Force—piloted by Gideon Magen, thirty-two,
and his navigator, Pini Nachmani, twenty-six.[1] The Phantom had been in IAF service for less than a year, but its
impact on the tactics and capabilities of the Israel Air Force
were profound. Able to fly at twice the speed of sound, the

F-4E Phantom could engage hostile aircraft in aerial combat with its 20mm cannon or its lethal array of Sparrow and Sidewinder missiles. The Phantom could carry over sixteen thousand pounds of bombs and rockets, a fact that made it deadly to ground targets. It was, is, and will continue to be the IAF's most potent piece of artillery. This spring day the IAF's prime artillery piece's gunsights targeted Syria.

Since July 1967 the War of Attrition had been fought primarily along the Suez Canal, where Egyptian and Israeli forces battled each other with brutal artillery barrages, air strikes, and commando raids. The conflict was also waged in the desert of the Jordan Valley, the mountainous hell that separated Israel from Jordan on the West Bank, where infiltrating Palestinian terrorists and IDF reconnaissance units fought a brutal campaign of wits, instinct, and death. The northern front, as Israel's border with Lebanon and Syria was called, remained relatively peaceful—quiet, that is, by Middle Eastern standards. There were Palestinian terrorist attacks emanating from Lebanese territory, and the Syrians occasionally shelled IDF positions on the Golan Heights plateau. In 1970, however, the Syrians upped the ante in an attempt to establish a third and decisively fatal front. They increased the ferocity and frequency of their artillery strikes and escalated their military support for Palestinian terrorists operating out of Fatahland, the crucible around Mt. Hermon connecting Lebanon, Syria, and Israel. Israel upped the ante as well. Air strikes were the IAF's ace in the hole.

The mission for Magen's and Nachmani's Phantom was to remove (an antiseptic term for "obliterate") a series of Syrian 130mm guns that had harassed new Israeli settlements atop the Golan Heights. The bombing run eventually turned into a chase against two Syrian Air Force MiG-21P Fishbeds that rose up for the challenge and the intercept. Over the skies of the lavish Damascus suburbs a dogfight transpired where 20mm tracer fire and subsonic roars filled the sky. Unlike most engagements between Arab and Israeli aircraft, this one would not end with only the MiGs being destroyed. Although the two MiGs were blown out of the sky by the Phantom, the F-4E also suffered a fatal hit and began to disintegrate in midair. The two airmen ejected successfully, landing in the hilly terrain just outside the Syrian capital. Hoping that a chopper from the IAF's Aeromedical Evacuation Unit would pick up their signal and pluck them out of harm's way in a brilliant rescue operation, the Israelis attempted to evade the scores of Syrian military units that raced to the sight of their descending parachutes. Since the advanced stages of their pilot's training Magen and Nachmani had been indoctrinated with horror stories of life in Syrian captivity. It was a much-feared element of IAF folklore, and preventing the torture and cruelty of a Muchabarat interrogation was the immediate concern for these two airmen. Other thoughts, however, slipped past their well-trained reflexes; after all, Nachmani's newborn was only two weeks old.

The choppers never came. The two were apprehended and taken into custody. Brutally questioned, beaten and tortured in barbaric fashion, both airmen seemed doomed in their newfound hell. In one of the many violations of the Geneva Convention of 1949 the Syrians committed against the IAF airmen, they forbade representatives of the International Red Cross to visit the captured Phantom crew. In another convention violation, Syrian TV actually broadcast live segments of the interrogation—including acts of violence committed against the two—to an eager audience. Oddly enough, this was seen as good news in IAF HQ in Tel Aviv. It was the first sign that the two men were alive. IDF Chief of Staff Bar Lev vowed to facilitate their release no matter what the cost. Patience, however, would be necessary.

On June 24, 1970, as part of what became known as Operation Cotton 10, massive armor battles transpired between Israeli and Syrian forces on the southern tier of the Golan Heights, the section that touches the Jordanian frontier. While the primary objective of the operation was Israel's removal of a massive Syrian artillery and armor buildup along the Golan, as well as the destruction of their extensive border fortifications, the underlying aim of the armored incursion into Syria was to capture as many prisoners as possible—human barter to be bargained off for the two Phantom crewmen held in the notorious el-Mazeh prison in Damascus.[2] In the fierce battles that took place for three days without respite, twelve IDF soldiers were killed and fifty-eight wounded. The Syrians lost 350 dead and 150 wounded, and twenty-six of their top-line main battle tanks were destroyed. Most importantly, the IDF seized thirty-seven Syrian soldiers. They were attended to in humane fashion, offered to the International Red Cross for inspection, and then offered to the Syrian government in exchange for the two IAF crewmen.

There was one small snag in Israel's grand scheme. During Operation Cotton 10, an IAF Mirage IIIC delta-wing fighter bomber—the French-built dynamo that virtually gave Israel the air victory in 1967—was shot down by ground fire while providing close-air support. The pilot, Boaz Eitan, was unable to maneuver his flaming jet back to friendly lines and was forced to parachute inside Syrian territory. He, too, was captured by the Syrians, showcased, tortured, and sent to el-Mazeh prison for a tenure of solitude and beatings.

Confident after their latest snare, the Syrians refused Israel's offer to exchange prisoners of war. A catch of thirty-seven Syrian conscripts, it appeared, was not worth three Israeli airmen.

June 1972. The spring of 1972 was a period of triumph and horror for Israel's war against terrorism. On May 8–9 the Chief of Staff's Boys struck in spectacular fashion in Operation Isotope 1, proving that decisive military action could defeat an equally decisive terrorist operation. Then, on May 30, terrorists would prove just how little Operation Isotope 1 had dented their ability and desire to exact blood from the Jewish state. Three Japanese Red Army terrorists working on behalf of Dr. George Habash's Popular Front for the Liberation of Palestine flew into Lod Airport on an Air France flight from Rome. After completing the passport control procedures without the slightest hint of suspicion, they proceeded toward the luggage belt to retrieve their bags, which had gone unchecked in Rome. From their cases the three produced a cache of Czech assault rifles and grenades, and they opened fire in a melee of death and carnage. Before Israeli policemen and border guards could react forcefully, twenty-nine passengers were killed and seventy-two injured; the majority of dead and wounded were Puerto Rican Catholics who were on a pilgrimage to the Holy Land.[3] Two of the terrorists were killed—one by an Israeli policeman who braved the barrage of automatic fire to cut one terrorist down with pistol fire, and one by his own hand. The third gunman, Kozo Okamoto, was captured and, following a sensational trial in Jerusalem, sentenced to life imprisonment.* The incident, known as the Lod Airport Massacre, became engraved in the minds of Israeli citizens as the embodiment of their nation's vulnerability to wanton acts of barbarity. The filmed newscasts of airport workers mopping up a tiled floor an inch deep in blood horrified the Israeli nation and outraged the Israeli leadership even more.

The Lod Airport Massacre, such a disastrous event for a nation still celebrating the "Angels in White" rescue of the Sabena hostages, warranted decisive action. Some form of retribution would have to be exercised.

The massacre at Lod was the culmination of a three-pronged wave of terrorist attacks against Israel that needed to be addressed. First, the spring of 1972 was the season of the letter bomb; eleven such deadly devices were mailed to Israeli and Jewish interests worldwide. Second came the Sabena hijacking—an operation that did not end as the terrorists had planned. Finally, there was the Japanese Red

---

*After going insane in an Israeli jail, where he tried to convert to Islam and then to Judaism (by attempting to circumcise himself with a spoon), Kozo Okamoto was released in May 1985 in a highly controversial human exchange engineered by the Popular Front for the Liberation of Palestine General Command (PFLP-GC) warlord Ahmed Jibril. The deal swapped three Israeli soldiers kidnapped by the PFLP-GC in Lebanon for 1,150 Palestinian and international terrorists held in Israeli prisons. Among those released in the deal were several men who three years later played a major role in the bombing of Pan Am flight 103 over Lockerbie, Scotland, in December 1988.

*Samuel M. Katz*

Army's killings at Lod. This new terrorist offensive demanded an Israeli retaliatory operation that would deter Palestinian terrorists and their international mercenaries from carrying out further such actions. Yet still on the back burner in the planning sessions at Operations Branch HQ was the fate of the three Israeli airmen languishing in the damp hell of their el-Mazeh prison cells. If one operation could combine these objectives, the interests of the State of Israel would be brilliantly served. The IDF chief of staff, Lieutenant General David "Dado" Elazar, knew exactly who to call. Lieutenant Colonel Barak's force of commandos was summoned at once.[4]

The matter of where to attack was simple: Lebanon. Since the Black September in Jordan, Lebanon had become the Palestinians' principal base of operations for "liberation missions" against Israel. What to strike, however, proved to be a more difficult choice. For months the frontier with Lebanon had been heating up: Katyusha rockets were fired against Galilee agricultural settlements; land mines were planted around the kibbutzim in the north; rockets were fired at Israeli patrols across the heavily fortified frontier; and RPGs were launched at a tourist bus in northern Israel. Lebanon was also proving to be the international terrorist mecca, the training capital for the world's political assassins and anarchists. Revolutionaries from South America, Europe, Africa, and Asia trekked to the refugee camps along Lebanon's Mediterranean coastline to learn the secrets of bomb-making, assassination, and politically inspired bloodletting from the true masters of the game: the PLO. Although the Lebanese government, fearing massive Israeli retaliation (especially following the Lod Massacre), went out of the way to disassociate itself from the Palestinian terrorists operating within its boundaries, the relationship between the Lebanese state and terrorism was irrefutable. Kozo Okamoto and his Red Army gunmen had trained in Palestinian camps in Lebanon.

Palestinian terrorist operations against Israel and the worrisome involvement of the terrorists in Lebanese affairs was increasing; oddly enough, for Operations Branch

112

planners, that was good news. It meant the Palestinians were assisted in their activities by sophisticated means—in Lebanon that meant the Syrians, and Syrian intelligence in particular. The connection between terrorism, Lebanon, and Syrian intelligence offered an enticing scenario for Israeli planners that would lay the groundwork for a classic commando operation that would not only secure the release of the three captive IAF airmen and restrain Palestinian terrorism but would also reap enormous espionage points. The contingency was known as Operation Crate.

The importance and remarkable nature of this operation were made evident by the fact that it required the authorization of Israeli Prime Minister Golda Meir; kidnapping so senior a group of enemy officers as was targeted that June evening required approval at the highest level. A nation-state is not an underground entity, and kidnapping is not an official state policy. Yet the circumstances in this case were different. Everyone involved understood that. Israelis are asked to sacrifice a great deal of their civilian existences to defend Eretz Yisrael (the Land of Israel): three years of conscripted service and a month-long yearly stint in the reserves until age fifty-five. Beyond the obvious sense of patriotism and duty and the back-against-the-wall psychology that makes Israelis into such fine combat soldiers, Israelis fight and take risks because they know that should they be hurt or captured, the IDF will do its utmost to extract them. The IDF's utmost meant military action to free them.

This is why Golda sanctioned the mission, and this is why the Chief of Staff's Boys were called in.

The Lebanese-Israeli border was a paradox of realities. The two warring nations were separated by a heavily fortified fence put up by the Israelis. The fence, which stretched from the Mediterranean shore at Rosh Hanikra to the reaches of the Golan Heights, near Mt. Hermon in Fatahland, consisted of rows of concertina, trip wires, mine fields, and electronic sensors; its most potent fortification was a thin, sandy strip of roadway patrolled by command cars. Each command car, staffed by heavily armed combat troops, was supplemented by a Bedouin, Druze, or Circassian tracker who, by reading marks on the sand road, could interpret whether or not infiltrators had crossed the fence and in which direction they were heading. If the tracker was really good, he could also determine what weight load they were carrying (the telltale sign for this was the imprint of the mark).[5] The border was one of the most heavily guarded in the world, yet through the barbed wire defenses Israeli forces could see Lebanese farmers tending to their fields, and Lebanese gendarmes could wave hello to small children at play in the kibbutzim. At many points the main Israeli civilian road along the frontier was separated from the main Lebanese roadway by only one hundred meters. This proximity would be ideally manipulated in the execution of Operation Crate.

Sayeret Mat'kal, according to published sources, was ideally suited for this task—trained for conventional and unconventional warfare, infiltration, and other covert activities that made their "Who Dares Wins" calling card so apt. One of the officers participating in Operation Crate was a young captain named Yonatan "Yoni" Netanyahu, one of the rising stars of the IDF. Although in 1972 his identity was a state secret of the highest order, the veteran reconnaissance officer would make an immortal name for himself in operations to come. Two other officers who clutched their AK-47s in the field during Operation Crate were Lieutenants Benjamin "Bibi" Netanyahu and Ido Netanyahu—making a brotherly triad that would reach fame and immortality in the years to come.[6]

On the night of June 9–10, 1972, it is believed,* Lieutenant Colonel Barak led his kidnap task force (the exact size of which remains classified to this day) across the frontier into the pitch-black abyss of Lebanon. Negotiating the rocky terrain, Barak led his heavily armed commandos to an advantageous ambush position in Fatahland, overlooking the main Lebanese roadway near the border. Once they were

---

*There have been several versions of what actually transpired in the series of moves that made up Operation Crate. The version presented here, along with names and dates, was compiled from interviews and reports in Israeli military journals and in the media.

in position, AK-47 gunsights and RPGs were directed toward the thoroughfare where vehicles—both soft-skinned and armored—that ferried Syrian "visitors" to the Israeli border would travel. A close-knit network of commandos armed with field glasses and field radios provided a hermetic surveillance cover for the attackers—any vehicle coming in from the north, west, or east would be picked up by the unit in time to set up the attack.

At a rather elaborate forward field command post hastily established just inside Israeli territory overlooking Lebanon sat the IDF chief of staff, Lieutenant General Dado Elazar, and the OC Northern Command, Major General Mordechai "Motta" Gur, himself a veteran paratroop and reconnaissance officer. They followed every step of the operation and listened to Barak's progress with anxious anticipation. Going through pack after pack of harsh Israeli cigarettes and Turkish coffee laced with cardamom, the two senior commanders sat glued to their earpieces, the chatter and squelch sounds adding unnecessary tension to an already electrified enclosed space.

Through a full night of surveillance and frayed nerves the expected convoy never reached Fatahland. Either intelligence was off or the Syrians had found something better to do with their time in Lebanon. Feelings of betrayal and disappointment began to grip Barak's commandos; after all, Yoni Netanyahu had confidently encouraged his fighters prior to the operation with the cocky words "Let's show these guys how we kidnap someone."[7] His men wanted action, they wanted to score this most important victory, and they wanted to secure the release of their comrades. Operation Crate 1 was history.

A few days later, on the night of June 12–13, another attempt was made to execute the kidnapping; this time it was known as Operation Crate 2. Lieutenant Colonel Barak commanded the primary ambush force, tasked with stopping and apprehending the convoy of vehicles. Replacing Yoni, and in command of the force assigned to block off any Lebanese reinforcements, was his younger brother Bibi, an officer of equal talent and charisma. This time the locus was an area of the volatile, terrorist-controlled Fatahland closer

115

to the heavily populated Mediterranean belt near the central area of the border. The commando force once again crossed the desolate frontier and assumed advantageous offensive firing positions overlooking a twisting and turning part of the road where the targeted vehicles would have to pass at lower speeds. Uzis were locked and loaded, and AK banana magazines were gingerly touched as gunsights were directed onto the road below. All that was needed was the green light.

Barak's task force found the thorny weeds and foliage perfect camouflage—too perfect, perhaps. Their radios were buzzing with coded passwords as commando leaders checked in with the Chief of Staff at the command post, when a herd of sheep and a shepherd suddenly stumbled across their position. The sheep began grazing at the feet of the commandos, sniffing their boots and innocently coming close to exposing the Israeli firing positions. The shepherd, intimate with the terrain, immediately knew something was wrong when he heard a telltale silence signaling impending trouble—no command cars on the other side of the fence and no IAF flybys. As the boy, wearing the traditional white *kefiyeh*, continued forward along the paved path he found a booby-trapped explosive device Barak's men had placed by the road to slow down any potential escape by the Syrian automobiles. A few seconds of chaotic anxiety overtook the commandos. Gunsights were directed at the boy, and commando knives were removed from their scabbards. But Barak ordered the shepherd seized, not killed, and one of the commandos raced out of his crouched position to grab the young boy. After struggling with the wily shepherd in a noisy fuss, Ido Netanyahu placed one finger over his lips and another finger across his throat in a menacingly cutting fashion—he passed his hand in a swordlike wave across his throat, warning the boy to keep quiet, or otherwise he'd be meeting Allah! The shepherd was retired with the help of some rope and a gag, and he sat in silence next to the Israeli commandos. Every ten minutes or so one of the Israeli fighters would give the poor lad the thumbs-up sign to indicate that he'd be all right after all.

Night slowly ground into morning, and still no action. Elements of the task force took a short nap, and others scouted the neighboring terrain for clues. At dawn's first light the convoy finally arrived, but there was a snag: it was escorted by a camouflaged Lebanese Army British-made Alvis Saladin armored car, and the vehicle's 76mm cannon was aimed directly at the commando's ambush position. The armored car placed Barak's men in a precarious position. This time they had only small arms; the heaviest weapon at their disposal was the 7.62mm FN MAG light machine gun, a weapon capable of fire support in an infantry assault but useless against armor. The Saladin was also escorted by a Land Rover filled to capacity with heavily armed Lebanese Army gendarmes. As the convoy of vehicles approached the ambush spot from a distance of seventy meters the choreography for a pitched battle was developing, and it did not look favorable to Israel. The soldiers' trigger fingers tensed, grenades were produced from khaki canvas ammunition pouches, and the adrenaline pumped at a fever's pace.

Barak radioed the details of the developing situation to Chief of Staff Elazar. The news was not encouraging. Elazar realized that this operation's success depended on lightning speed, secrecy, and the prevention of casualties. Both Bibi and Barak urged the Chief of Staff to persevere—they could handle it, they assured him over the radio. Barak even described how he had ordered one of his commandos to jump out along the road and take care of both vehicles with grenades, but their confident pleas to continue the mission fell on deaf ears. Fearing a large-scale engagement, Dado aborted the mission, ordering his boys back home. After the convoy proceeded past the commandos' position they pulled back in disgust. Operation Crate 2 was history.

No one was angered more by Elazar's order to abort the operation than Barak, who felt a painful sense of frustration. A golden opportunity to grab Syrian officers and exact the release of the three Israeli airmen seemed to be lost. The wily lieutenant colonel was livid. This was an extremely bitter pill for the commando unit to swallow, as they looked at the task of liberating their comrades as a sacrosanct mission; many of Barak's commandos personally knew one of the flyers, Nachmani, who had once worked with the force.[8]

For several days A'man lost track of the Syrian officers. Their disappearance heightened the sense of a lost opportunity in the commando camp and raised their anger at Chief of Staff Elazar. Why did they exist as such a highly touted unit if they were not even allowed to execute the type of mission only they could perform? The commandos were an extremely proud group of warriors. They were told from day one in the military that they were the best, that they were a cut above everyone else, and that they would be performing spectacular acts of military daring vital to national security. In reality, it appeared to them that one lousy Lebanese Army armored car had spoiled their efforts. Following the rescue of the Sabena hostages at Lod a month earlier, the callback order in Operation Crate 2 was seen as an ominous insult.

Amid the controversy and anger among the commandos was a remarkable footnote—one that threatened the operation much more than an armored car sporting a Lebanese Army battalion flag. The Lebanese shepherd remained a captive until the Syrian convoy was well out of range. Realizing that the border area with Israel was becoming extremely dangerous, concerned villagers set out to look for him in a desperate and anguished search—with so many armed Palestinians, Lebanese, Syrians, and Israelis roaming the region, they naturally feared the worst. Although Syrian intelligence officers and the Lebanese Army could not find the Israelis lying in ambush, the villagers did. After careful negotiations conducted with respect and Middle Eastern tribal deference, Barak and Ido Netanyahu, both wearing full battle gear and toting their AK-47 7.62mm assault rifles, negotiated with the group of men while their coveted flocks of sheep and goats continued to graze at the commandos' feet. Clearly, the incident with the villagers proved to be a most serious violation of operational security—but still Operation Crate was a go. Even after the plight of the shepherd appeared in a French newspaper a few days later, the Israelis were adamant about executing the operation.[9] The Syrians, intelligence reports learned, had either failed to read the article or were ignoring the potential risk of Israeli action. They continued their work along the frontier. So did the Israelis.

The respite between the second attempt and what was hoped to be the closing chapter of the mission provided the commandos with the coveted opportunity to refine their tactics. The first two failed attempts to apprehend the precious Syrian officers were haphazard assaults: set off a booby-trap device; rush onto the roadway; kill, only if necessary, the accompanying bodyguards; and bring the officers back to Israel. It was a routine task. The delay between the second and third tries, however, afforded the squad the chance to add a degree of sophistication to the attack and to call in for reinforcements should heavier firepower be required; this, it was hoped, would lend a degree of confidence to the frightened top brass, especially Chief of Staff Elazar. To ensure that no bureaucratic order would end this third and, hopefully, final try, Barak attached himself to Elazar's and Gur's command post. He traveled with them, sat with them, ate with them, and if he had been allowed, he would probably have followed them to the latrine. He was determined to impede any decision to cancel the raid yet again. Although only thirty-one years old, Barak was the owner of a notorious reputation as the guiding light of the IDF. Already one of the most decorated officers ever to wear the Tzahal name tape across his fatigue's left breast pocket, he was a confident maverick unwilling to digress from his view of how things should be done. It was a concept he had learned from day one, when Major Avraham Arnan recruited him into the fold and turned the "lock-picking bastard" into Israel's most feared and capable soldier. The unit did whatever it wanted to—it answered to no rules or regulation of regular military service. Now, as commander of the nation's best soldiers, Barak was determined to have his way in this operation. These were his men on the line—Chief of Staff be damned.

For the next foray across the fence Barak's unit would be

enhanced by a formidable array of men and weaponry from other units. For starters, several Centurion MBTs and M3 half-tracks positioned just inside Israeli territory were parked right alongside the fence. The tank unit was one of the best in the IDF and had distinguished itself in special operations in both the 1967 Six-Day War and the subsequent fighting in the war of attrition. Batteries of self-propelled 155mm howitzers, mounted on the backs of Sherman tank chassis by innovative IDF Ordnance Corps personnel, assumed firing positions a few kilometers in the rear; their deadly shells would provide impressive cover fire should a serious engagement develop.

A fleet of M3 World War II–era half-tracks were also parked right alongside the fence. They were manned by reconnaissance paratroopers from Sayeret Egoz, the territorial airborne reconnaissance element of IDF Northern Command.[10] Sayeret Egoz was one of the finest *sayerot* in the IDF and had years of experience operating in the dangerous stretch of territory separating Israel from Lebanon. Although many in Egoz reconnaissance felt that *they* should have been tasked with Operation Crate, they realized certain operations should be delegated to certain units. They were, however, determined to provide a deadly display of speed and automatic fire support should their Mat'kal brothers require assistance.

A force of conscript paratroopers was also mobilized for this operation. They were placed on full battle alert and were ready to be ferried into the melee. Should anything go wrong, these conventional forces would be the ones to engage in the fighting. The IDF was not about to have its best fighters get caught in a death trap so close to Israeli territory.

Opeation Crate 3 was carried out on June 21, 1972.[11]

The size of the Mat'kal force was larger than the one fielded in the two previous attempts. There would be three elements to the raid. Two—one to the west, the other to the east of the site—were cover and blocking forces, while the third and largest force was to execute the kidnapping. Each force would assume ambush position atop a hill command-

THE ELITE

ing not only the main road but large stretches of Lebanese territory as well. This way, should the Lebanese Army be called into the fighting—though it was hoped there would be no fighting—the commandos could act as artillery spotters or call in air strikes. With Barak holding Chief of Staff Elazar and OC Northern Command Gur hostage in the CP, Captain Yoni Netanyahu was given the lead role as commander of the central unit.

The location of the raid was ideal. The Syrian convoy would be traveling along an axis between the Mediterranean and the Israeli town of Metulla. It was a point along the Israeli-Lebanese frontier where only one kilometer separated the road the Syrians would be traveling from the primary road holding Israeli armor.

Yoni's orders were clear and simple. If at all possible, he was to seize the Syrian officers without any gunfire; the purpose of the mission, Barak told him, was to capture them all alive and bring them back to Israel. If this was an impossibility, or if he sensed even the slightest hint of danger to his men, Yoni was to order terminating firepower into the fold.

In the early morning hours of June 21 Yoni's force cut across the frontier into Lebanese territory. While several commandos placed their FN MAG light machine guns in full battle readiness, the commandos were to ward off any potential counterattack. Yoni and his men scanned the roadway for land mines, trip wires, and other defenses. After nearly three hours of this exhaustive and dangerous toil Netanyahu radioed to Barak that all was clear. Barak then ordered three vehicles—two M3s and a civilian car— to proceed to a predetermined point where the Israeli fence had been cut open to facilitate passage of heavy and armored vehicles. The two M3s would assume positions along the road that commanded approaches from both east and west. The third vehicle would also be placed on a strategic stretch of road, but it was to act as a decoy. Its hood would be open, shielding Yoni's squad from view while they milled about it as if the car had overheated. The sight of men attending a sidelined vehicle would not produce suspicion; it would indicate that the frontier was quiet and draw the Syrian and Lebanese column further into the trap.[12]

The hours passed in what seemed like a full day of hurrying up and waiting. Still no convoy was sighted. Fighters became anxious lying in wait for so many hours. Chief of Staff Elazar, a Pal'mach and armored unit veteran, began to express his overt concern that yet another mission had gone wrong.

At 12:00 hours, however, a scout stationed a few klicks up the road radioed Yoni. Civilian vehicles—an Austin and a Chevy Impala—were exiting the village of Ramish, in the north; they were escorted by a Land Rover full of Lebanese gendarmes. Yoni called in his three half-tracks and ordered them to cross the frontier and race the three hundred meters to the Lebanese roadway, setting themselves for the ambush. When they reached a small ditch at the side of the road the commandos, having left their engines running, cocked their Uzis and AKs one final time. Operation Crate 3 was a go.

In the Murphy's Law equation of military operations, something had to go wrong. An Israeli scout waiting to the east of the ambush position failed to notice a Volkswagen Beetle heading straight into the danger zone. In a surreal and comical moment the Lebanese civilian driving the VW gazed out his windshield to see a large force of armed men and sandy gray half-tracks positioned alongside the road; instinctively, he waved at them. Immediately Yoni began to fear that their cover had been blown and the mission compromised. The VW was heading straight down the road, right toward the Syrian convoy, and there was nothing the commandos could do about it. Killing a civilian would ruin the element of surprise and would be a violation of the IDF's Tohar Ha'neshek policy—a moral policy that dictates the use of deadly force and is meant to prevent avoidable civilian casualties. A civilian death might also prove to be politically embarrassing for Israel.

When the VW stopped alongside the Syrian officers and a loud discussion transpired, the order came to spring into action. Yoni ordered the vehicle drivers to floor the gas pedals of the half-tracks and race toward the column before the Syrians could turn tail and escape into the Lebanese countryside.

From the eastern and western flanks commandos raced up the roadway, their weapons at the ready. Yoni's men caught the Syrians as they attempted to flee. Twenty meters away the half-tracks banked sharply and slammed on the brakes, and the fighters jumped out of their rear holding pens. Racing along the roadway toward the Syrian generals, several of the commandos fired warning shots into the air; more commandos soon appeared racing up the paved path, weapons at the ready. At first the Lebanese bodyguards were transfixed in shock—they stood motionless atop their vehicle in a deliberate stare, not really understanding what was happening. The commandos yelled in Arabic, *"I'mdu!"* ("Raise your hands!") The command in Hebrew-accented Arabic brought the Lebanese soldiers back to reality, and they reached for their weapons. A small one-sided firefight broke out. The Lebanese fired wildly, aiming, for some reason, into the tree line, while the Israelis fell into prone firing position and demonstrated their marksmanship. Within seconds five Lebanese lay dead beside their vehicle (four gendarmes and a Lebanese Muchabarat officer). They were cut down by deliberate four-round bursts aimed at their hearts. Two Syrian officers managed to cut and run in the confusion of the exchange, escaping in a green Mercedes limousine that joined the column seconds before the ambush.[13] As the commandos raced to their vehicles to secure the hostages, one of the Syrian officers shouted "No blood" in a deliberately heavy Arabic accent. The five staff officers were rounded up, placed inside the M3 half-track commanded by Captain Botzer, and driven quickly back to Israel. The other M3s and the captured vehicles followed in close pursuit, filled with the joyous commandos. One Syrian officer was wounded in the firefight, as was one Mat'kal commando. Lieutenant D. was also hurt, shot in the leg by pistol fire. Chief of Staff Elazar leaned over to Barak, slapped him on the shoulder, and offered a reassuring and apologetic pat on the back.

When the ensemble returned to Israeli territory, their retreat covered by IDF tank units searching the nearby Lebanese villages for additional Syrian military personnel, the magnitude of the operation became shockingly clear. The five captured Syrians included Brigadier General Adham al-Ra'ani, Colonel Radwan Alush, and Colonel Nazir Jerach (the OC of Syrian Army Field Intelligence), all from the Operations Department of the Syrian Army General Staff. More important, however, were the two lower-ranking officers seized, Lieutenant Colonel Rafik Shurbaji and Lieutenant Colonel Walid Aba'asi. Both were senior commanders in Syrian Air Force Intelligence, the principal military intelligence service the Syrians employed to keep tabs on developments both overseas and internally—developments Syrian Air Force Intelligence controlled brutally.[14] Also seized were Captain Josef Nadif, an intelligence officer in the Lebanese Army General Staff, and three gendarmes. The catch was, in fact, remarkable—even Chief of Staff Elazar had a hard time comprehending the implications stemming from the men his boys had seized. It was as if during World War II British commandos had captured senior officers of Hitler's High Command, or as if German paratroopers had seized staff officers of Eisenhower's command. These were the men who made the Syrian Army work, directed its operations, and gathered and analyzed its intelligence data. These were the men whose talents and positions allowed Syria to threaten Israel. Thanks to Lieutenant Colonel Barak's commandos, they were now in Israeli hands.

Immediately upon learning of what the IDF had done the Syrians offered to exchange the three IAF airmen for their captured top brass. Now it was Israel's turn to refuse to barter. The human bazaar was temporarily closed. A'man was too busy interrogating the high-ranking prisoners to relinquish them immediately, and Israel was now increasing its demands: It wanted the Syrians to convince their friends in Egypt to release several IAF airmen they were holding. The Israelis were stalling for time. They knew the pilots were now safe. They would be spared beatings, sensory deprivation, and psychological torture. They would be allowed visits from the International Red Cross. Back in Israel the five officers provided inquisitive A'man officers with an unbelievably intimate look at the Syrian military, its thought processes, and how the Syrian soldier thought and was trained to operate. Such intelligence rewards had been the basis for the creation of Sayeret Mat'kal in 1957. The five offered their inquisitors invaluable tidbits of information on the psychological makeup of the Syrian soldier, his training, and his capabilities. It was an extraordinary view of an enemy fighting machine; very few armies in the history of war have been able to obtain such a picture of their opponents. The intelligence obtained was used with great skill and success sixteen months later in the Yom Kippur War.

The five Syrians were exchanged for the three Israeli airmen in June 1973, following intensive negotiations.

Operation Crate 3 achieved secondary objectives as well. Hours after the Mat'kal commandos brought their human booty back to Israeli territory flights of IAF warplanes struck Palestinian terrorist targets in southern Lebanon. The air raids, known as Operation Cut-Up, retaliated for a series of Palestinian attacks against Israeli civilians, including the Lod Airport Massacre; over fifty terrorists were killed, and seventy more were wounded. Ten bombs, however, tragically fell on the Druze village of Hasabiya, killing ten civilians. Operation Crate 3 initiated a forceful Israeli campaign to root out Palestinian terrorist bases from Israel's northern frontier. There was Operation Nuisance, a day-long artillery barrage against Palestinian positions in Fatahland; Operation Cat, a large-scale infiltration of Sayeret Egoz reconnaissance paratroopers into Fatahland; and Operation Honey and Thorn, a naval ambush of Palestinian seaborne elements off the coast of Sidon. On June 27, 1972, one week after the Lebanese border erupted into full-scale war, the Lebanese government ordered the Palestinians to cease and desist their terrorist operations from the northern frontier. For the time being, at least, Galilee was safe.

Operation Crate 3 was a remarkable achievement for Sayeret Mat'kal. It achieved all primary and secondary objectives, it was executed without a single Israeli casualty, and the rewards it produced were of monumental proportions. Like most wars in the Middle East and most IDF special operations, Operation Crate 3 could not, in all its glory, achieve any broader goals of peace through deterrent actions—it only gave the Israeli north a brief respite from terrorist attack. The Palestinians' war against Israel and Israel's war against the Palestinians would, of course, continue. June 1972 was the opening burst of summer—a season that would climax with the Olympics in Munich.

The Chief of Staff's Boys would have very little time to revel in their success. There was still much work to be done.

# NOTES

1. Tamar Golan, "Shirei Herut Be'Kele Damesek," *Ma'ariv Shabat,* April 19, 1989, 1.

2. *Ibid.,* 1.

3. Yechiam Fadan, ed., "Bitachon Yisrael: 40 Shana Lu'ach Eru'im," *Skira Hodshit,* 1988, 66.

4. Yosef Argaman, "Hatifat Ha'Generalim Ha'Surim," *Bamachane Hu'l,* September, 1987, 67.

5. The trackers (or *gashashim,* as they are known in Hebrew) are truly Israel's first line of defense against terrorist infiltration. Uncanny in their abilities to read the terrain, their forty-plus years of courageous service along the Egyptian, Jordanian, Syrian, and Lebanese borders have become legendary. When a terrorist infiltration is identified and contact is made with the enemy, the trackers race ahead of their officers in the engagement. As a result, they are usually the first to fall in battle. Such was the case in April 1988, when, in a pursuit of Palestinian terrorists infiltrating

into Israel near Mt. Dov along the Lebanese frontier, Sergeant Ramzi Wachsh, a tracker in the Giva'ati Infantry Brigade, was killed in a fierce firefight; he was the fifth Wachsh brother to fall in the line of duty. In February 1991, at the height of Operation Desert Storm, a Bedouin tracker serving along the border with Jordan, Master Sergeant Mohammad Shibli, was killed in a battle with Islamic Jihad terrorists.

6. Yitzhak Ben-Horin, "Ha'Hamisha Ha'Potachat," *Ma'ariv Shabat*, April 19, 1989, 3.

7. Yosef Argaman, "Hatifat Ha'Generalim," 68.

8. Yitzhak Ben-Horin, "Ha'Hamisha Ha'Potachat," 3.

9. Yosef Argaman, *Ze Haya Sodi Be'Yoter* (Tel Aviv: Ministry of Defense Publications, 1990), 38.

10. Yitzhak Ben-Horin, "Ha'Hamisha Ha'Potachat," 3.

11. *Ibid.*, 3.

12. Yosef Argaman, *Ze Haya Sodi*, 38.

13. Uri Milshtein, *Ha'Historia Shel Ha'Tzanhanim: Kerech Daled* (Tel Aviv: Schalgi Ltd., Publishing House, 1987), 1599.

14. Yosef Argaman, "Hatifat Ha'Generalim," 68.

15. *Ibid.*, 68.

# 6

---

# *The Mother of All Operations*

---

*Operation Spring of Youth*
*April 9–10, 1973*

It was the year of terror, 1972, and nothing would hinder the Palestinians' quest for distinction and publicity. Undaunted by their first two failures—a letter-bomb campaign in January 1972 and the foiled Sabena hijacking—Black September retreated into the cold, but its battle plan was clear, bold, and awakening. In terms of a comprehensive offensive to bring the plight of the Palestinian people to the world's attention, the letter-bomb campaign of January 1972 was a probing action, a test of the enemy's resolve; the Sabena hijacking was a mere skirmish, a test of the enemy's defenses. Operation Berim and Ikrit, however, was to be the surprise attack that would cripple the enemy and prime it for the kill. Named after two Arab Christian villages that had treacherously surrendered to Israel in 1948 without putting up a fight, Operation Berim and Ikrit was the assault on the Israeli compound at the Munich Olympic Village—an operation that would emblazon the name of Palestine in the world conscience. According to PFLP warlord Dr. George Habash, in an interview given to the Arabic journal *As-Sayyed,* "A bomb in the White House, a mine in the Vatican, the death of Mao Tse-tung, and an earthquake in

128

Paris could not have echoed through the consciousness of every man in the world like the operation at Munich. . . . It was like painting the name of Palestine on a mountain that can be seen from the four corners of the earth."[1]

September 5, 1972. Just before the long summer's sun appeared in the skies of Munich eight athletically-built men clad in blue and white Adidas track suits scaled the flimsy security fence that separated the Olympic Village from the rest of the world. Although laden down with unusually heavy travel bags, the eight had little difficulty negotiating obstacles in their path, including security guards who thought them to be track stars returning from a night out with the frauleins. They headed toward 31 Connolly Strasse, the living quarters of the small Israeli team. Their paramilitary training in Lebanon had served them well. They slinked around the building, locating a series of connecting rooms bristling with the sound of snoring athletes. The eight men produced AK-47 7.62mm assault rifles from their bags, locked and loaded their weapons, and attempted to knock down the room doors with sharp kicks; twenty-two athletes and coaches were housed in the complex.

The ruckus woke up the Israelis, including wrestler Joseph Romano and his coach Moshe Weinberg. The Israelis, realizing immediately what was happening, reacted quickly. Romano and Weinberg raced to the door, trying to keep the terrorists out as eleven of their comrades shattered windows with chairs and climbed through, escaping. The Palestinians opened fire through the door with an AK-47 7.62mm assault rifle, and Romano and Weinberg were killed in a flurry of automatic fire. The Palestinians stormed the room, weapons in hand, and took nine athletes hostage. Looking at his hostages and at the bullet-ridden room and bodies of Romano and Weinberg, Muhammad Masalhad, the terrorist leader, smiled at his comrades and said, "Black September has scored a monumental victory." He was being modest.

Within moments of the gunfire Bavarian police units began to reach the Olympic Village. Masalhad, an architect turned terrorist, was quick to state his demands. Addressing an assembled contingent of police and journalists with a ski mask covering his face, Masalhad proclaimed that the hostages would be released—alive—in exchange for Israel's turning free two hundred Palestinian terrorists in her jails, including Kozo Okamoto. The West Germans were also ordered to free Red Army Faction leaders Andreas Baader and Ulrike Meinhof.

The Israeli public and government were stunned by the hostage-taking. The Israeli cabinet, led by Prime Minister Golda Meir and Defense Minister Moshe Dayan, weighed the political consequences of the hostages getting hurt against negotiating with terrorists. In the end, the cabinet came down in favor of Israel's ironclad policy of non-negotiation for the reasons the policy was established in the first place. Negotiation and acquiescence only encouraged further acts of terrorism and hostage-taking. Besides, the Israelis agreed, this was taking place in German jurisdiction, making this a German matter.

Unfortunately, the Germans were ill equipped emotionally and militarily to cope with this crisis. Covered by over six thousand journalists who hours earlier had been witnessing the feats of American swimmer Mark Spitz and Soviet gymnast Olga Korbut, the terrorist attack was now taking center ring in an Olympic-size media circus. The Germans stalled for time, and the terrorist deadlines were pushed back and back. The Palestinians grew resilient and Bavarian snipers carrying submachine guns staked out the roof and the floors below, awaiting their order to free the captives. Hours passed into an eternity as the ordeal continued. In a final plea for reason, the West Germans naïvely offered the Palestinians money and vivacious blond beauties in exchange for an end to the ordeal. They were willing to do anything in order to prevent Jewish blood from being spilled on German soil. After all, the games in Munich were meant to put *that* tragic chapter of history aside.

Realizing that the Germans did not have the stomach to storm 31 Connolly Strasse, Golda Meir ordered her Mossad chief, Major General (Res.) Tzvi "Tzvika" Zamir, to Munich at once; he was joined by an Arabic-speaking Shin Bet officer expert in Black September tactics and psychology. According to foreign reports, Moshe Dayan asked the Germans if the IDF could send a force from Sayeret Mat'kal to Munich to end the crisis in a quick and deadly military operation.[2] Bonn refused the request. They would handle it.

The ensuing events could fill a military manual titled *How to Screw Up a Hostage Rescue*. Although West Germany was politically required to refuse Sayeret Mat'kal permission to operate *overtly* on her sovereign soil, in light of the brilliant hostage-rescue success of Operation Isotope 1 it was militarily the sole choice to be made at the time. Nevertheless, the Bavarian police opted to ambush the terrorists themselves, when the Palestinians would be at their most vulnerable point—on open ground at the Furstenfeldbruk NATO Airfield, moments before they were to fly off to an Arab capital as victorious warriors of Palestine. The West Germans hoped to ensure that the terrorists would never make it out of the country alive. It would be the last time the world underestimated the abilities of Black September.

The terrorists and their hostages were ferried to Furstenfeldbruk in two West German military Bell 205 choppers. As the helicopters' rotor blades sliced a path for the ten-minute hop to the NATO airfield the Bavarian police prepared their gauntlet. Tragically, the events of the next few hours were utterly terrifying, confusing, and deadly. The German snipers, armed with single-shot bolt-action rifles, had insufficiently prepared for the ambush; they failed to establish lines of fire and had been briefed that there were only a couple of terrorists. The police marksmen had no military backup, a desperate error when facing an adversary armed with automatic weapons and grenades, and they had no night-fighting capabilities whatsoever. Tzvi Zamir, a retired general, and the Shin Bet officer offered their anguished opinions in frustrated attempts to help ensure that all the hostages would live through the battle. The Germans, however, did not take kindly to the outside suggestions. It was to be a night that would haunt the Mossad commander forever.[3]

The Germans attempted a snare for the terrorists, hoping to pick them off one by one when they would be most exposed: traveling from the chopper to the Lufthansa airliner that was supposed to ferry them to an Arab capital. Masalhad emerged from the Bell-205 and sprinted in a crisscrossing pattern—to avoid the sniper's cross-hairs in case of an ambush—en route to conduct a personal inspection of the Lufthansa jet. Minutes later a confident Masalhad emerged from the Boeing 727. He placed his two fingers up in a "V for victory" sign. This was, indeed, a victory for Palestine. Operation Berim and Ikrit was a brilliant success.

As he walked slowly and surely back from the jet, confident that German goodwill was genuine, he carried his AK-47 loosely, sure that it would not have to be used. Seconds later, however, an impudent lone shot rang out from the administrative building and control tower at Furstenfeldbruk. It was followed by four additional gunshots. The Bavarian attempt to remove all of the terrorists with surgical precision had been a haphazard effort. Not only were the German snipers outgunned, but they were outnumbered as well.

The German snipers had mistakenly taken out a terrorist walking alongside Masalhad, exploding his head with a shot above the ear. The wily terrorist leader managed to dive in a Rambo-like commando move and take cover in the shadows. The tarmac was in silence for a few seconds until Masalhad fired a wild burst of 7.62mm fire at the control tower, knocking out the principal spotlight and killing one German policeman. For the next six minutes the Germans battled the terrorists in a futile firefight. The German police were outgunned, and the Palestinians had nowhere to go—except to martyrdom.

A stray bullet sliced through an electrical transformer, engulfing Furstenfeldbruk in total darkness. A standoff ensued while the nine hostages remained behind, inside the helicopters, their hands and legs tied to ensure they went nowhere without Black September approval.

For the next ninety minutes a "quiet chaos," in the words of one of the German officials, ensued on the tarmac. Shouts in Arabic were heard emanating from the darkened runway, while bombastic orders in German engulfed the control tower; a few curses in English, directed at the Bavarian officials, were also uttered quite loudly by Mossad Chief Zamir and his Shin Bet aide. Then, suddenly, the Palestinian terrorists emerged from the black abyss, fell into firing position, and raked the two helicopters (still holding the hostages tied firmly to their seats) with magazine-emptying bursts of AK-47 fire. The athletes had no chance to survive the melee, but for good measure incendiary grenades were tossed in. As the two helicopters and their precious human cargo erupted into a fiery ball of orange flame, Zamir wept. The Shin Bet officer was less diplomatic, nearly taking out his rage on the German officials for allowing the cold-blooded killings to transpire.[4] For the next several hours West German military forces, brought into the fray too late, battled the remaining Palestinians, killing four and capturing three. The Games of Peace were shattered by the cold-blooded reality of terrorism.

The objective of the Munich Olympics massacre was to show the plight of the Palestinians to the world. It was to serve as a desperate act of publicity that would spark world leaders into pressing Israel into a state of submission and appeasement. In this respect, the mission failed miserably. Europeans were horrified by the wanton carnage. Arabs were beaten in the streets of Munich and Cologne; protests were mounted against Palestinian offices in Paris and Brussels; and in hundreds of letters in the international press the terrorists were labeled "scum of the earth" and "degenerate heroes of the sewers."[5]

Clearly, this was not the outcome Yasir Arafat—the head of the PLO, el-Fatah, and, concurrently, Black September—wanted when he dispatched his commandos into Western Europe. Another objective, however—the killing of Jews—was carried out meticulously. The eleven Israelis who died in Munich—innocent athletes who had trained for much of their lives for the peaceful competition between nations—were brought home to Israel on board a special flight, their coffins draped in the Star of David flag of the Jewish state. A period of national mourning overcame the Israeli psyche.

Israeli response was immediate and lethal. The IAF was called in to destroy ten separate Palestinian terrorist training camps inside Lebanon; the raids were known as Operation Rigidity 6, and they proved the deadly abilities of the F-4E Phantom fighter bomber to any doubters. The air raids—an IAF version of carpet bombing—were meant to prove to the PLO leadership that such acts of murder as had transpired in Munich would be avenged tenfold. Black September, however, was undaunted, even cocky. The size of the Israeli air operation indicated to the Palestinians that revenge had developed into an Israeli obsession. Eight men in track suits had caused more pain, anger, and vulnerability than hundreds of Syrian and Egyptian brigades in conventional combat. Their war would continue in equally audacious style.

On September 10, 1972, as the flags at all Israeli installations worldwide were flown at half mast in honor of her eleven slain, Black September struck again. This time the target was Tzadok Ophir, a low-level diplomat at the Israeli embassy in Brussels. Ophir was an undercover Mossad agent in charge of, among other things, infiltrating the Palestinian terror networks of Western Europe.[6] A double agent pumped four 9mm bullets into the Mossad spook, but Ophir miraculously survived. A few days later, on September 13, a Syrian radio reporter in Paris, Khader Kanou, was murdered in a wild rampage of bullets by a Black September assassination squad. Kanou was rumored to be a Mossad informer.

These attacks against Israeli intelligence personnel displayed a certain degree of skill and professionalism in the Black September game plan; the attacks, coming so soon after the Munich operation, indicated that it was a force to be feared and respected. It was an entity that had declared total war against the Jewish state and would stop at nothing to achieve its goals. For Israel, Black September was an organization that had to be destroyed.

On September 16, 1972, the IDF struck in southern Lebanon in an attempt to root out the bases in which Black September squads had learned their deadly crafts. A mini-invasion of southern Lebanon ensued in a search-and-destroy mission known as Operation Turmoil 4; air, armor, artillery, and infantry elements swept into southern Lebanon to root out the terrorist infrastructure in a dazzling blitz. Although the week-long operation was a military success—damage to Palestinian interests was acute—Black September was not the type of revolutionary phenomenon that could be defeated by conventional means. Less than two weeks after the Munich massacre Black September initiated the second of its letter-bomb offensives. On September 18, 1972, Black September operatives in Amsterdam dispatched over seventy letter bombs to Jewish and Israeli interests worldwide; the most successful effect of the campaign was the killing of Ami Shachuri, the agricultural attaché at Israel's London embassy. Audaciously, one week later Black September operatives in Israel sent a series of letter bombs to American President Richard M. Nixon, Secretary of State William P. Rogers, and Defense Secretary Melvin Laird in an attempt to bring the Palestinians' war to a new field of fire.*

Yet what prompted Israel into decisive and historic action was the fact that the crimes in Munich would go unpunished. On the morning of October 29, 1972, a Lufthansa Boeing 727 on a routine connecting flight from Beirut to Ankara was hijacked by two anonymous Black September terrorists. The hijackers' demands were simple and unyielding: The surviving Munich gunmen were to be released immediately. In Germany, hours later, the three surviving Munich gunmen were rushed from their maximum-security

*The perpetrators of the attack turned out to be a mixed network of Palestinian and Jewish sleeper agents working for Black September and Syrian Air Force Intelligence, their eventual arrests were made easier by the rewards of Operation Crate 3.

Bavarian cells and transported to Furstenfeldbruk; they were loaded onto a privately hired executive jet and flown to Tripoli, Libya, where they would receive a hero's welcome. Palestinian terrorists had committed an act of mass murder in front of an internationally televised audience of nearly one billion people, and they had gone free. The fact that Germans were involved in releasing the killers of Jewish athletes added greater historical tragedy to the Munich massacre. Jewish blood was cheap. Israel, however, was determined to raise the price dramatically.

Black September was not a tangible and stationary target that could be destroyed in an air raid (or series of air raids) by armed-to-the-teeth Phantoms, nor could it be crippled in a hit-and-run assault by heliborne Israeli commandos. It was a highly capable force, honed in its skills of terror by the best experts the Soviet Union, Czechoslovakia, East Germany, and North Korea had to offer.[7] It was a force proficient in espionage and counterintelligence, and it was a cunning foe that knew how to cut and run rather than face a determined military might on the battlefield. For Black September, the world was a battlefield; the capitals of Europe, Asia, and North America were the stage on which the destruction of Israeli security would be played out. The only way the Jewish state could defeat this most serious threat was to respond in kind. One of the most fascinating periods in Israeli history had begun.

The Munich Olympics massacre might have polarized world public opinion on the Palestinians, but it galvanized the political will of Israel Prime Minister Golda Meir to destroy Black September. Prime Minister Meir had long viewed herself as something of an Israeli mother figure, an icon who could protect her citizens from harm and comfort them in troubling times. Munich embodied her failing as a national maternal guardian. She took the events in Bavaria personally and vowed to terminate this new terrorist presence once and for all.

According to published reports, Meir ordered the formation of a joint A'man/Mossad task force led by Aharon Yariv, the outgoing A'man director, who was given the mysterious and all-inclusive title of "special advisor for terrorist matters." Through his work with Mossad Chief Zamir, the result of Israel's yearning for vengeance became the infamous hit teams. Beyond vengeance, Black September's termination was meant to prevent future Munich massacres from taking place, as well as to illustrate to the other Palestinian terrorist organizations with the blood of their comrades that there was a fine line not to be crossed. The Israeli campaign began in the streets of Rome and ended months later at the shoreline, slums, and luxury flats of Beirut. It would be one of the State of Israel's most spectacular intelligence and special forces operations.

The hit teams succeeded in eliminating most of the architects and messengers of the death in Munich. Made up of Mossad, A'man and—according to foreign reports—on-loan Sayeret Mat'kal gunners, they were led by a mysterious man known simply as Mike. (Years later Mike was identified as veteran Mossad agent Mike Harari, a man who would become Mossad station chief in Mexico City and, eventually, the controversial right-hand man to deposed Panamanian strongman Manuel Noriega.[8]) The targets the hit teams addressed were removed by typical Israeli means: .22-caliber gunshots or ingeniously designed explosive devices. Among those dealt with were Wael Zwaiter, the Black September operations chief in Rome, killed on October 16, 1972, by anonymous gunmen in the Italian capital; Doctor Mahmud Hamshari, the Black September second-in-command in Paris, killed by an explosive device placed inside his telephone, on January 9, 1973; and Abd el Hir, the Black September station chief in Nicosia, Cyprus (he was also a high-level KGB agent), killed by an explosive device planted under his bed, on January 24, 1973. The man they were truly after, however, was Ali Hassan Salameh, the infamous Red Prince and Rasd leader.* He was hunted mercilessly throughout Europe, but—unfortunately for the Israelis—the hunters were becoming the hunted.

On January 26, 1973, Baruch Cohen, the Mossad station chief in Madrid, arranged to meet with an informant,

---

*Ali Hassan Salameh was killed on January 22, 1979, by, according to foreign sources, a Mossad car bomb in Beirut.

a Palestinian student who was to provide the Israeli spy with invaluable intelligence concerning Black September's extensive network in Western Europe. The meeting was, in fact, an ambush. The Rasd, one of the most sophisticated intelligence forces operating in the Arab world, had succeeded in infiltrating Cohen's network. As Cohen sat inside a popular student café awaiting his contact two gunmen pumped three 9mm slugs into his body from an automatic pistol fitted with a silencer. He died less than three hours later.

The Palestinians had upped the ante. The Israelis, however, would raise the stakes enormously to a level the Palestinians could not afford to meet. This time Israel would not strike the terrorists in their European haunts or in their backyard. Instead the IDF would assault Black September's front porch—Beirut. The IDF had just the force to kick in its door: Sayeret Mat'kal.[9]

A preemptive raid in Beirut had been in the files of Operations Branch for several years. Initially the raid was to be a minor operation meant to destroy several Palestinian terrorist facilities that were producing indigenous weapons and munitions. Although it was not a heavily defended city and the abilities of the Lebanese Army were suspect, Beirut was not a soft target. Although Operation Gift had gone off without incident four years earlier, this was a very different Beirut. Now home to a large and heavily armed Palestinian guerrilla presence, the once-peaceful shores of Beirut were in the first stages of becoming a hellish fortress. Any raid in Beirut was to be small, covert, and without major incident. After all, the political fallout from the destruction of the Arab airliners on the tarmac at Beirut International Airport had been very costly.

Munich changed everything, however. It made Black September fair game, and it made their home base, Beirut, fair game as well. The IDF's special forces were capable of combining the logistical and combat talents of several smaller units into a cohesive offensive element; their combined firepower was, in fact, devastating. As the size and scope of the Beirut operation grew in heated General Staff meetings, so did a list of potential targets. Intelligence sources were tapped and pressed for the whereabouts of many of the PLO's most important terrorist leaders—Habash, Jibril, Salameh. Lieutenant Colonel Shmuel Pressburger, an influential officer who had great impact on the handling of the Chief of Staff's Boys, was Brigadier General "Manno" Shaked's deputy as second in command of the IDF Paratroop and Infantry Branch. He came up with an aggressive plan that would snare PLO chieftain Yasir Arafat and several of his top aides.[10]

Then, as if by divine intervention, two fascinating addresses were uncovered by Israeli intelligence. The first, a seven-story building on West Beirut's fashionable rue Khartoum, served as headquarters for the Democratic Front for the Liberation of Palestine, one of the more capable Palestinian terrorist factions, commanded by Nayif Hawatmeh; the building also served as a living facility for over 150 of Hawatmeh's most senior commanders.

The second address was even more endearing: two adjacent blocks of luxury apartments on the fashionable rue Verdun in the ultra-exclusive Ramlat al-Bida section of the city, which housed three of Black September's top leaders. Topping this list was Muhammed Najer, better known by his terrorist nom de guerre, Abu Yusef. He was a leader of Black September, a principal planner of the Munich Olympics massacre, and the el-Fatah operations and intelligence chief for worldwide operations against Israeli installations. The second resident of rue Verdun was an equally important figure in the Palestinian revolution; his name was Kamal A'dwan, and he was responsible for running terrorist operations inside Israel. His cells all originated in the West Bank and the Gaza Strip. Finally there was Kamal Nasser, a poet by profession and a cold-blooded executive in the Black September hierarchy by trade; he was their official spokesman. News of the three officials living *so* close to one another brought new life into the planned IDF foray into the Lebanese capital. Israel's policy of retribution for the Munich horror was being extended to a conventional, albeit spectacular, level. Not only was Israel going after the heart of Black September, but the targets in Beirut were its brain and soul. In Tel Aviv, as IDF units were summoned for the task at hand, three death warrants were being signed.

There had been severe debate within the IDF general staff as to which target would be hit in Beirut and which unit would execute the mission. Naturally, Chief of Staff Dado Elazar wanted his boys to carry out the delicate undertaking, but the Ha'Kommando Ha'Yami OC Colonel Shaul Ziv—who owned the unique reputation of being a very well-liked officer in the competitive special forces arena as well as a commander who could get the job done—urged the general staff to consider *his* men for this most awe-inspiring challenge. The Mat'kal commandos had come off the two known successful operations of rescuing the Sabena hostages and kidnapping the five Syrian staff officers; the naval commandos, on the other hand, had come off several very successful covert missions of their own, in addition to the brilliantly executed Operation Hood. Prospects for a raid on Beirut obsessed Colonel Ziv. It sparked much uncharacteristic infighting between the commanders of several *sayerot* and even led to numerous and extremely loud (even by Israeli standards) shouting matches. When the primary target of a Beirut operation was the el-Fatah explosives factory in the el-Ouzai section of the city, located in the southern slums adjacent to the Sabra refugee camp, Ziv even went so far as to construct a model of the target at the naval commandos' home base. Ziv argued that since the facility at el-Ouzai produced homemade limpet mines it was a naval target, and worthy of his unit's talents! All other operations were discarded in favor of training for this highly coveted mission. His men were trained nearly twenty-four hours a day, seven days a week.

Before the weekly Sabbath leave Ziv ordered his men to carry out a dress rehearsal of the Beirut raid. It was to fill their thoughts and concerns even as they ventured home for a two-day leave.[11] Beirut was to be a proud chapter in the history of Ha'Kommando Ha'Yami. In fact, when the raid against Beirut was approved and awarded to Ziv's underwater warriors, the first man to shake his hand was Colonel

Menacham Digli, the former commander of the elite unit in direct competition with the naval commandos (he was at the time the head of A'man's ultrasecretive Intelligence Collections Department).[12]

The expansion of objectives in Beirut eliminated the need for interservice rivalry; the mission's importance and grand scale dictated the need for cooperation and cohesion. It was to be the largest and most important commando operation in the IDF's twenty-five-year history, and nothing would be left to chance. Along the lines of the highly successful February raid against Tripoli, this venture was to be a combined arms undertaking, an operation incorporating several elements of various paratroop formations, the IAF, the IDF/Navy, the IDF Communications and Signals Corps, A'man, and the Mossad. Entrusted with the most delicate portion of the raid would, of course, be Sayeret Mat'kal.[13] In March 1973 the IDF's operations computer spit out the code name for this aggressive undertaking. The attack against Beirut would be called Mivtza Aviv Ne'urim, or Operation Spring of Youth.

Operation Spring of Youth consisted of five objectives, each with a female code name: Gilah, the destruction of the DFLP's apartment complex in rue Khartoum by a force of reconnaissance paratroopers commanded by Lieutenant Colonel Amnon Shahak Lipkin, a future A'man director and deputy chief of staff; Vardah, a two-pronged objective that included the destruction of the el-Fatah headquarters responsible for terrorist operations inside Israel and the el-Ouzai explosives and ordnance factory, which would be carried out by Colonel Shaul Ziv's naval commandos; Tzilah, the destruction of a major el-Fatah ammunition storage facility located at the northern tier of Beirut harbor, by a force of naval commandos; Yehudit, a diversionary raid against an el-Fatah storage facility north of Sidon, south of Beirut, by a force of reconnaissance paratroopers under the command of Lieutenant Colonel Amos Yaron.

Lastly, there was objective Avivah, the assassination of Muhammed Najer, Kamal A'dwan, and Kamal Nasser by the Chief of Staff's Boys.

One of the most fascinating aspects of the Sayeret Mat'kal portion of Operation Spring of Youth was the fact that Lieutenant Colonel Barak was supplied only with a target and scenario. Everything else—the blueprint of the raid, the exact style of attack, and how he'd accomplish his assignment—was all left to Barak and his equally capable staff of commanders. For a small unit, this displayed enormous trust and flexibility. In an army a unit is usually presented with a mission, told how to accomplish the assignment, and then expected to execute the operation as planned and ordered. Barak proved his brilliant and innovative military vision when he presented his final plan to Chief of Staff Elazar. Dado's words were to the point: *"Kadima . . . le'hit'amen!"* ("Forward . . . start training!")[14] On paper, at least, Barak's plan was an impressive success.

Even before training commenced for Operation Spring of Youth it was clear to all involved that this was a most ambitious and dangerous undertaking. There were five separate objectives, five separate task forces, and the possibility of five separate forces of the IDF's finest soldiers being cut off inside an enemy capital—vastly outnumbered, hopelessly outgunned, and possibly stranded for a gruesome fate.

Beirut in 1973 was a very different city than the chaotic tidbit of hell it turned into during the civil war. Beirut was Lebanon—its capital, financial center, and site of the greatest concentration of Lebanese Army forces anywhere in the country. It was a city that still had two years left before it committed fratricide, as Muslims and Christians still lived in what could now be considered relative peace. It was a Beirut where the Israelis had no ally to turn to. It was years before Mossad and A'man developed close political and military ties with Lebanon's various Christian militias.

Should anything go wrong, there was little hope that the Israeli task force would come home alive.

The dangerous nature of this planned endeavor was not lost on Prime Minister Golda Meir—a woman who, although not a "military man," understood what a suicide mission looked like when she saw it on paper. Golda Meir was always concerned that Israel's image be kept clean in such affairs; that its forces were not involved in particularly brutal operations; and that these operations always be conceived, planned, and executed so that Israeli casualties would be kept to an absolute minimum. Brigadier General Emanuel Shaked was given authorization to begin training exercises only when he promised the Israeli prime minister that he would do all in his power to make sure that all the boys would come home. It was a difficult promise to make and an even harder one to keep.[15]

Training for the operation was extremely serious business. The reconnaissance paratroopers and the naval commandos retreated to their home bases, where models of their targets were constructed from plywood and cinder blocks. In between the long hours dedicated to perfecting assault techniques to split-second precision, as well as to the commandos' own very high standard of excellence, lengthy intelligence briefings were carried out. Gigantic wall maps of Beirut were produced before the assembled groups of soldiers, and key avenues, streets, and landmarks in the city were highlighted and memorized. Unit commanders pressed and quizzed their legions on a daily basis so that they'd be as familiar with the Lebanese capital as if they'd be driving in the streets of Haifa, Tel Aviv or Jerusalem. Brigadier General Shaked often made it a personal point to quiz the conscript fighters himself. He was not about to send Israel's finest fighters to Beirut unless they were fully prepared.

For Lieutenant Colonel Ehud Barak, commander of Sayeret Mat'kal, training on a wooden mock-up of an urban target was an important part of the preoperation maneuvers. But Barak knew his men could not gather the proper feel for engaging an enemy inside the confines of concrete and steel towers while dancing about in a secluded desert facility. He opted for more a realistic setting: Tel Aviv.

The Ramat Aviv suburb of Tel Aviv is one of the city's most exclusive neighborhoods. Located a few kilometers north of the city near the coastal road, it was an ideal choice for an ad hoc stand-in of the Lebanese capital; located near the sea, it was suitable for an amphibious approach. Made up of luxurious high rises, it looked very much like the target area of rue Verdun. With an intelligence photo in his lap Barak drove around Ramat Aviv for several hours until he discovered an ultraluxurious block of flats under construction. Leaving his unobtrusive white Peugeot IDF staff car, he cased the location in greater detail with several of his officers, including Majors Yoni Netanyahu and Muki Botzer. Both approved. A few telephone calls later it was decided that the residents of northern Tel Aviv were about to endure an eventful night.

The March night was cold and damp—typical winter fare for the Mediterranean. Just off the coast of Tel Aviv, as the city's residents braved the cold weather to sit and gossip off the seaside promenade, a silhouette appeared in the distance. It was a *Sa'ar* (Storm) class missile boat of the IDF/Navy, and although stationary in friendly waters it was operating under total battle conditions: radar was tuned out, lights were extinguished, and radio silence was maintained. As Tel Aviv went about its business several Zodiac craft were lowered from the missile boat and loaded with men—all wearing dark sweaters and olive fatigue trousers—and equipment. The boats hummed in the rocky surf for several minutes till they reached shore and were met by three unobtrusive cars parked along a seaside promenade, usually known as the "meat market" for Tel Aviv's ladies of the evening. The commandos headed quietly for the "targeted" building, which was under construction on a Ramat Aviv neighborhood side street. The men exited the cars in slow and deliberate fashion, each hiding something underneath his clothes. Speaking in flawless English, they split into two groups. One stood outside, looking suspiciously at any movement by vehicle or pedestrian, while the second group entered the building; their brown leather jump boots made harsh sounds on the scaffolding and loose boards. One man, a short stocky fellow, sat near the lead vehicle gazing at a stopwatch.

Israelis are naturally suspicious, and the sight of unsavory characters milling about a well-to-do neighborhood was not lost on its residents. One old gentleman, in fact, feared there was a robbery or terrorist attack taking place. Nervously he dialed 100, the police emergency number, and demanded action. A squad car was on the scene several minutes later.[16]

What the police found when they arrived was a mock military exercise transpiring in the streets of Israel's largest city. They were dumbfounded. When they asked for an explanation and tried to take some of Barak's men down to the local station house for questioning, they were warned off with the simple comment, "I wouldn't if I were you!" After a few anxious radio calls to headquarters the policemen realized that they had stumbled onto something they were clearly not meant to know about; although a policeman's thirst for knowledge is a legendary trait of the job, national security concerns were of paramount importance. One of the commando officers supervising the training along with Lieutenant Colonel Barak winked at the departing policemen and said, "Maybe one day you'll read about it . . . MAYBE!" Following the incident, the residents of Ramat Aviv, still telephoning the 100 police emergency line, were told to go back to sleep and mind their own business the next time they saw mysterious armed men milling about construction sites.[17]

Training for the Avivah objective was, in fact, carried out in the Tel Aviv area on numerous occasions. Preparations for the assault had to be divided between two separate locations. While Ramat Aviv proved to be an ideal replica of the streets of Beirut, there were obvious constraints. Due to security concerns, fellow commandos could not masquerade as local civilians and Palestinian gunmen to add the much-needed element of realism, and very senior IDF commanders could not oversee the training as it progressed —they were public figures and would almost certainly be recognized by neighborhood residents. And most importantly, the commandos could not be expected to train with live ammunition in a Tel Aviv suburb.

Although ideally the assassinations were to be executed with silenced weapons, it was quite unsafe to train with live fire in an area so congested with civilians. As a result, Barak's men split their training between Ramat Aviv and a wooden mock-up built in a secluded training ground on the West Bank. Here the *tachlis* of the operation was carried out: what type of weapons, how many shots, the kind of explosives to be carried, etc. Logistics such as the time it would take to be ferried from the missile boat to the homes on rue Verdun were tested time and time again on the streets of Tel Aviv. All kinks were ironed out to ensure that once inside Beirut nothing preventable would go wrong.

Training continued for over five weeks—an enormous amount of time to prepare for a few hours of action, but this was no routine venture. Barak's commandos were reminded daily that should they encounter difficulties in Beirut or be forced to engage numerically superior forces in a firefight, they could not count on any help whatsoever—nothing from the Armored Corps, no artillery support, and, it was assumed, probably not even an air rescue from the IAF. If there were any screw-ups, they'd be on their own.

Objective Avivah was the sole target in Operation Spring of Youth that *could* be deniable. Assassination was a dirty game. The world was not to know that the deaths of the three Black September leaders came as a result of an Israeli government–sanctioned military operation. As far as Tel Aviv was concerned, they could let the world think that the Arabs had done this to one another—the events of Black September in Jordan were proof that such fratricide was common in the brutal Palestinian camp. To preserve the covert nature of the raid, Barak's commandos could not wear Israeli army fatigues; could not speak Hebrew; and could not use weapons identifiable with the IDF. Accomplishing the most difficult of assignments without getting caught was, after all, a Mat'kal trademark.

As for not speaking Hebrew, most Israelis learned English as a second language, so this was no problem. Yoni Netanyahu, one of the principal actors in the mission, had been educated in the United States. Although the IDF favored the sturdy Uzi 9mm submachine gun for special work, it was clearly not a weapon that could be used if the force was to cover up Israeli involvement. As a result, the American Ingram MAC-10 .45 ACP-caliber submachine gun was to be deployed. Used for covert assignments, the MAC-10 was a simple, robust, and deadly weapon. It came with a built-in silencer, which made it particularly useful. It was relatively light, and although it lacked an effective range beyond close quarters, it was particularly lethal for the point-blank task at hand. To ensure security, the weapons' serial numbers would be carefully filed down.

It was finally decided that Barak's men would wear civilian clothing—blue jeans, leather jackets, and other garb favored by the hippie generation. Since most of the commandos considered gym shorts and sandals as fundamental elements of fashionable attire, they were ordered to enjoy extravagant shopping sprees in the poshest shops of Tel Aviv. The men all bought clothing in extra-large sizes in order to accommodate weapons and ammunition. Many of the fighters bought outrageous and colorful outfits. Some commandos, including Barak, bought dresses and makeup. The Tel Aviv shopkeepers, a sarcastic bunch as it was, wished their oddball customers much fun in their Halloween-type outing.

The assortment of clothing was bizarre but effective. In late March, at an anonymous location in central Israel, a full dress rehearsal of Operation Spring of Youth/Objective Avivah was carried out for the general staff. Several commandos even appeared in drag, including Ehud Barak, who gallivanted around the mock target on rue Verdun carrying an AK-47 and wearing an elegant evening dress, long-haired brunette wig, and falsies that would have made even the bustiest of women feel flat-chested.[18]

Spring of Youth was a go. D-Day was the night of April 9–10, 1973.

On April 1, 1973—a typically beautiful spring day in the Paris of the Middle Eastern Riviera—a thirty-five-year-old Belgian named Gilbert Rimbaud arrived in the Lebanese capital and hired a cab driven by a friendly young Palestinian. Eventually Rimbaud checked into the Sands Hotel, a modest Beirut lodging, telling the clerk he was in need of a few days of rest. Hours later a West German tourist named Dieter Altnuder checked in as well.[19] The two men never crossed paths in the hotel lobby, did not appear to know each other, and spent their days in total anonymity. Rimbaud, in particular, enjoyed long walks throughout the city—especially along the coastline—and Altnuder was quite fond of fishing, especially at a secluded spot along the city's Dove Beach. These visitors to the Lebanese capital operated in too frugal a manner to arouse suspicion as intelligence operatives. Since the days of Kim Philby Beirut had possessed a reputation as the Middle East's spy capital. Foreign espionage agents tended to frequent better hotels, part with foreign currency (and tips) with greater generosity, and entertain the finest and most expensive Levantine beauties for hire. Modesty, it appeared, was not an element of Lebanese tradecraft.

Six days later, on April 6, the Sands Hotel received three new visitors—a Belgian, Charles Boussard, and two Englishmen, Andrew Whichelaw and George Elder. That same day Beirut's Atlantic Hotel received an eccentric British guest, Andrew Macy, a Briton who characteristically asked about the weather several times daily but—unlike most Englishmen—was a very good tipper. The seven visitors to Beirut rented several strong and sturdy vehicles—three Buick Skylarks, a Plymouth station wagon, one Valiant, and one Renault. The seven were, of course, seasoned Mossad agents sent to Beirut to lay the groundwork for Operation Spring of Youth.[20]

Security constraints for such an operation are fanatically observed. They have to be. In such a large-scale and dangerous undertaking, in which the cream of the Israeli military and intelligence would be operating together in the field, early detection by the enemy would probably have resulted in the appearance of a heavily armed Palestinian reception committee. The results might have damaged Israeli security capabilities for generations. In fact, any indication that Operation Spring of Youth had been compromised might have prompted the IDF chief of staff to order its cancellation. Oddly enough, such a scenario transpired only hours before the first Zodiac craft were about to hit the beaches of Beirut.

April 9, 1973, Nicosia, Cyprus. On Nicosia International Airport's main runway three gunmen from the Arab Nationalist Youth Movement, an obscure cover group for Black September and el-Fatah, attacked an Arkia (a small Israeli domestic and charter airline) aircraft as passengers prepared to board for the quick flight to Tel Aviv. Two armed Israeli security guards acted decisively, pulling their Beretta 9mm pistols from their backside holsters to engage the Palestinians in a wild shootout on a tarmac crowded with aircraft, fuel trucks, and passengers. The Israeli security agents killed two of the Palestinians (a Cypriot policeman was also killed) in the firefight. Remarkably, the Cypriot authorities arrested the two Shin Bet trained guards before seizing the Arab gunmen.

A few minutes later, also in Nicosia, a powerful explosive device detonated in the home of the Israeli ambassador to Cyprus, Rechamim Timor, as he departed his official residence to help bail out the two Arkia guards. Clearly, the terrorist attacks were meant to serve as a warning.[21] Had Israeli security been lax? Had Operation Spring of Youth been compromised? The possibility of a connection between the terrorist attacks and the planned Israeli operations troubled many in the general staff.

The events in Cyprus were troubling, but the latest intelligence reports originating from Beirut indicated that security arrangements in the Lebanese capital were routine. Additional army units were not on the city's streets, and forces were not manning defensive barricades along the shoreline. Spring of Youth was still on.

On the morning of April 9, at the IDF/Navy's sprawling Haifa base, IDF Chief of Staff Elazar sat with Chief Paratroop and Infantry Officer Manno Shaked in a quiet last-minute briefing. Elazar was extremely concerned. He warned that one minor glitch could create a web of uncontrollable events that would expose the elite troops to certain death. Shaked, who spent much more time with these men and knew exactly what they were capable of, was more confident. Sayeret Mat'kal's esprit de corps matched their training and combat skills. *"Lo lidog, ye'hiyeh beseder"* (Don't worry, it'll be all right"), he said. "Each soldier knows the odds and knows what he has to do."[22]

A few hours later, just after noon, a mini-armada (nearly the entire IDF/Navy) of nine missile boats and two smaller Dabur (Bee) coastal patrol craft departed Haifa harbor bound for Beirut. Two missile boats, the I.N.S. *Mivtach* and *Ga'ash,* ferried Lieutenant Colonel Amos Yaron's force of reconnaissance paratroopers to Sidon (Objective Yehudit); the I.N.S. *Akko* brought the joint force of naval commandos and reconnaissance paratroopers commanded by Lieutenant Colonel Shmuel Pressburger to northern Beirut (Objective Tzilah); the I.N.S. *Sa'ar* and *Miznak* positioned Brigadier General Shaked's command and control force, as well as an emergency rescue force of paratroopers, just off the Beirut coastline; and the I.N.S. *Herev, Eilat, Sufah,* and *Misgav* set anchor off the southern Beirut waters. These four missile boats held the brunt of the Spring of Youth task force, including Colonel Ziv's naval commandos, Lieutenant Colonel Shahak's paratroopers, and, of course, Lieutenant Colonel Barak's Mat'kal commandos. The entire task force had been addressed by the chief of staff prior to boarding the vessels and were wished good luck and the obligatory "be careful!"

Each force then split into separate groups and went over the latest intelligence information, including last-minute aerial reconnaissance photographs of the Lebanese capital and other bits of highly classified information, portions of which were even kept from the commandos—no need for added bits of classified data being heard by too many people. These briefings were held in closely guarded quarters, far from the prying eyes of IDF/Navy personnel not cleared for such top-secret data. IDF/Navy men are usually awarded considerable security clearances, but the missile boat and *Dabur* crews were supplied with little information concerning their springtime cruises to Beirut. Even the commandos were kept in the dark until the very last minute. Only in open waters, as the mixed force of Mat'kal, Sayeret

Tzanhanim, and naval commandos sat inside the constricting confines of the missile boats, were the men informed that it was D-Day.[23]

At 21:00 hours the armada reached the waters off the Beirut coast. Radars were turned off, radio silence was maintained, and the sailors manning cannon and machine-gun positions were placed on full battle alert. From the sides of the largest missile boat contingent, ferrying the Avivah and Gilah task forces, twelve grayish-black Zodiac craft were lowered into the choppy black waters. Little emotion was displayed—little fear and little excitement. The missile boat officers, more concerned about their own ships sitting helplessly in hostile waters than the well-being of the commandos units, looked on in silent respect. The missile boats were moored just off southern Beirut, close to the fashionable Dove Beach.

Operation Spring of Youth was a test of the IDF's analytical approach to special operations. Each objective was to be attacked separately, and in order of importance. Objective Avivah, naturally, was first.

Just before midnight the twelve outboard motors of the Zodiac flotilla could be heard from Dove Beach. This was welcome noise to the seven Mossad agents who had brought their rented cars to the seaside promenade, usually reserved for romantic liaisons and ladies of the evening. As the rubber craft approached the beach the Mossad agents ignited their headlights for a brief second—a signal responded to with the shining of Ehud Barak's service flashlight. The coast was clear. While several of the agents continued their surveillance of the secluded beachfront, nervously watching for any military or police patrols, the commandos disembarked from their Zodiacs and placed them at a well-camouflaged spot until the naval commandos could return the crafts to shallow waters. The rubber boats were the task force's only means for returning to ship.

A brief exchange transpired between lieutenant colonels Barak and Shahak and one of the Mossad agents. After a cold and emotionless handshake the force split into two. Shahak's men traveled in three cars toward objective Gilah, the DFLP headquarters, while Barak's force went in the three remaining automobiles toward rue Verdun.[24]

The streets of Beirut were bustling with life and activity that evening. Two years later civil war would turn this thriving cosmopolitan city into a war-ravaged hell, but now the sidewalk cafés of the Lebanese capital were filled to capacity with diners and lovers; parents brought children out to amusement parks and playgrounds; and the soldiers milling about were on leave rather than manning a checkpoint where religious affiliation equaled an entry visa. Colorful lights washed the city's sidewalks. That night, however, there was a large presence of heavily armed gendarme units. They patrolled the streets vigorously but were positioned at key intersections to ward off student protestors who had plagued the city; these armed units were definitely not expecting a visit from Israeli commandos.

At 01:29 hours on the morning of April 10 the three Mossad cars slowly approached the targeted house on rue Verdun. Weapons were closely clutched inside the roomy American-made sedans, but the lead Mossad driver suddenly released some pressure from the gas pedal and pointed to his left. A gendarme vehicle with a .50-caliber machine gun was positioned at the entrance to rue Verdun—probably protecting the Iraqi consulate. Undaunted but considerably more cautious, the Israelis did not park on rue Verdun but instead came to a halt on adjacent Ibn Walid Street. A mechanic working at a nearby gas station was suspicious of the three vehicles, but his fears were allayed when he saw several young men carrying travel bags and suitcases— hippies, he thought—and two very sexy females wearing dresses that barely held in their luscious breasts.[25] One "woman," Ehud Barak, wore a dirty blond wig and walked hand in hand with her lover, Major Muki Botzer, who was whispering sweet nothings into her ear.* As the mechanic looked at this scene with jealous pangs of passion he failed

---

*Following the raid, a Beirut resident who observed the entire operation from his balcony told an Italian newspaper that the commandos were led by a vivacious blonde beauty, "the type of woman of which fantasies are made of."

to notice Botzer's right hand holding the trigger mechanism of a MAC-10. Disguises *did* work.

Two squads of the Mat'kal force remained behind in their automobiles, along with the Mossad agents, to delay any Lebanese or Palestinian interference while the hit squads entered the high rise on rue Verdun. The first house entered was where Abu Yusef lived. Its downstairs glass door was left unlocked, and the civilian watchman, who usually sat at his post, was nowhere to be seen. Once safely inside Barak returned to the street for overall tactical command of the situation and to see why the other hit teams had yet to spring into action. He then discovered that the Black September leader had positioned two cars, manned by Force 17 gunmen outside his residence for added security.

Barak and a few other commandos closed in on the vehicles and, after producing silenced .22s from their pockets or purses, they pumped several rounds into each car. The guards, attempting to flee, were killed by the thudding explosions of .22 projectiles slamming into their bodies.[26]

But all was not well. One bullet sliced through the car's mechanical system and caused the horn to wail uncontrollably, its sound muffled somewhat by the throbbing disco beat emanating from the Gold Room disco located a few yards away. The authorities and terrorists stationed nearby were alarmed. The mission had to be executed as quickly as possible. The sounds of small-arms fire and Lebanese gendarmes shouting orders to one another in Arabic were heard in the street below.

Major Yoni Netanyahu, Major Botzer, and two other commandos proceeded quickly up the staircase toward the sixth floor. The suitcases were filled with explosives that, it was hoped, would break through any locked door; the cases were also to carry back any valuable documents found lying around in the target's apartment. The four-man squad reached the apartment and quickly placed the charges by the door's lock and hinges. Uzis and MAC-10s were produced and readied for service. The explosion was loud but not debilitating. The force burst through the apartment but found Abu Yusef's son, Yosef, instead. Yoni went down nervously on one knee and asked the lad in Arabic, *"W'en abu'k?"* ("Where is your father?"). The boy, frightened by the men invading his home, raced to the terrace while the commandos slowly and methodically entered each room in search of the terror master. The Israelis burst into his bedroom and came across his wife, Maha. Immediately realizing what was transpiring, she began to plead for her husband's life with kind words of respect. When she saw the armed men continuing their search and clutching their weapons closer to their chests she began to curse them in Arabic barrages of indignation.

Yoni eventually found Abu Yusef in an adjacent guest room. The mustached man, still in his pajamas, was looking frantically for his trusted AK-47. As Yoni raised his MAC-10 to let off a magazine-emptying volley Maha jumped in front of her beloved husband to act as a dedicated human shield. It was a fatal mistake. Twenty .45-caliber rounds ripped through both their bodies. Abu Yusef's last word was "Cowards," uttered as he slid into a lifeless form on the shiny marble floor.

A thorough search of the apartment was quickly attended to as hundreds of loose papers, many bearing PLO letterheads, were placed in the large cases for later analysis at A'man and Mossad headquarters.[27] Yoni's men went through Abu Yusef's desk drawers, safe, and other hiding places one final time and then proceeded downstairs to help Barak.

Meanwhile, the second and third Mat'kal hit teams sprang into action in the adjacent building on rue Verdun. The second squad, commanded by "N." (identity protected for security reasons), raced up the staircase to the second floor and then broke Kamal A'dwan's door in with a sharp kick—"just like in the movies," as one of the commandos would reflect later in an interview with the Israeli press.

Inside the fully lit apartment adorned with paintings of Palestine and exotic tropical plants, N. found A'dwan attempting to hide behind a lavish row of Persian curtains. A'dwan was carrying a fully loaded AK-47, which he fired wildly, even managing to wound one of the Mat'kal commandos slightly. Amid the blinding flash of 7.62mm projectiles N. calmly dropped to one knee in a picture-perfect firing position and laced the terrorist leader with a violent volley of 9mm bullets, striking him in the chest and head. His wife and child were found motionless in an adjacent room frozen in fear. Before departing the A'dwan apartment N.'s commandos filled two suitcases with documents. Two down, one to go.

Kamal Nasser was next. As the commandos raced up the staircase toward his flat Nasser was at his desk, working on the first draft of a speech he was to give the following afternoon to a group of senior el-Fatah officers. After blowing his door off its hinges, the commandos searched his flat quickly. "G.," one of the younger Mat'kal commandos to participate in the raid, found Nasser and emptied a full MAC-10 magazine into him. As Nasser struggled in the last seconds of life G. quickly changed magazines and emptied another magazine for good measure. "T.," the squad leader, ordered G. to see "if this was, indeed, our man," but .45-caliber rounds to the neck and head made proper identification impossible.

As the commandos attempted to identify the corpse further a shout was heard coming from the staircase ordering them to get their asses back to the street. Files were seized and placed in several suitcases as the four-man squad hurried onto the street below.[28]

Rue Verdun was becoming a very dangerous place. As Lieutenant Colonel Barak nervously waited outside, keeping in constant radio contact with his three hit teams, a Lebanese Army Land Rover with half a dozen soldiers suddenly veered onto the street, apparently on a routine patrol responding to the muffled sounds of gunfire. Not taking anything for granted, Barak's men opened fire. In the opening bursts of the firefight three Lebanese soldiers were killed. The MAC-10s the Mat'kal commandos carried proved to be big disappointments, however. "R.," one of the commandos on rue Verdun with Barak's mobile CP, said, "I aimed my weapon at the driver's compartment from a range of fifteen meters and fired a full magazine, in short bursts, and I failed to hit anything."[29]

During the chaos Barak, his wig discarded, ordered his men back into the cars on the double. Half a dozen Israelis, all firing short, stubby weapons, battled heavily armed Lebanese Army units. The gendarmes, daunted by the gunfire, immediately took shelter—after all, this was not their battle. The three rented cars reversed into the intersection at Ibn Walid Street and headed toward the sea. The commandos had been at rue Verdun for all of twenty-nine minutes!

The drive back to the Mediterranean shore was tense. The Mossad agents remained calm, but the commandos appeared apprehensive. They were lightly armed and feared a full-scale firefight they knew they had no hope of winning. Approximately two hundred yards from shore the Mossad/Mat'kal convoy passed several Lebanese Army jeeps loaded to capacity with soldiers, all carrying French 9mm MAT 49 submachine guns and Belgian 7.62mm FN FAL assault rifles, heading towards rue Verdun.

Once on the beach the Mossad agents and the commandos descended onto the sands in deliberate groups. Barak and five of his officers remained on the roadway, determined to stop any uninvited Lebanese Army units, while the remainder of the force proceeded to the sands below. Barak and his men aimed their weapons in a 180° radius; they were veteran warriors who realized that if anything went wrong in an operation, it usually happened in the closing minutes.

The naval commandos were called in from their mid-sea mooring, and the missile boats were told to expect returning guests. In the only snag during the operation, one of the commandos left two suitcases filled with documents in the rented car. He requested permission to return to the promenade and retrieve the coveted papers, but Barak refused. They were playing on borrowed time as it was. The naval commandos arrived seconds later. The Mat'kal commandos boarded the six Zodiacs and headed out to the blackened horizon. Objective Avivah was executed brilliantly.

The remaining objectives of Operation Spring of Youth

were attended to according to schedule. Of all the targets, objective Gilah, the attack on the DFLP complex, was the site of the stiffest Palestinian resistance and the most brutal fighting. Lieutenant Colonel Shahak's task force arrived at rue Khartoum five minutes ahead of schedule and immediately established a CP across the street from the DFLP headquarters.

All the commandos wore a grab-bag mixture of civilian clothing, ranging from hippies' peace-symbol T-shirts to Yuppie business suits, and carried Uzis and AK-47s. These forces was split into four teams of two, plus a command section consisting of Shahak, the unit's chief medical officer, and an observing Mossad operative. The lead team approached the building by asking one of the DFLP guards for a light. Seconds later, after silenced Berettas were produced, two of the terrorists were dead, two others wounded. Within a few more seconds, however, the house at rue Khartoum was ablaze with automatic fire. DFLP gunmen fired incessant bursts of 12.7mm machine-gun fire from the windows above, as well as lobbing grenades onto the street below. Shahak's men responded by firing antitank rifle grenades, fitted to the barrels of 7.62mm FN FAL assault rifles, which they brought along for good measure when they entered the seven-story complex. The Israelis pinned down the Palestinians with short, accurate bursts of gunfire. Seconds after the firefight began, two Israelis were already dead.

Palestinian resistance was determined, but Shahak's *sayeret* operated brilliantly. They threw several smoke grenades into the building's staircase, forcing the Palestinians to use the building's elevator to get to street level. As the doors of the lift opened the Palestinians were met by the murderous hail of Israeli machine-gun fire. The scene was chaotic. Time and time again the Palestinians used the elevators, even as bodies of their comrades littered the lift's carpeted floor.[30]

After a five minute firefight—a battle often fought hand-to-hand and with brutal ferocity—Shahak ordered the building prepared for explosives detonation. Casualties had forced Shahak to radio in an IAF medevac chopper to remove two dead and three seriously wounded. The call for

Samuel M. Katz

help removed the veil of secrecy and deniability from the operation.* The Israelis could no longer deny complicity in Operation Spring of Youth when a helicopter sporting the IAF's blue Star of David emblem was seen flying over the Lebanese capital. Dozens of West Beirut residents had watched the battle from their terraces.

As Shahak's force headed into their vehicles for the quick ride back to Dove Beach a thunderous explosion—the DFLP headquarters collapsing in a cloud of fire and debris —covered their retreat. They reached the shore and frantically ordered in their naval commando escorts to get them back to ship. Objectives Vardah, Tzilah, and Yehudit were all carried out as planned and without incident.

Operation Spring of Youth is considered one of the IDF's most spectacular *known* special operations. It made Israel an object of the world's awe as a David among Goliaths, able to strike all her enemies anywhere in the world.

On April 10, 1973, back in the Haifa base, Lieutenant Colonels Barak and Shahak met their chief of staff in a cocky postmortem celebration. The officers felt that there was nothing their men could not achieve. The raid in Beirut was such a success that it would be copied exactly fifteen years later, on enemy soil much farther from Israel than Beirut—in Tunis by, according to published reports, virtually the same cast of characters.

# NOTES

1. David Hirst, *The Gun and the Olive Branch* (London: Faber and Faber, 1977), 314.

*For his cool and decisive leadership under fire, Lieutenant Colonel Shahak was awarded his second red-ribboned I'tur Ha'Oz courage medal. His first had come in Operation Hell, the paratroopers' large-scale raid against the major Palestinian training base in Karameh, Jordan, on March 21, 1968.

2. Leroy Thompson, *The Rescuers* (New York: Dell Publishing, 1986), 157.

3. Yosef Argaman, "Zamir Medaber," *Bamachane*, January 27, 1987, 7.

4. Ya'akov Erez and Oded Granot, "Rosh Ha'Mossad," *Ma'ariv Yom Ha'A'atzma'ut*, May 9, 1989, 2.

5. David Hirst, *The Gun and the Olive Branch*, 315.

6. Samuel M. Katz, *Guards Without Frontiers* (London: Arms and Armour Press, 1990), 37.

7. Roberta Goren, *The Soviet Union and Terrorism* (London: George Allen and Unwin Ltd., 1984), 130; Dr. Yuval Arnon-Ochana and Dr. Arieh Yodfat, *Asha'f Diyukono Shel Irgun* (Tel Aviv: Sifriat Ma'ariv, 1985), 135; and Guy Bucher, Lexicon Asha'f (Tel Aviv: Ministry of Defense Publications, 1991), 247–248.

8. For Noriega's connection to Mike Harari, see Yossi Melman and Dan Raviv, *The Imperfect Spies* (London: Sidgwick and Jackson, 1989), 374. In addition, numerous accounts have insinuated a Sayeret Mat'kal connection with the infamous (although denied by the Israeli government) hit teams. Among those sources where the mention of a possible Mat'kal/Mossad connection is implied are Neil C. Livingstone and David Halevy, *Inside the PLO* (New York: William Morrow, 1989), 49, and Edgar O'Ballance, *Language of Violence* (San Rafael: Presidio Press, 1979), 172–173.

9. Samuel M. Katz, *Follow Me! A History of Israel's Military Elite* (London: Arms and Armour Press, 1988), 43.

10. Uri Milshtein, *Ha'Historia Shel Ha'Tzanhanim: Kerech Daled* (Tel Aviv: Schalgi Ltd., Publishing House, 1987), 1611.

11. *Ibid.*, 1616.

12. *Ibid.*, 1616.

13. Christopher Dobson and Ronald Payne, *Counterattack* (New York: Facts On File, Inc., 1982), 88–89.

14. Uri Milshtein, *Ha'Historia Shel Ha'Tzanhanim*, 1617.

15. *Ibid.*, p. 1618.

16. Michael Bar-Zohar and Eitan Haber, *The Quest for the Red Prince* (New York: William Morrow, 1983), 168.

17. *Ibid.,* 169.

18. Uri Milshtein, *Ha'Historia Shel Ha'Tzanhanim,* 1618.

19. Yossi Melman and Dan Raviv, *The Imperfect Spies,* for further elaboration as to the close-knit working relationship between West German intelligence and the Mossad.

20. Michael Bar-Zohar and Eitan Haber, *The Quest for the Red Prince,* 189.

21. Yossi Argaman, *Ze Haya Sodi Be'Yoter* (Tel Aviv: Ministry of Defense Publishing, 1990), 359.

22. Uri Milshtein, *Ha'Historia Shel Ha'Tzanhanim,* 1623.

23. *Ibid.,* 1623.

24. In the motion picture *Black Sunday,* a film depicting a fictitious attempt by Black September to kill thousands of Americans at the Super Bowl, the opening sequence of an Israeli commando raid in Lebanon was copied from the pages of Operation Spring of Youth. It is also believed that the lead in *Black Sunday,* played by Robert Shaw, was based on Ehud Barak (not to mention the unique resemblance of actor Shaw to Ehud Barak!).

25. Uri Milshtein, *Ha'Historia Shel Ha'Tzanhanim,* 1624.

26. Uri Dan, *Etzba Elohim: Sodot Ha'Milchama Be'Teror* (Tel Aviv: Masada Publishing House, 1976), 115.

27. Michael Bar-Zohar and Eitan Haber, "She'Ehud Barak Paratz Be'Bgadei Isha Le'Dirat Ha'Mechablim," *Yediot Sheva Yamim,* November 30, 1990, 9.

28. Uri Milshtein, *Ha'Historia Shel Ha'Tzanhanim,* 1627.

29. *Ibid.,* 1627.

30. Uri Dan, *Etzba Elohim,* 121.

# 7

## Years of Bloodshed and Loss

*The 1973 War and Terrorist Attacks at Ma'alot and the Tel Aviv Shore*

Revenge is as fundamental an element of the Middle Eastern landscape as are the rolling hills of Galilee, the desert abyss of the Arabian peninsula, and the sectarian hatred that unites all of the region's inhabitants into an infrangible web of conflict. On October 6, 1973, Egypt and Syria acted on their long-anticipated opportunity to exact payback from the Jewish state.

At 13:50 hours on that fateful Yom Kippur day, the holiest day in Judaism, Israel found itself under surprise attack in a coordinated assault by the Syrian and Egyptian armies. Israel's frontiers were under siege, and its confidential psyche was blasted into chaotic disarray.

In the north the Syrian army had launched an all-inclusive bid to recapture the ultra-strategic Golan Heights in a massive armor and infantry assault; the Syrians' opening move, interestingly enough, was a heliborne commando assault on Mt. Hermon—according to foreign reports, a top-secret Israeli intelligence-gathering post. The Syrian onslaught was supported by an extensive umbrella of Soviet-produced surface-to-air missile batteries, or SAMs, which forced Israel's ground forces—not fully mobilized in

161

light of the surprise blitz—to fight without air support against an enemy that enjoyed a vast numerical advantage.

In the south the picture was equally bleak. Through cunning and skill the Egyptians had managed to overcome the great Suez Canal barrier, to isolate and overrun the IDF's Bar-Lev Line fortifications, and to rush hundreds of thousands of their best armored and infantry soldiers into the Sinai wasteland. Here, too, Israeli air power was temporarily neutralized by the dreaded SAM. Israel's qualitative edge in tanks was also nullified by Egyptian infantrymen firing hand-held rocket grenades and wire-guided missiles.

Just as the 1973 War caught the State of Israel and the IDF by deadly surprise, so did it catch Sayeret Mat'kal off guard. In fact, many of the unit's most famous fighters were not even *in* Israel when war erupted. When many of these men, such as Major Uzi Dayan, Moshe Dayan's nephew and one of the most flamboyant fighters to ever serve in Sayeret Mat'kal, returned home and to the unit's home base, they found their comrades playing cards and sipping Bedouin coffee laced with cardamom. Israel's best fighters were waiting for an operational assignment—any assignment! When the call to action finally came the unit was initially attached to Ugdat Sharon, a mixed armored and infantry division commanded by Major General (Res.) Arik Sharon, which fought the Egyptians in Sinai, along the Suez Canal.[1]

Later Sayeret Mat'kal was sent up north to assist the Golani Brigade in recapturing Mt. Hermon; the mission, it appeared, was to infiltrate Syrian lines and promulgate chaos and confusion in the enemy's rear while the main attack force inched its way up the steep cliffs.[2] The unit fought a bloody hand-to-hand battle against the Syrian commandos, who—dug in and equipped with Soviet SVD 7.62mm sniper's rifles, RPGs, and generous supplies of F-1 antipersonnel grenades—proved to be unyielding, desperate foes. The battles, fought along the harsh, mountainous rock, were conducted with unheard-of ferocity, even by Arab-Israeli standards. The Syrian commandos attempted to intimidate the Sayeret (and Golani) fighters with taunting cries of *"I'tbach al-Yahud"* ("Slaughter the Jews"!)—shouts that were answered by magazine-emptying bursts of 9mm Uzi fire. Fighting was so fierce, in fact, that the reconnaissance commandos assaulted many Syrian emplacements with a blazing weapon in one hand and a razor-sharpened dagger in the other. Knife fights, similar to the turf wars fought by street gangs in urban America, were carried out inside bunkers and atop boulders amid the sonic-boom backdrop of dive-bombing jet fighters and the lurching whine of incoming artillery support. The Israelis' M26 fragmentation grenades proved particularly effective when lobbed inside the confines of the Syrian's hastily assembled bunkerlike firing positions.

After hours of incessant bloodletting with no quarter given, the Golani Brigade finally arrived; they had waged an epic battle of their own against determined Syrian commando units dug in throughout the mountain. The Mat'kal commandos requested permission to raise the Israeli flag over the shell-tattered position, but OC Northern Command Major General Yitzhak Hofi (a future director of the Mossad) vehemently refused. This was Golani's show. After all, Sayeret Mat'kal did not officially exist.[3]

The 1973 Yom Kippur War, like all of the Arab-Israeli conflagrations, ended in a decisive Israeli military victory. Anything else would most likely have meant the destruction of the Jewish state. Things were so desperate in the eighteen days of furious combat, however, that Israel, according to foreign reports, came close to using its arsenal of nuclear weapons in a true and horrifying Armageddon. Unconventional weapons were never deployed, even though the war went to desperate stages suffered by both sides: The Syrians nearly recaptured the Golan Heights, and the Israeli counterattack nearly got them to Damascus. The Egyptians crossed the Suez Canal, yet so had the IDF. After a military rout of the Arabs seemed imminent, the Soviet Union placed its airborne forces on full alert, threatening to intervene militarily should Israel continue its winning ways; Washington responded in kind by placing the 82nd Airborne Division on full alert and raising the prospects of a superpower showdown and nuclear confrontation in the

Middle East—the closest the world has come to annihilation since the Cuban Missile Crisis.

The Arabs, however, had achieved *their* revenge for 1967. The war, which lasted only eighteen days, had cost the IDF over two thousand dead and over ten thousand seriously wounded. Israel's shield of invincibility had forever been shattered. Yet the quest for vengeance was not complete. Operation Spring of Youth had been a painful and costly embarrassment for Nayif Hawatmeh's Democratic Front for the Liberation of Palestine. Not only had dozens of his most senior commanders and most trusted legions been killed in a pitched battle with Sayeret Tzanhanim commandos masquerading as hippies and European tourists, but his headquarters on rue Khartoum, in West Beirut, had been obliterated courtesy of a few dozen kilograms of well-placed high explosives. The DFLP's next attack against the hated "Zionist entity" would be one that could never be forgotten. It would expose Israeli vulnerability to attack in much the same way that Operation Spring of Youth had proved that the Lebanese capital was not a safe haven from IDF retaliation. For the second time in nearly a year, the paths of the DFLP and Sayeret Mat'kal would once again clash in a bloody engagement.

Contrary to the belief of many self-vaunted "experts," terrorists tend to lay low during full-scale conventional wars; terrorism is not a viable tactical tool during combat. It achieves virtually nothing in the political arena, with the exception of inspiring hatred and anger against the perpetrating party, and militarily it has no value at all. The destruction of an airliner, the rocketing of a bus full of schoolchildren, or the murder of an ambassador during war tends to remove the restraints from a fighting force prosecuting a conflict as hatred and a thirst for revenge mixes with the tactics and structure of combat. Terrorists are also looked upon as dishonorable mercenaries by true soldiers. Palestinian terrorist attacks did not coincide with the fighting in June 1967, nor was terrorism evident in October 1973. Even in the Persian Gulf war of 1991, Saddam

Hussein's much feared army of car bombers and hijackers never materialized.

The gray period of a cease-fire following a conflict is an opportunity to witness the blood and horror of terrorism. It is here, in the midst of clandestine negotiations and removed press coverage, that the shadowy warriors make their bold and cowardly moves. It is a time when the targeted army is battle-weary and the civilian public more inclined to feel vulnerable, insecure, anxious; as a result, governments may acquiesce to terrorist demands in order to prevent the spilling of more blood. Such was the case following the Yom Kippur War, when Israel's confidence was already shaken following the collapse of its intelligence capabilities and the horrific human toll.

As a bitter war of attrition was waged between Syrian and Israeli commando forces along the Golan Heights, a new front was opened toward the west, on the Israeli-Lebanese border. On April 11, 1974, one week after Lieutenant General Mordechai Gur was named the IDF's tenth chief of staff, three terrorists from Ahmed Jibril's Popular Front for the Liberation of Palestine General Command (PFLP-GC) crossed the heavily fortified frontier and infiltrated the border town of Qiryat Shmoneh. Jibril's plan was to attack a schoolhouse, take a class hostage, and barter children's lives in exchange for jailed comrades in Israeli prisons. But Jibril, a terrorist warlord known for meticulous planning, had grossly miscalculated. It was Passover, the feast of redemption for the children of Israel, and the school was closed. Undaunted, and now seeking a target before being discovered, the three terrorists had decided to head for an adjacent block of flats when they heard the sounds of families gathered for the morning meal and children playing. The terrorists, trained in world-class facilities near Damur, just south of Beirut, systematically searched each apartment, killing anyone they found. One family was massacred as it sat at the breakfast table.

Eventually units from the Golani Brigade, responsible in

part for security duties along the northern frontier, were called in. The terrorists, seeking refuge from the overwhelming firepower brought to bear against them, found brief sanctuary in a top-floor apartment. After several rounds of recoilless rifle fire pushed them downstairs, the three men were cut down by incessant and unforgiving bursts of Golani fire. The terrorists' toll, however, was grisly. Sixteen civilians lay dead, as did two Golani infantrymen.

From a storefront office in Beirut a pudgy PFLP-GC spokesman named Abu Abbas (famed in later years for hijacking the *Achille Lauro* and embracing Saddam Hussein, and commander of the PFLP-GC breakaway group known as the Palestine Liberation Front) declared that the attack against Qiryat Shmoneh was "the beginning of a new campaign of revolutionary violence and revolutionary suicide inside Israel."[4] Abu Abbas's statement was prophetic, as Hawatmeh tried to exact his own brand of vengeance for Operation Spring of Youth.

In the early morning hours of May 15, 1974, on Israel's twenty-sixth birthday, three DFLP terrorists wearing IDF fatigues slipped across the Lebanese border into Israel, bypassing the fortifications, mine fields, concertina obstacles, and electronic sensors. Laden down with explosives and ammunition, they slinked alongside the underbrush of a main roadway staying clear of routes IDF patrols were known to frequent with varying degrees of regularity. They were en route to Ma'alot, a northern town along the Lebanese frontier. Ma'alot was their target, but this was not going to be an indiscriminate display of death and destruction to the hated "Zionist entity," like the debacle at Qiryat Shmoneh. Hawatmeh, a Greek Orthodox Christian and dedicated communist, was a bold and tenacious planner. He was an operational genius who relied on accurate intelligence reports from his spies and informants, and on the ruthlessness of his men in the field—one-time commandos whose suicide was as much a tactical statement as deciding what to hit. As the IDF had struck him where he lived in Beirut, he would devise a similar fate for the Israelis. May

15 was the day the DFLP was to seize an entire schoolhouse and barter off helpless children in exchange for a few incarcerated comrades and headlines in the international tabloids.

The three terrorists—Ali Ahmed Hassan, Ahmed Saleh Nayef, and Zaid Abdul Rahmin—were ideally suited to the task at hand. All three had been born in Israel proper, all three spoke flawless Hebrew, and all had light complexions, meaning that they could pass for Jews; with their olive "Israeli" uniforms and light skin tone, they were sure to pass as IDF personnel with little difficulty.

After entering the sleepy border town of four thousand inhabitants at 03:50 hours they encountered Ya'akov Kadosh, a sanitation worker in the Ma'alot municipality. In impeccable Hebrew they asked, "Where is the school?" Unaware of any danger and assuming them to be lost reservists, Kadosh pointed with his left hand signaling that the building was further up the road. Ali Hassan, the group's leader, then asked Kadosh if there were any children in there now and, finally and fatefully, if he was a Jew or an Arab. "Jew, of course," responded a proud Kadosh, but it was an answer rewarded with a burst of 7.62mm fire directed at his chest. As a screaming Kadosh lay bleeding profusely in the gutter the three armed men continued on their way, their pace intensifying only slightly.

Their next stop was the home of Yosef and Zachina Cohen, a target chosen at random. They knocked on the door, yelling madly in Hebrew about needing the phone to contact police and summon an ambulance. When the sleepy couple came to answer the call they were met by wild bursts of AK-47 fire. Both parents—Zachina was six months pregnant—and a daughter, Baya, were hit and fatally wounded. Two other children were seriously hurt. Leaving the small home engulfed with the choking stench of cordite and spilled blood, the three Palestinians continued up the road.[5]

The sound of two separate volleys of gunfire served as a warning to the sleepy town. After all, gunfire in northern Israel could mean only one thing—a terrorist attack. The town had been the target of frequent Katyusha rocket attacks in the past, and each residential area was equipped with its own well-stocked bomb shelter. The explosive percussion of automatic gunfire also awoke several nervous adults and 103 groggy-eyed children, students from the Safed Religious School who were bivouacking in the Ma'alot schoolhouse during a three-day nature outing in the Galilee region. The sleeping children, dispersed throughout the three-story building, were ripe targets.

At 04:10 hours the three DFLP gunmen broke into the building, pumping nearly a dozen warning shots into the loosely plastered ceiling. Many of the teachers, some of the students, and a Gad'na (Youth Battalion) instructor managed to leap out a ground floor window and race into the surrounding trees, but the majority remained trapped behind. Speaking a slow and deliberate Hebrew, the terrorists then gathered the children into controllable locations. Amazingly, one student recognized Zaid Rahmin from his days as a public works laborer in Safed and angrily asked him how he could be involved in such a thing.[6]

Operation leader Hassan told the children that nobody would be hurt if they behaved and cooperated—but would the IDF cooperate? They would most certainly have been summoned by now! Large bundles of explosives were placed at a strategic position inside the main entrance, and all the classrooms were wired to detonators.

A few minutes after the three had burst into the school the first police vans and IDF jeeps arrived. The policemen pulled pistols from their holsters, and soldiers, unsure of what was transpiring in front of them, crawled into advantageous firing positions with their gunsights aimed at any window where movement was noticed. A high-ranking police officer carrying an Uzi and a megaphone established preliminary contact. The talks were carried out in Hebrew and mixed with the odd gunshot thrown in for good measure. Sniping was a bad way to start negotiations, but Israel, it must be remembered, did not negotiate with terrorists.

It was clear from the onset that this was a very serious

situation. This terrorist act was not a bomb left in a crowded market nor a suicidal murder spree in a residential area. This was not even the Sabena hijacking, where adults held other adults hostage. The future generation of the State of Israel was being held captive by desperate men who were more than ready to die for their cause. The hostages were innocent children whose fate was to be determined by trained gunmen schooled in the art of cold-blooded killing at the best facilities the PLO could afford, and by the skill and courage of the IDF's best unit. Less than half an hour later several IAF helicopters adorned in a dazzling three-color camouflage scheme landed at a nearby soccer field. Through the churning dust and thumping symphony of rapidly beating rotor blades, a group of heavily armed men wearing olive fatigues, brown leather paratrooper boots, and full battle kit disembarked from the choppers and raced toward the hastily assembled command post. It was the Chief of Staff's Boys, Sayeret Mat'kal.[7]

Clearly, the Mat'kal commandos had unique experience in hostage-rescue operations—more experience, that is, than anyone else in the IDF and, probably, the world. But the Ma'alot schoolhouse was a much tougher nut to crack than an isolated Boeing 707. There could be no disguises and no invisible entrances. The schoolhouse was not a controlled environment like the Sabena liner at Lod. It was a terrible place to stage a covert rescue mission. Amid the senior commander's conferences, soldiers readying their gear, and terrorists sniping at anything in olive that moved in their direction, hundreds of Ma'alot residents trekked to the embattled hilltop to observe the unfolding drama. Some wanted to see the destruction of the murderers of the Cohen family; some were Golani Brigade soldiers on leave who brought their weapons just in case their services would be needed. And then there was the most emotional group to reach the scene: hundreds of anguished parents and family members, crying in uncontrolled bursts of grief, praying that their babies would not be harmed. The occasional sounds of gunfire emanating from inside the school were not encouraging signs for those watching.

At 06:00 hours IDF Chief of Staff Lieutenant General Mordechai Gur arrived. A veteran Na'ha'l reconnaissance officer and the man who, as commander of the 66th (Res.) Paratroop Brigade, liberated Jerusalem in 1967, Gur was a highly respected no-nonsense commander. It was his task to stall the bloodshed and prevent a massacre until the rescue plan was in place.

The terrorists' demands were modestly ambitious and were hand delivered to Chief of Staff Gur by a released female IDF lieutenant, one of the Gad'na instructors who had accompanied the Safed students. Typed on official-looking stationery prepared in Damascus, it stated that in exchange for the lives of the students Israel was to release twenty-six convicted Palestinian terrorists in her jails—one for each year of her independence. Half the children would be released when the twenty-six freed fedayeen arrived safely in Damascus on board a Red Cross transport, while the remainder of the hostages would serve as human shields to protect the terrorists from harm as they flew to an Arab capital in a jet provided by the Israelis. According to the terrorist demands, the French and Romanian ambassadors to Israel were to oversee the prisoner release. Accordingly, Hawatmeh had dispatched letters of instruction to French and Romanian diplomats hours before the three-man squad had even crossed the border into Ma'alot. A deadline of 20:00 hours was issued. If by then either the French or the Romanian ambassador had not delivered the coded message from Damascus, the terrorists would blow up the school and everyone in it. Not a single Israeli on the scene doubted their determination, will, or ability to execute their bloody mission.

Slowly the Mat'kal commandos had inched their way as far forward as they could get without making their presence known. Mishmar Ha'Gvul (Border Guard) units secured a perimeter, and police officers did their best to keep outraged parents from foolishly taking matters into their own hands.

It was a classic standoff until 07:30 hours, when additional strains of excitement and tension reached Ma'alot. As the terrorists were in the process of reiterating their demands to the assembled Israeli authorities Defense Minister Moshe Dayan arrived, together with the OC Northern Command, Major General Raful Eitan. Dayan had been visibly shaken by the events of the last year; many considered the intelligence failure of the 1973 War *his* failure, and many in the apolitical IDF called for his resignation. The once-mighty icon of the Israeli military establishment was now a self-doubting symbol; his actions, once unwritten law, were now discussed and even debated at the brigade commander level. Raful, however, emerged from the war one of the most respected and capable of all IDF generals. Commander of Ugdat Raful, a division that had held the Golan Heights against the Syrian army, his decisive leadership turned imminent rout into breathtaking counterattack twenty-two miles into Syria proper. A few days after his heavily fortified headquarters at Nafekh were nearly overrun by an unstoppable and unending line of Syrian armor, his guns were in range of the Syrian capital. His brilliant leadership brought victory to the north.

Raful was not one to mince words or delay in the execution of decisive military action. After twenty years of combating terrorists, Raful knew their minds with a mixture of cunning respect and contempt; he knew their abilities, their psyche, and, most important, their shortcomings. Perhaps more than anyone else in the IDF, Raful also knew the capabilities and determination of Sayeret Mat'kal. Because he was OC Northern Command, this operation would be Raful's call.

For the next several hours the desperate standoff continued. For Raful, the order to wait until Defense Minister Dayan returned from a cabinet meeting in Jerusalem (he had left the embattled schoolhouse) was very hard to swallow; had the incident transpired at a truly isolated location, he might have ordered in the assault teams immediately. Yet the order to wait was even harder for the commandos who had crawled at a snail's pace ever closer to the schoolhouse gates, inching their way forward and finding cover behind anything that would shield them from the 7.62mm rounds being peppered in their direction. These men were trained to act in explosive fashion—to strike the enemy hard and without respite, to execute the objective in haste, and to depart even faster. This "hurry up and wait" business was hard to adjust to and harder to accept—especially when the terrorists laced the school grounds with bursts of automatic fire at every mood swing. The cries of terrified children and the inability to alleviate their fright and suffering was heart-wrenching to the Sayeret Mat'kal commandos, many of whom entertained brief thoughts of doing something, anything, with or without top-brass authorization. They were, however, professionals and stood fast in their firing positions with their fingers gently caressing the K'latch trigger housings.

Between 09:00 hours and noon a mini-battle of sorts was under way at the schoolhouse—it was a war of nerves as the terrorists continued to fire at anything that moved in their direction. Negotiations to stall for time continued, but they consisted of pleas shouted through megaphones to spare the hostages. Occasionally the commandos returned sniper fire in self-defense, but that was it. They were under extremely strict orders not to use automatic fire; that might indicate the commencement of the rescue assault and result in the terrorists' detonating the explosives and killing the children.

At 13:10 hours, minutes after releasing four ailing students in a surprising display of humanity, one terrorist barricaded by the third-floor window exposed his AK barrel long enough to squeeze off a burst of 7.62mm fire. He was an accurate shot, and his volley killed a Mat'kal commando creeping closer to the school—close enough, perhaps, to squeeze off a shot at one of the "bandits." A valiant attempt by his comrades to remove his body met with an impassable hail of gunfire, and the bleeding soldier was left exposed on the dry grass lawn until the rescue was ordered.[8]

The DFLP gunmen meant business and had what appeared to be an endless supply of ammunition. It was clearly the time to act, but the government debate in Jerusalem caused a deadly delay—one that removed the element of surprise from the commandos' hands and allowed the terrorists to accept gradually their status as martyrs for Palestine.

As the sniping continued at Ma'alot a full-scale conflagration was under way in Prime Minister Golda Meir's office in Jerusalem. Numbed by the Yom Kippur War, the Israeli cabinet was in no mood to witness further carnage—especially involving children. In a heated cabinet debate, vicious even by the cruel and crude standards of Israeli politics, it was decided to release twenty Palestinians in exchange for the lives of the Ma'alot children. (Later both Prime Minister Meir and Defense Minister Dayan vehemently declared that they had voted against the exchange deal with the DFLP terrorists.)[9]

The consternation of the Israeli government was all-encompassing. To prove to the terrorists that they were sincere about acquiescing to their demands, the government ordered two imprisoned terrorists brought to the schoolhouse as a sign of good faith. The two men, handcuffed and blindfolded, were brought up to the main entrance for a look. Clean-shaven and resilient, the incarcerated men braved the taunts of the local Ma'alot residents gathered at the area—mainly immigrants from North Africa who intimately understood the Arab mentality—to show themselves off as stoic soldiers of Palestine; in Arabic they shouted, "Soon we will be in Damascus to fight another day." It was a promise of hope that would not be kept.

The logistics of Hawatmeh's intricate demands, however, proved to be more of a challenge than the political will to make the deal. The Israeli government was not about to risk an Israeli-flag aircraft, since it was argued that the Syrians would shoot it down either before or after it arrived in Damascus. No other foreign carrier was willing to make the trip, and a United Nations aircraft in Jerusalem's small Atarot airport was under repairs and could not be ready until well past the terrorist deadline. Both the French and Romanian ambassadors were playing with tied hands; the French ambassador did not have the required code word to end the ordeal, and when Bucharest offered Romania as an alternate destination to Damascus, the terrorists thought it a stalling move and, as a result, stood fast in the refusal to extend their deadline.

It was clear, as Defense Minister Dayan returned from Jerusalem unable to meet the transportation demands of the terrorists, that a military solution would be required. Slowly the order was issued over the radio network for the commandos to regroup at the ad hoc CP, while snipers were to remain in position; although the actual weapon used by the Mat'kal sniper is still classified, foreign reports indicate that it was either an M-16 5.56mm rifle fitted with a scope or a captured Soviet 7.62mm SVD.[10]

What happened next remains one of the most controversial and painful chapters in the history of Israel's war against Palestinian terrorism. At 16:00 hours, after an extensive and anguished briefing of the various generals assembled at the CP, the Sayeret Mat'kal commander, and his top officers, the commandos were ordered to begin their final crawl to destiny.

Infantry ballistic helmets were worn for protection against shrapnel penetration, each head covering camouflaged with tan netting and supported by black rubber tubing. The principal weapon carried was, of course, the trusted K'latch. Almost every weapon was equipped with two magazines taped together, offering sixty immediate and available rounds of firepower. Since the battle inside the building was expected to be fierce, several commandos also carried the FN MAG 7.62mm light machine gun, bringing a weapon capable of firing between six hundred and one thousand rounds per minute into a closed-quarter, confined combat environment. Each commando carried additional grenades—mainly fragmentation grenades, but white phosphorus (the famed "Willy Peter" canister) was also carried as part of the conventional kit.[11]

Casualties were expected to be very heavy. Almost every other commando carried a stretcher strapped to his back, and the unit's medical officers were placed in the vanguard of the assault. Ambulances were readied, and a squadron of IAF choppers was also prepared to bring the critical cases to the more advanced trauma centers located in northern Israel. Some of the IDF secular officers assembled at the schoolhouse—men who on Yom Kippur, a day of fasting, ordinarily barbecued meats at the beach—began to pray. An eerie sense of peace engulfed the gathering. It was quiet and frightening—truly the calm before the storm.

As the seconds ticked closer to 17:00 hours the commandos began their final crawl toward the schoolhouse. In the minds of each commando, every inch traveled brought him that much closer to rescuing the hostages; leg muscles, cramped and tired in the nearly twelve hours of waiting, were poised to coil and leap into action. At 17:25 hours the team's point sniper was issued the green light to engage a target; his ripping shot was to signal the commencement of the raid. The plan was simple: Race through the building and kill the terrorists before they could detonate the well-placed explosive charges. At most the commandos would have sixty seconds to assume control over the building; anything more would allow the surviving terrorists the time needed to detonate strategically placed dynamite. There was nothing scientific to the plan, nothing bold or innovative. The tools for implementing the military solution were equally primitive: the courage of an individual soldier and the accuracy of his aim.

The Mat'kal chief sniper located a terrorist walking past a window on the third floor. The man, a handsome individual with striking features, was carrying his AK-47 in a manner indicating he was about to empty a magazineload of rounds into the grassy courtyard below. A lone shot shattered the anxious silence as a tracer round ripped through the brain of the DFLP gunman. Immediately the olive-clad force burst into action. In seconds the commandos entered the building, bursting through the main door, racing through the main hallway, and purifying each room in dire haste, supported by indiscriminate firepower. The laden-down Mat'kal fighters looked like choreographed pinballs bouncing off bumpers as they propelled themselves off walls to burst into room after room. The commandos, however, had mistaken the location of the terrorists and hostages—an

175

error that led to tragedy. First, they raced to the third floor instead of the second; this alerted the terrorists to the attack and gave them time to turn their gunsights on the students instead of the Mat'kal commandos. The second mistake was equally costly. The use of white phosphorus grenades meant that each blast was followed by a blinding cloud of smoke— one that had to clear before the commandos could see what they were doing. By the time they reached the second floor and waited for the choking white cloud to dissipate, the horrific destruction had been committed. The two surviving terrorists had killed twenty-two children with gun and grenade fire, and over sixty were critically wounded before the terrorists were silenced by Mat'kal bursts of lead. When they finally encountered the terrorists, the Mat'kal commandos made it a point to empty enormous volleys of ammunition into the DFLP martyrs.

The much-anticipated code word, Al-Aksa—the name of the beautiful and majestic Jerusalem mosque that is Islam's third-holiest shrine—was never heard.

The Ma'alot Massacre was one of the saddest days ever endured by the State of Israel, a nation exposed to tragedy on a daily basis. The death of so many children was an outrage of historic national proportions. The sight of weary Mat'kal commandos carrying bleeding children on their backs to ambulances sent a paralyzing shock wave through the Israeli public, a population already in mourning after one of the costliest military conflicts in its short and bloody history. The enemies of Israel appeared to be cold-blooded and capable, and the IDF—the guardians of the Jewish state—failed to keep the nation's children from the evil of Middle Eastern treachery. Some families lost two children;* some families were destroyed forever. Many of the children had been so deformed by the gunfire of the terrorists that

*The Mader family of Safed lost their daughter Yehudit and their son David in the massacre. Eight years later their eldest son Haim, a senior master-sergeant in the Border Guard, fell in the line of duty while combating Palestinian terrorists in Lebanon following the 1982 Operation Peace for Galilee.

they could only be identified days later. Following the funerals of the Ma'alot fallen, Prime Minister Meir stated, "I cannot promise that the terrorists will allow us to live in peace. But I can and do promise that every government of Israel will chop off the hands of those who want to cut short the lives of our children."[12]

The Ma'alot massacre also proved that Sayeret Mat'kal was not perfect; its men were human and fallible. Israel's supermen had *not* achieved the impossible. They had used inappropriate weaponry, failing to employ such high-tech and revolutionary tools as electronic sensors and stun grenades to locate the terrorists and temporarily disarm them. They had executed the rescue in a slow, deliberate, and unsuccessful manner.[13] According to Sayeret Mat'kal's Major Uzi Dayan, "It was the worst carnage I had ever seen. It was the first time I had ever seen a room soaked in human blood and the remains of small children caked to walls. It was a tragedy we should have averted."[14]

Israel responded to the Ma'alot massacre with routine air strikes against various terrorist targets in southern Lebanon, but Israel, the IDF, and Sayeret Mat'kal had been changed forever. For the prime minister, Ma'alot was an ominous sign. She had used the 1973 War as main justification for her decision, and Ma'alot proved to be the straw that broke the camel's back of her political career. She announced her resignation along with Dayan's letter of self-removal.

A government inquiry was duly ordered, and it came up with startling revelations that illuminated the reasons for the debacle. One interesting finding was that Israeli radio was providing a play-by-play description of the events to a live and captive audience. Each terrorist carried with him a portable transistor radio as a staple element of his equipment; they, too, followed the unfolding events with uncanny real-time insight.

Ma'alot was a historic turning point for the antiterrorist policy and strategy of the Israeli Defense Ministry. The seizure of the children proved that counterterrorist operations had to be conducted by a highly specialized force, a unit whose sole task was hostage rescue. A purely military unit trained in the most sophisticated aspects of cross-border intelligence gathering and commando assaults could not be used in domestic security details. To do so would risk death in operations that should be handled by other, more conventional forces and lead to public exposure and scrutiny. A unit such as Sayeret Mat'kal was created in order to operate purely under a veil of anonymity—its victories were never to be known to the public, and its defeats were not supposed to become the subject of mass-media (or even government) examination and review. After all, Sayeret Mat'kal's mandate was as a covert intelligence force. But its unique abilities made it the ideal antiterrorist unit—a quality and operational legacy that brought on unwanted publicity.

Ma'alot led to change in Israeli counterterrorist strategy as special internal security duties were removed from sole IDF domain and allocated to the police and border guards. The creation of a special counterterrorist hostage rescue force was the culmination of this governmental decision.[15]

In early 1974 the national police had been toying with the idea of creating a special commando force of its own, although the Ma'alot massacre drastically changed the force's character and eventual mandate. Much like the West Germans' much-vaunted Grenzschutzgruppe-9 (GSG-9), Western Europe's elite antiterrorist strike force (attached to the Federal Border Guard, which had been created in the bloody aftermath of the 1972 Munich Olympics massacre), the new Israeli unit's sole mandate was hostage rescue and delicate arrest operations. This would include, according to foreign sources, the seizure, with Shin Bet supervision, of high-ranking terrorists in the West Bank and Gaza Strip. Unlike the various *sayerot* in the IDF, however, this new border guard force would not have to endure a persistent changeover in manpower due to the termination of the conscription service periods of its soldiers, and it would not have to train for both conventional military objectives and irregular counterterrorist operations. The new border guard force would be organized along the lines of the GSG-9, a professional force; it would only receive volunteers who were chosen following a rigorous selection process. It was to be manned primarily by veterans from the IDF's various *sayerot*—mainly conscripts possessing superb combat skill and dedication, but unable to acclimate to the mundane day-to-day existence of Israeli civilian life. This new and top-secret force took a mysterious acronym as its name—Ya'ma'm (Yechida Meyuchedet Le'Lochima Be'Terror, or Special Unit for Combating Terrorism)—and its existence was known to only a select group of high-ranking officials.

The Ya'ma'm was supposed to be the sole force entrusted with hostage-rescue operations inside Israel. Yet a force of this nature took time to staff, man, and train—a lot of time. Unfortunately for Sayeret Mat'kal, time was not on Israel's side.

Encouraged by the DFLP's success in attacking Israel and bringing the nation's sense of vulnerability to panic proportions, Yasir Arafat's el-Fatah faction embarked on an ambitious terror offensive of its own. This time, however, frontier towns and border villages would not be hit—that was, after all, the domain of the amateur. Arafat and his operations chief, Abu Jihad—a man who would, according to published reports, meet Sayeret Mat'kal in the future—would strike the heart of Israel: its population and cultural center, Tel Aviv.

March 5, 1975, off the coast of Tel Aviv. On the damp deck of a rusting freighter eight men clad in lizard-pattern camouflage fatigues, laden down with rucksacks filled with explosives and web gear pouches loaded to capacity with ammunition and grenades, saluted the red, green, black, and white Palestinian flag as it waved violently in the mid-sea air. Moments later two Zodiac rubber dinghies were thrown into the water as the first sign that a masterful terrorist operation was under way. The eight men were members of the Abu Yusef Commandos (an ad hoc title honoring the slain Black September leader) in this, the PLO's version of Operation Spring of Youth. It was an operation, their commanders in Beirut hoped, that would make the Ma'alot incursion seem like an old lady's kaffeeklatsch.

At 23:15 hours the Zodiacs landed undetected at a

deserted Tel Aviv beach—it was the last moment of winter, and too cold for the city's lovers to be sitting along the romantic promenade. After assembling their gear and wrapping their AK-47 slings around their shoulders in attack position, the eight slinked their way to Hayarkon Street, a seedy boulevard quite popular with Tel Aviv's ladies of the evening. The terrorists raced in and out of the shadows in the hope of eluding discovery. They were successful. Yet upon reaching the Hayarkon Street intersection they decided to forgo stealth and announce their arrival to all within range—they went wild, firing their weapons in a 360° radius, lobbing grenades onto second-floor terraces, and looking for any moving target. They found the filled-to-capacity Cinema 1 and tossed several grenades into the crowded movie house before exiting for greener pastures; they headed toward the seaside Savoy Hotel, located at 5 Geula Street. After attempting—unsuccessfully—to take an entire wedding party hostage at an adjacent catering hall, the terrorists burst into the sleepy hotel lobby, a dimly lit room where old women were busy drinking cups of hot water, sugar, and thinly sliced lemon, and shot dead the pensioner desk clerk for good measure. They immediately barricaded the entrances and raced throughout the four floors to assemble all the guests, who now found themselves hostages.

During the assault on the sleepy Tel Aviv waterfront, between frenzied barrages of tracer fire and exploding fragmentation grenades, the terror squad managed to pass an undercover police car on a stakeout (the policemen were expecting an underworld shootout, no less), and within minutes dozens of police cars sealed off the area. The sound of gunfire awoke the sleepy neighborhood, and a soldier on leave, Private Moshe Deutshman, grabbed his FN FAL 7.62mm assault rifle and raced toward the fray. Courageously, he engaged the terrorists alone, opening fire on the men racing through the streets; but he was fired upon as well. Several rounds ripped through his body, and he was fatally wounded.

The operation proceeded just as Arafat and Abu Jihad

THE ELITE

had planned in their Beirut war room. Less than a year following the twenty-two deaths at Ma'alot, Israel was bracing itself for yet another tense hostage standoff.

The slumbering Tel Aviv night had been shattered by the bursts of machine-gun fire, and soon hundreds of heavily armed police officers arrived carrying Uzis with two magazines taped together. Border Guard police units (including, it has been reported, assault teams from the newly created Ya'ma'm), military police units, and elements from Sayeret Mat'kal appeared, too.[16] Also at the scene were the top commanders of the Israeli defense establishment; the Savoy Hotel was, after all, a five-minute car ride from the Kirya. The emergency signal had been sounded inside the Kirya compound, as a terrorist attack on Israel's most sensitive piece of real estate was a possibility that could not be ignored. Military police perimeter guards now cocked their pistols and automatic rifles; only essential personnel were allowed inside the bustling mini-city. The lights in both the Operations and Intelligence Branch buildings were turned on, their coffeepots filled, and the "need to know" personnel contacted.

Back outside the Savoy, alongside the jeeps, command cars, and ambulances, several staff cars began to arrive, ferrying the who's who of Israel's defense establishment. Early on it was apparent to the assembled leadership that this attack was a turning point of some kind—either for the good or, it was feared, for the bad. So soon after the Yom Kippur War and the Ma'alot tragedy, a successful terrorist strike in the heart of Tel Aviv could cause acute damage to Israeli confidence in its defense forces and its political leadership. This was most obvious to Shimon Peres, who, although as lackluster a politician as the Israeli Labor Party had ever produced, was a brilliant strategist and long-range planner. His orders that evening to the Chief of Staff and the Sayeret Mat'kal commander assembled at a street corner were: "Evacuate all the nearby homes in a calm and panic-free environment while preparing the makeup of the rescue team in dire haste. There is to be no acquiescence to their demands, no compromise. Just toy with them in negotiations and then strike them when they least expect it with as few casualties as possible."[17]

Once again casualties were expected to be heavy; Tel Aviv's two largest hospitals, Ichilov and Hadassah, were readied for the expected catastrophe.

Also present at the Savoy battlefield was Colonel Uzi Yairi, a staff officer in the Intelligence Corps and onetime commander of Sayeret Mat'kal.[18] Yairi reached the scene on his own, dressed in full battle kit and carrying a legendary AK-47, a souvenir awarded to him from a captured terrorist following the February 1973 IDF commando raid on Tripoli, Lebanon. He attached himself to the pre-assault briefing and offered himself as the assault's point man. According to "A.," the assault commander, "Yairi said that since he wasn't laden down with web gear, bulletproof vest and other top-secret bits of equipment which the commandos wore, he was lighter and faster than anyone in the unit—he was, indeed. He would mark the positions toward which the commandos would direct their well-aimed bursts of gunfire and lead the way."[19] Nobody dared to refuse Colonel Yairi when he was adamant about leading an operation—he lived for his men and for the security of his country!

The terrorists' demands were quite modest, considering the audacious nature of their attack. They demanded the release of ten jailed terrorists and safe passage to Damascus. While the politicians and hostage negotiators talked to the terrorists, pushing back deadlines and promoting a false feeling of security, the commandos refined their assault plan. The terrorists were holding, it was assumed, no more than ten hostages. A lightning strike into the building, preceded by a stun attack of some kind, could terminate the bandits with limited loss of innocent life. The attack was to be shorter than a couple of minutes. Prime Minister Rabin was briefed and was impressed with the contingency plan. Rabin, however, ordered that the rescue take place before the day's first light and before the nation awoke and went to work.

As the dawn's first rays of sunlight burst over the city, police and border guard personnel inched their way closer to the building—they were to provide cover fire if needed. At 05:12 Colonel Yairi, clutching his beloved K'latch in his left hand, raced along Geula Street into the building as dozens of heavily armed men, weighed down by heavy loads, followed in close pursuit. Upon their explosive entry into the hotel, where hails of grenade and gunfire had preceded the attack, a fierce firefight erupted inside the hotel lobby. Yairi, A., and several of the commandos had managed to kill three terrorists with sharp bursts aimed at their heads and torsos; taking prisoners might be good for intelligence, but now it was a secondary objective. As the rescue force made its way through the hotel, toward a cloakroom where the majority of the hostages were being held, a thunderous blast was heard throughout the city. The terrorists had placed huge quantities of explosives throughout the building and had exploded the floors above the commandos. A large section of the hotel collapsed in what looked a falling house of cards. The choking smoke of debris created mass confusion and chaos. Shots were heard emanating from all directions.

The Mat'kal commandos continued their purification of what remained of the hotel undaunted—after all, it would take much more than a collapsing building to deter them from their mission. As the commandos continued to purify the decimated facility a terrorist emerged from behind a partly open door and laced Sergeant Itamar Ben-David, a veteran Mat'kal NCO, with a volley to the head, killing the young squad leader instantly. A few moments later Yairi and A. closed ranks toward a room—one of the few remaining that had not yet been searched and secured—from which the thuds of automatic fire had come. A. warned Yairi that the room was not yet secure, but Yairi continued his approach. As he positioned his body against the wall, preparing to toss in a grenade, Yairi gingerly stuck his head around the corner to see if there were any hostages in the room. A three-second burst of fire struck the sturdy colonel in the head and neck, and he collapsed with an anguished cry of pain. He died hours later on the operating table at Ichilov Hospital.

By 06:00 hours the ordeal at the Savoy Hotel was history. Eleven Israelis, including the three soldiers, had been killed, and twelve were seriously wounded. Seven of the terrorists were killed in the assault, and one, identified as Musa Juma, survived the melee and was found emerging from the rubble hours later. For the next several hours, as curious onlookers came to gaze at the destruction, nervous sappers from the IDF Combat Engineers' elite Bomb Disposal Unit raked the rubble for further explosive surprises.

Colonel Uzi Yairi, thirty-nine, a father of five, was laid to rest later that day. His coffin was carried by six colonels, all personal friends in the joys of peace and comrades in the dire heat of battle. He was a unique IDF commander, a man who had begun his military career in the idealistic ranks of the Na'ha'l farmer/fighters, then gone on to the paratroopers, and then to the unit. He was a powerful and charismatic figure, a man for whom courage was a fundamental element of life. Following Operation Spring of Youth, for example, he went to the home of Avida Shor, a reconnaissance paratrooper killed in the assault of the DFLP HQ, and remarkably told the fallen soldier's mother, "It was me who sent your son on the operation!"[20] The 1973 War changed him, however. As commander of the paratroop brigade he lost forty paratroopers killed and one hundred critically wounded during the Chinese Farm battle, and something died in him as well. He opted, until convinced otherwise, to leave the IDF altogether. Eulogizing the former Mat'kal commander, Chief of Staff Gur said, "He felt compelled to join in on the assault—he just couldn't sit quietly by on the sidelines."[21] Colonel Uzi Yairi was the first Sayeret Mat'kal commander, either retired or on the job, to die in the line of duty. He wouldn't be the last, however. Terrorism, it appeared, had won the day once again.

The fighters in Sayeret Mat'kal vowed revenge for the killing of two of their own, but where and when? Terrorism was becoming bloodier, and it appeared that the Chief of Staff's Boys' skills were not capable of the task at hand. Some commandos even spray-painted the word *nekama* (revenge) on the walls of their home base. On July 4, 1975,

Ahmed Jibril's PFLP-GC planted a powerful bomb inside a refrigerator abandoned outside a store in Jerusalem. The blast killed thirteen and wounded seventy-eight. One year to the day after this "victory" for Palestine, Sayeret Mat'kal would, indeed, receive its long-anticipated chance for revenge against terrorism. It would not come outside a terrorist-held schoolhouse or a two-star hotel along the Mediterranean coast. It would come thousands of miles from the Israeli frontiers in the dark abyss of Africa, in an operation of which the world is still in awe.

# NOTES

1. Emanuel Rosen, "Uzi: Ha'Klaf Ha'Chazak Shel Shoshelet Dayan," *Ma'ariv Sof Shavua*, February 5, 1988, 8.

2. For Uzi Dayan's connection to Sayeret Mat'kal, see Yossi Melman and Dan Raviv, *The Imperfect Spies* (London: Sidgwick and Jackson, 1989), 200; for Uzi Dayan and Sayeret Mat'kal's operations during the 1973 Yom Kippur War, see Emanuel Rosen, "Uzi: Ha'Klaf Ha'Chazak," 8.

3. Emanuel Rosen, "Ha'Klaf Ha'Chazak," 8.

4. Edgar O'Ballance, *Language of Violence: The Blood Politics of Terrorism* (San Rafael: Presidio Press, 1979), 231.

5. Hamital Tzur, "Be'Hazara Le'Ma'alot," *Bamachane*, September 27, 1990, 22.

6. *Ibid.*, 24.

7. For a confirmed reference to the arrival of the elite unit, see *Ibid.*, 24; for foreign mention as to Sayeret Mat'kal's arrival at the scene, see Christopher Dobson and Ronald Payne, *Counterattack—The West's Battle Against the Terrorists* (New York: Facts On File, Inc., 1982), 90, and Leroy Thompson, *The Rescuers: The World's Top Antiterrorist Units* (New York: Dell Publishing, 1986), 157.

8. Hamital Tzur, "Be'Hazara Le'Ma'alot," 23.

9. Edgar O'Ballance, *Language of Violence*, 233.

10. Interview with anonymous Western intelligence officer, June 22, 1991.

11. See Christopher Dobson and Ronald Payne, *Counterattack,* 91.

12. Edgar O'Ballance, *Language of Violence,* 233.

13. Christopher Dobson and Ronald Payne, *Counterattack,* 92.

14. See Emanuel Rosen, "Uzi: Ha'Klaf," 10.

15. Tzvi Zinger, "Ya'ma'm," *Ha'aretz,* April 7, 1978, 8.

16. Sarit Yeshai Levi, "Lo Rotza A'aravei Zicharon," *Ha'dashot,* March 30, 1990, p. 39.

17. "Dramat Ha'Damim Be'Savoy," *Bamachane,* March 10, 1985, 59.

18. For a mention of Colonel Yairi as the commander of Sayeret Mat'kal, see Shlomoh Slotzky, "Lama Paratz Uzi Yairi Be'Rosh," *Mosaf Hadashot,* March 30, 1990, 39, and Orah A'rif, "Elohim Yarad Ve'Hofiyah Al Ha'Adamah," *Yediot 24 Sha'ot,* April 16, 1991, 12.

19. *Ibid.,* 39.

20. Orah A'rif, "Elohim Yarad," p. 12.

21. Shlomoh Slotzky, "Lama Paratz Uzi Yairi," 39.

# 8

## The Longest Ninety-nine Minutes Ever

*Operation Thunderball/Yonatan*
*Entebbe, Uganda*
*July 3–4, 1976*

Air France Flight 139 was the daily flight connecting Tel
Aviv and Paris, with a brief stopover in Athens. Since
Israelis usually saved up all year for an annual lavish
shopping trip abroad, the flight was filled to capacity with a
mixed bag of Israeli consumers and returning French tourists. The stopover in Athens was a selling point of the flight,
as it allowed a few more moments of inexpensive duty-free
shopping.

On June 27, 1976, Air France Flight 139 was once again
full—any empty seats were to be filled by connecting
passengers in the Greek capital. At Ben-Gurion International Airport, in Lod, the pre-dawn check-in went on in
typically chaotic fashion. Since this was Israel, El Al security
was in place as all bags were searched; passengers were
quizzed by Shin Bet–trained personnel and put through a
body search, X-ray machine, and metal detector. Even
though Flight 139 was not El Al, who could harm a flight so
vigorously protected? At 08:59 hours the flight finally took

off as heavily armed border guard policemen stood guard on the tarmac.

The Airbus A-300B was not the only aircraft making a connection in the Greek capital that morning. At 06:45 hours Singapore Airlines Flight 763 landed in Athens from Bahrain via Kuwait; four unassuming passengers awaiting a connecting flight headed to the transit area, where they went to the Air France service desk, checked in for Flight 139, and settled down for a long wait with cigarettes, coffee, and, it is believed, amphetamines.¹ Patience was something in which they had been carefully schooled.

When Flight 139 landed in Athens, at 11:30 hours, fifty-eight new passengers boarded the aircraft. Among the travelers struggling with parcels and travel bags were the four passengers from Singapore Airways: an Aryan-looking male, Wilfried Bose; a blond Scandinavian-appearing woman, a West German Baader-Meinhof terrorist named Brigitte Kuhlmann (her PLO nom de guerre was Halimeh); and two dark-skinned Middle Eastern males, Abu Walid el-Haliali and Ali el-Mi'ari, both longtime PFLP veterans.

Flight 139 took off as scheduled at 12:20 hours. Eight minutes and 31,000 feet later, just as the no smoking lights were extinguished and the mad dash to the toilet and galleys began, Bose, Kuhlmann, and the two Arabs rose from their seats. They produced handguns and grenades from their possessions and took control of the aircraft. While the sadistic Kuhlmann and the two Arabs seized control of the 244 passengers and 12 crewpersons, Bose, armed with a pistol and clutching an F-1 fragmentation grenade with its ring already pulled, burst into the unlocked cockpit. He ordered the flight's captain, Michel Bacos, to head toward Benghazi, Libya. Gleeful in his victory, Bose took the microphone from the control panel and announced to his captive audience that Flight 139 had been hijacked by the Che Guevara cell of the Haifa unit of the PFLP, and that it had been renamed Arafat.

One of the most bizarre and spectacular acts of terrorism and counterterrorism in the State of Israel's history had just begun.

If the Palestinian cause had one man capable of initiating a bold new front against the Zionist entity, it was Wadi Haddad. Dr. Haddad, Dr. Habash's longtime special operations chief, was behind some of the PFLP's most spectacular operations. Most important, he was the instrumental player in creating a cohesive Palestinian alliance with the various terrorist, revolutionary, anarchist, and "crazy" groups that sought an armed solution to the world's ills on the four corners of the globe. In the PFLP's "Ivy League" terrorist training facilities in Lebanon an international roster of men and women who dreamed of emulating Che Guevara were trained in the art of bomb-making, cold-killing, and hostage-taking. The groups the PFLP trained included the Japanese Red Army, the Basque ETA, and the Irish Republican Army, as well as assorted individuals from Armenia, Turkey, Iran, Puerto Rico, the Philippines, Western Europe, South America, Africa, and Asia.[2]

Yet the PFLP's most important terrorist alliance existed with the West German Baader-Meinhof Group and, as it was later known, the Red Army Faction (RAF). The Baader-Meinhof gang and the PFLP shared almost identical ideological beliefs: Both groups supported a worldwide Marxist revolution, both groups enjoyed KGB support and backing, and both groups avidly promoted and practiced violence to achieve their political agendas. The Baader-Meinhof terrorists relied on the PFLP for training, weapons, and, in many cases, targets, while the Palestinians needed the Baader-Meinhof Group's Western European safe houses and their blond anonymity to transport arms and do their murderous bidding. Yet the German anarchists provided Dr. Habash and Dr. Haddad (both known by the affectionate name of el-Hakim (Wise Man) with a devastating psychological weapon. Germans killing Jews brought back historical nightmares no government or news agency could ignore. Old hatreds and painful memories did, indeed, die slowly.

By the summer of 1976 the time was ripe for action. Lebanon, the Palestinians' military exile, had erupted into full-scale civil war a year before. Heavily armed Christian militias first fought even more heavily armed Palestinian factions before it became a full racial conflagration of barbaric and chaotic proportions. At first the war had gone well for the Palestinians and their Muslim allies. The poorly led and undisciplined Christian forces, who before the conflict were little more than Mafia-type enforcers protecting smuggling and drug-running routes, were no match for the battle-hardened PLO forces. Each side massacred the other with untold butchery and ferocity. Yet just when it appeared that a two-thousand-year-old Christian presence in Lebanon would be wiped out forever, the Syrian army invaded the Levantine hell and came to the Christians' rescue. Damascus, more concerned about historic claims to Lebanon as a part of "Greater Syria" than the plight of their Palestinian brothers in arms, intervened in a bold and decisive stroke. The tide slowly turned as the Syrians and Christians, who were eventually covertly supplied by Mossad and A'man funding and assistance, began to maul the Palestinians in battle—a scenario that prompted the Syrians to switch sides once again and fight on the side of the PLO.[3]

At a time in its history when Christian gunners laid siege to the sprawling Tel Za'atar refugee camp near Beirut in an artillery bloodletting of indescribable horror, the Palestinian cause needed a decisive action of its own that would, like the Munich Olympics massacre, spread the name of Palestine to the four corners of the earth. Most of all, it needed an international incident that would allow the world to forget intra-Arab conflict and return its attention to the issue of Palestine.

Dr. Haddad had just such an operation in mind.

The Wadi Haddad faction of the PFLP was formed in mid-1975, when Libyan leader Colonel Muammar Qaddafi, upset that the world revolution he had been financing for so long had yet to take place, offered a limitless supply of weapons, support, and, above all, funding to any group willing to perpetrate more aggressive acts of international terrorism against Israeli and Western interests. This greatly appealed to Dr. Haddad, who, as the PFLP's operations and foreign liaisons branch director, was often hampered by a frugal budget and limited logistical means. Haddad formed his own small though extremely efficient terrorist army, which, with such infamous foot soldiers as Carlos the Jackal, was determined to wreak havoc worldwide—the world, that is, with target Israel as its center.

To execute his grand scheme Haddad chose East Africa as a field of operation. Beyond the range of the terrorists' historic nemesis, the IAF, East Africa was Muslim and pro-PLO; a forward observation post was even established by Haddad's men in Mogadishu, Somalia, a nation that was a member of the Arab League and a Soviet ally and client state.[4] After a long search of airline traffic patterns throughout the Mediterranean and Middle East, airline routes, and, of course, airport security systems, Haddad's intelligence agents uncovered an ideal target. Finally the venue and production were coming together—all that was needed were actors.

Wilfried Bose was a low-level Baader-Meinhof hanger-on who had worked for a small leftist publishing house in Frankfurt; he had occasionally provided logistic support for revolutionary operations in France and West Germany. In May 1975 he was recruited for larger tasks by none other than Carlos the Jackal (Euzkadi Ta Askatasuna) himself and was dispatched on an intelligence-gathering mission on behalf of the Basque ETA movement in Spain.[5] Although arrested by French police, he was mistakenly let go, and he quickly submerged in the underground of Europe's revolutionary armies. He would surface one year later in Athens.

Within minutes of Flight 139's seizure Ben-Gurion Airport, the point of its departure, had learned that radio contact with Captain Bacos had disappeared. The Air France station manager contacted Paris, while his counterparts in Lod placed emergency telephone calls to Jerusalem. The news eventually reached Prime Minister Yitzhak Rabin, himself a former IDF Chief of Staff, and Defense Minister Shimon Peres. The missing Air France flight became the main, albeit unscheduled, order of business at the regularly scheduled Sunday cabinet meeting. Obviously there were many Israeli citizens on board that aircraft, and the loss of radio contact indicated two alternatives: Flight 139 had crashed, or it had been hijacked. When radar contact with "Arafat" was reestablished shortly after 13:00, the Israelis had their answer.

The Israelis, infamous pessimists, had a well-rehearsed contingency plan for such an emergency. The procedures had been scripted into the Defense Ministry's operations manual following the Black September hijacking of the Sabena jet to Lod on May 8, 1972. At 13:27 hours Aga'm, IDF Operations Branch, put into motion the procedure for dealing with an emergency at Ben-Gurion International Airport concerning a hijacked airliner. It was believed this hijacking might be a repeat performance of the Sabena affair, even though most intelligence officers in A'man HQ thought the Palestinians would not try this type of operation again. A forward command post was set up inside the airport's main building. Civilian traffic was tightly controlled by border guard police units, which rolled out armored cars and donned web gear for possible action. And of course, an elite unit was summoned to prepare for a possible rescue attempt. IDF Chief of Staff Lieutenant General Gur placed the call for his boys and ordered them to assemble at the airport at once. Shortly after the call went through, Major General Yekutiel "Kuti" Adam, the Operations Branch director, and Defense Minister Peres were inspecting the *yechida muvcheret* (chosen unit) at Lod. Mat'kal was readying its gear for potential action while Peres and Adam conferred with the unit commander, Lieutenant Colonel Yonatan Netanyahu.[6]

Lieutenant Colonel Netanyahu had assumed command of Sayeret Mat'kal in the summer of 1975, after a two-year stint in the Heyl Ha'Shirion (Armored Corps). There he commanded a battalion of Centurion MBTs protecting the Golan Heights from Syrian attack.[7] Like many other elite-unit commanders—men who led daring special operations raids by reconnaissance infantrymen or paratroopers into the heart of enemy territory—Yoni flirted with tanks. Yoni's departure was meant as no act of disrespect to the ethics of commando warfare, but rather as an acceptance of reality. There *was* life after Sayeret Mat'kal.

Upon his return to the unit, this time as its commander, Yoni set about remaking Sayeret Mat'kal in his own image —cocky, capable, and cohesive.

Yoni was one of the unit's most charismatic leaders, calm and confident, introspective yet endearing. His American upbringing and Harvard schooling made him different from the unit's other commandos. His personality was a magnet, and when his men were asked to perform on the battlefield they did it for Yoni as much as for anything else.

On the afternoon of June 27 Yoni was inside a gigantic hangar at Ben-Gurion Airport, adorned in a full battle-kit briefing, and clutching his K'latch as he pointed to a chalk-written chart that divided his men into assault squads. Initially the discussion was a history lesson in which the do's and don'ts of Operation Isotope 1 were religiously examined.

Unfortunately for Mat'kal, from a logistics standpoint a storming of Arafat would be very different from Operation Isotope 1. Flight 139 was an A-300B Airbus, not a Boeing 707. This was a serious problem, considering that El Al did not fly the Airbus. No foreign carrier—for practical as well as security reasons—could be approached and asked that silly question, "Can we borrow your plane for a few hours?"

Without a plane the commandos were forced to examine photographs of the aircraft, as well as diagrams quickly assembled by Intelligence Corps personnel. If Flight 139 was to land in Israel, it would not be an easy nut to crack. Additional briefings were carried out by the unit's number two, Major Muki Botzer, who returned with additional intelligence data from the Air France office in Tel Aviv.

At Lod the hours stretched into an eternity as the commandos waited for news—any news! They had been kept in a secluded portion of the airport so they would not be seen by anyone. But the art of hurry up and wait was not a

Sayeret Mat'kal specialty. "Where the hell are the bastards?" several commandos uttered to themselves as they cleaned their weapons and nervously toyed with the AK-47 folding stocks.

At 14:58 hours some questions regarding Flight 139 were answered when Bose radioed Benghazi, Libya, demanding that Arafat be refueled and that PFLP representatives meet them at the airport. According to foreign reports, A'man had intercepted the Benghazi radio transmission. The Libyan connection posed some problems. A rescue attempt in Libya, while possible in theory, would be extremely difficult to execute and could potentially spark a new regional conflict. Libyan leader Muammar Qaddafi maintained a small but lavishly equipped military. As a result, any IDF operation in Libya would entail the destruction of the several hundred MiGs and Mirages of the Libyan air force, the Libyan air defense network, and much of its navy. For A'man and Aga'm the prospect of such an operation was daunting. When the aircraft landed it was met by a full Libyan political delegation and protected by a brigade-size force of mechanized Libyan troops.

Some passengers, expecting Benghazi to be their final stop, arose to assemble travel bags and coats tucked into the overhead racks. Halimeh, however, brutally quelled their hopes by beating several of the passengers with her pistol and promising that their ordeal had just begun. After a terrorist chin-wag between Bose, Kuhlmann, and several men who briefly came on board wearing poorly fitting suits and jet-black sunglasses, Arafat took on forty-two tons of jet fuel and was readied again for takeoff.

Before departure one passenger was released. A British woman named Patricia Heyman faked the early signs of a miscarriage and, in a show of compassion, was released. She was taken to a Libyan hospital, then ushered onto the next flight to England. Her release afforded French and Israeli authorities the first invaluable insight into what was actually transpiring on board the hijacked airliner. When news arrived at A'man HQ at 21:50 hours that Flight 139 was airborne once again, it was greeted with some trepidation, but with relief as well.

Flight 139's final destination was Entebbe, Uganda, located off the shores of Lake Victoria. The aircraft touched down near the Ugandan capital just before the brilliant dawn's sun exposed to the weary and frightened passengers peering out the window scores of heavily armed black men aiming their weapons at the aircraft. The Ugandans were joined by three other men, senior Wadi Haddad faction officers who would help Flight 139's hijackers in guarding, controlling, and, if necessary, executing the hostages. Indeed, Entebbe was the final stop for the French aircraft and an obvious location for the hijacking ordeal to come to a victorious or bloody conclusion.

Once, when the Israeli flag flew proudly in many African capitals, Uganda was one of the Jewish state's most loyal supporters on the continent. Ugandan President Milton Obote had established an overt friendship with Israel, but in 1969, after a violent coup in neighboring Sudan, a Muslim nation, Obote's amiable policies toward Jerusalem cooled considerably. The Ugandan army's chief of staff, General Idi Amin, was also a staunch supporter of Israel and a great admirer of the IDF. In 1968 he traveled to Israel and underwent military training and even a parachutist course in a goodwill gesture. The much coveted IDF *knafei tznicha* (jump wings) were placed upon Amin's chest at the conclusion of his instruction. He returned to Uganda with several Soviet-produced BTR-50PK armored personnel carriers the Israelis had captured from Egypt in 1967, which were offered to the African nation as another token of goodwill.[8] The Israelis helped to establish the nucleus of a small Ugandan air force; IDF officers were covertly dispatched to Kampala to train Ugandan officers; the Shin Bet helped create a special security force; and when Idi Amin seized power in a 1971 coup (which some foreign accounts have insinuated was engineered and supported by the Mossad), the Israelis provided him with an indigenously produced Westwind commercial jet and even a pilot. In fact, Israeli engineers and construction personnel built much of Entebbe Airport to afford it the prestigious international status Amin coveted.

Israel's Ugandan honeymoon ended when President Amin began to make absurd requests of the Israeli Defense Ministry for a grandiose scheme on the continent. These demands included a request that IDF/Navy provide him aid in crossing Lake Victoria and attacking Tanzania and, in March 1972, the insistence that the IAF dispatch a squadron of F-4E Phantom fighter bombers to Uganda so that Tanzania could be carpet-bombed. Israel ignored this flirtation with insanity, and Amin sought allies elsewhere. He found Libyan leader Qaddafi and PLO Chairman Yasir Arafat. Uganda soon became a Soviet-supplied fortress in Africa, a Libyan-financed armory where "justice for Palestine" became a national obsession. Never before the hijacking of Flight 139 had Amin gone so far to act out his pro-Palestinian policies.

Legally and morally it was the French government's responsibility to secure the release of the Air France plane and its passengers. Yet the Israelis had doubts about France's will or capabilities; Israeli-French ties were not strong and had been strained since 1967. There was historic animosity between France and Israel. In the Six-Day War Israel "disrespected" the honor of the French republic by ignoring President DeGaulle's demand that the IDF not draw first blood. France, Israel's principal arms supplier, responded by imposing an all-inclusive arms embargo on the Jewish state, including canceling delivery of fifty paid-for Mirage V fighter bombers and a mini-fleet of missile boats.*

On June 28, the second day of the hijacking ordeal, with negotiations going nowhere and the French vacillating, it became clear to the planners in IDF Operations Branch that a military solution would be the incident's only remedy. As a result, contingency planning for an Entebbe rescue opera-

---

*The Sa'ar class FAC, known as "the boats of Cherbourg," were eventually "liberated" in a brilliant Mossad/A'man/IDF/Navy operation reminiscent of a James Bond novel.

tion were being drawn up in the Kirya. Major General Adam ordered his chief of operations in the general staff, Colonel Ehud Barak, to begin gathering intelligence data and background material for a rescue raid in Uganda.[9]

Barak's plan initially called for several commandos to be parachuted into Entebbe and, with the support of intelligence operatives infiltrated past the airport perimeter, systematically eliminate the terrorists one by one. When all the terrorists had been eliminated, the Israeli task force would call on the Ugandans for help.

When it became clear that the Ugandans were operating in collusion with the terrorists, Barak's plan grew in size and scope. He now planned to parachute a large force of commandos (including elements of Sayeret Mat'kal and the naval commandos) into Lake Victoria and have them deploy from folding rubber craft. Such deployment would achieve a defensive beachhead and permit entry with absolute surprise into Entebbe Airport. His plan was a brilliant display of tactical innovation, but it had one very serious flaw. An intelligence officer on Barak's staff—a man who just happened to have a lifelong interest in African nature—pointed out at a planning meeting that Lake Victoria was teeming with crocodiles. Lake Victoria was crossed off all memos, and Barak's plan was quickly modified to be a more conventional assault on the airport itself.[10]

Operations Branch Director Adam came up with his own unique plan to secure the hostages' release. Recalling the brilliant success of Operation Isotope 1, Major General Adam conceived of a combined French-Israeli operation in which the French would agree to all of the terrorists' demands on the condition that, for security reasons, the prisoner exchange transpire on Israeli soil. Once the terrorists and their hostages landed at Lod—or perhaps at a secluded IAF air base somewhere in the Negev Desert—a repeat of the Isotope rescue could be performed.[11] It was an audacious thought that few Israeli leaders, let alone the French, could count on. But when there was nothing on the table, anything seemed better than nothing!

The IAF OC, Major General Binyamin "Benny" Peled, a

man known as a rogue military thinker with a brilliant track record in the field, came up with a way to outdo Major General Adam. Peled, an influential and controversial voice in general staff meetings, asserted that the rescue could succeed only if the IDF committed to a large-scale operation involving thousands of fighters and dozens of aircraft. Peled argued that the entire city of Entebbe should be seized while the terrorists and their Ugandan associates were terminated, the hostages freed, and the airport used to facilitate the refueling and maintenance of all the transport aircraft involved.

The hijacking was considered so serious to Israeli national security, reports Eilan Kfir in his semiofficial history of the IDF paratroopers, *Tzahal Be'Heilo: Tzanhanim Ch'ir Mutznach,* that another plan was considered for resolving the Entebbe crisis: the kidnapping and eventual ransoming of Idi Amin himself. The solution was considered too politically risky by Defense Minister Peres, and it was subsequently shelved.

While the generals were tossing out wild ideas at closed-door meetings, the OC Paratroop and Infantry Branch, Brigadier General Dan Shomron,* was busy planning a rescue of his own. Shomron was a confident officer who had commanded several paratroop reconnaissance formations as well as an armored brigade during the 1973 War in Sinai. By elite forces standards he was conservative in his thinking, but his cool head under fire and his exhaustive planning were legendary. So were his audacious self-confidence and his trust in the men under his command. According to Shomron, in an interview on Israeli Army Radio, "I knew from the onset that any rescue mission would be a big operation, and I knew that *I* would be its overall commander."

Shomron's thinking centered on the notion that the hostages were being guarded in a three-ring setup, with inner, middle, and outer circles of defense. The inner ring was, of course, the terrorists; the middle ring was the

---

*Lieutenant General Dan Shomron was the IDF's thirteenth Chief of Staff from April 1987 to April 1991.

Ugandan soldiers guarding the old terminal perimeter; and the outer ring was the Ugandan battalion that defended Entebbe Airport itself.

Naturally, the terrorists had to be removed first. Once they were terminated and the hostages secured, the Ugandan soldiers in the middle and outer rings could then be neutralized while the exfiltration of hostages and fighters was executed. It would be Shomron's blueprint for a rescue that would be used at Entebbe.

Uganda was certainly within the IDF's operational range. In October 1971 the IAF took delivery of its first two Lockheed C-130H Hercules transports—aircraft that would become the IAF's principal heavy transports for over two decades. Up until March 1972, in fact, IAF Hercules had flown regular supply flights for the Israeli training mission in Uganda. The C-130 could ferry nearly a hundred soldiers or several vehicles and could easily use Entebbe's runways as a springboard for a rescue operation. Even though information on the situation was sketchy at best, a rescue was, indeed, possible. At least there was hope.

Shomron's planning was in its preliminary stages—so preliminary, in fact, that it was not even presented to the Israeli cabinet, which had been meeting around the clock to try and resolve this unexpected nuisance as soon as possible. On June 28, however, the French government formally announced that it was assuming total responsibility for the crisis. Yet, according to several Israeli officers involved in preparing the groundwork for a rescue (including Lieutenant Colonel Netanyahu and Operations Chief Major General Adam), this ordeal would eventually end with Israeli action. Major General Adam proved prophetic—it would indeed be an Israeli matter.

At 21:00 hours on the night of June 28 the terrorists finally released their demands to the Israelis. The hostages would all be released unharmed if Israel released forty jailed freedom fighters, including Lod Airport mass killer Kozo Okamoto and Archbishop Capucci, a cleric turned PLO gun runner; West Germany released six terrorists; Kenya set free five Palestinian terrorists who had tried to shoot down an El Al airliner over Nairobi; freedom was given to one named terrorist in Switzerland, one named terrorist in France, and one Palestinian held in South America. Last but not least, France had to pay the Wadi Haddad faction a nominal U.S. $5 million ransom—money that would certainly finance operations in the future.[12]

It was clear to most senior officers in the IDF general staff that military action was required, and soon. The lights burned all night in both Colonel Barak's and Brigadier General Shomron's offices. Israel would certainly not release any terrorists, and Germany tended to shy away from putting convicted Baader-Meinhof thugs back on the streets. In any event, the hijacking of Flight 139 was such an audacious move that it demanded punitive action executed in an equally audacious fashion.

In the early morning hours of June 29 the hostages, now moved from the confined hell of a sun-baked airliner to the airport's old terminal building, were ordered to pay close attention to Wilfried Bose, who was sitting in the center of the large hall at a coffee table guarded by an AK-47–toting Brigitte Kuhlman. The 256 hostages had already been through extreme misery, fear, and bizarre theater. Not only had they been seized in an act of aerial piracy and forced to sit on an aircraft for nearly twenty-four hours, but they had been visited several times by Big Daddy himself, President Idi Amin, who gave a rambling speech in support of African unity, German engineering, and, of course, the PFLP's heroic action on their behalf. On the morning of the 29th the *selektion* began!

Sitting at his desk with a stack of passports, the blond terrorist slowly read off the names of his captives one by one. Those with Israeli passports were, of course, singled out. The Israelis were ordered to fetch their belongings and walk to a small hall prepared for their stay. No explanation was given, and none was needed. Later, the names of non-Israelis with Jewish-sounding names were called. As the dozens who were ordered to scamper into the small room collected their belongings and passed the ring of terrorists and Ugandan soldiers, the group in the hall soon swelled to nearly a hundred people. Memories of Dr. Mengele at Auschwitz deciding who would live and who would die ripped through the blood-chilled bones of everyone in the room. The fact that Bose, a New German, was continuing the ways of his fathers added to the sense of tragedy.[13]

In all, ninety-one Israelis and Jews were singled out. Gallantly, Captain Bacos and his eleven-person crew remained behind. They could not leave in good conscience while the fate of so many of their passengers remained in question.

As the 103 Entebbe captives looked on, those fortunate enough not to have been born Jews were fed, rested, loaded onto a jet, and rushed off to Paris in two separate groups.

From a political point of view, the release of the 153 non–Israeli/Jewish hostages freed Israel's hands. Israel did not have to rely on the benevolence of a foreign power to secure the release of its own people (according to the Israeli Law of Return, all Jews are considered Israeli citizens); Israel did not have to worry any longer that a failed rescue mission would kill scores of French or European nationals and develop into an embarrassing and painful diplomatic snafu. From a military standpoint, the release of 153 hostages made any Israeli operation much simpler: it lessened the logistical nightmare by more than fifty percent, as there were now fewer people who needed to be transported to safety. Yet it was from an intelligence point of view that the release of the non-Jewish passengers turned out to be a fatal mistake for the Entebbe hijackers.

When Flight 139 eventually turned up in Entebbe, A'man files on Uganda—very slim files, it must be stressed—were pulled out of the vault and studied. The files produced very little useful information. The hijacking had caught the soldier spies of A'man completely by surprise, as there was no advance warning that the Wadi Haddad faction was up to something major in Europe or Africa. Forty-eight hours into the crisis, very little was known of the hijackers, the airport, or the Ugandan military. To pull off any stunning military moves the IDF General Staff required two forms of intelligence: first, aerial reconnaissance and data for flights to and from Uganda, and second, field intelligence on the layout of the airport, the deployment of the Ugandan soldiers, the number of terrorists, etc. This information was crucial for the commandos to have a chance of pulling off the rescue quickly and successfully. Most important, the intelligence had to be accurate!

On the aerial front, the most important bit of information obtained was the fact that the Entebbe Airport was still open for business, as cargo and passenger flights were still touching down and taking off. This would allow the fleet of C-130s a window through which to land unannounced. Naturally, the IAF Intelligence Department studied international flight patterns and schedules with great zeal. The IAF also took into consideration the possibility that Entebbe Airport might be under a military blackout at night, and that a blind landing would have to be performed by the C-130 pilots. The Procurement Department had to obtain powerful beacons that could be either pre-positioned or planted along the runway. A blind landing also meant that aerial photographs of the landing strip had to be memorized by the Hercules pilots so that any unique obstructions, landmarks, or physical oddities could be avoided without being seen. El Al pilots who had flown the African hubs were called in to IAF HQ to be debriefed, as were retired C-130 pilots who had flown transport sorties to Entebbe in 1972.

From the onset it was clear that Yoni's commandos would be in the crucible of any rescue attempt, be it at Ben-Gurion International Airport, Benghazi, or Entebbe. Yet these men were only as good as the intelligence they received, and feverish attempts were made to bring the attack forces up to date on the situation at Entebbe. Once Entebbe became the target, anyone who had ever had contact with Uganda was summoned to IDF HQ and drilled for information. Travel agencies along Tel Aviv's fashionable Ben Yehuda Street were systematically approached; any brochures or information regarding Uganda were seized by nondescript men wearing Intelligence Corps unit tags and offering little explanation. IDF officers who had served in Uganda as part of the IDF's military assistance program were also questioned. Many of their personal photographs from the good old days in Uganda were borrowed, to be returned at a later date; it was hoped that something innocent in one of these fading black and whites might provide a bit of information—a background shot of an ammunition dump, storage shed, or barracks. Veteran Mossad agents were quizzed; ex-diplomats who had served on the African continent and El Al pilots who flew those routes were all summoned and interrogated in ad hoc field briefings.[20]

Many valuable sources of intelligence, however, were no longer in the security community; anonymous men of the shadows who had risked their lives in covert operations were now husbands, office managers, and retirees. During the late night hours many phone calls were placed from the Kirya to locations throughout Israel, from the *kibbutzim* of Galilee to the Gulf of Aqaba resort town of Eilat. "Is your daddy home? Tell him it's an old friend from the army on the line." "Come to HQ at once. Use the side entrance, where I'll be waiting for you. Don't tell anybody where you're going!" A nation like Israel relies on her citizen soldiers for the defense of the country, and this crisis was no exception. Secrecy was also an absolute priority, as a slipped word could escalate into a rumor that, if heard by the wrong people, could jeopardize any military operation.

The most valued chunk of intelligence the IDF received came from the non–Israeli/Jewish hostages released from Entebbe, who were arriving through Paris. The first group of forty-seven flew out of Uganda on a chartered Air France flight on June 30. Prime Minister Rabin's special advisor on terrorist matters, Major General (Res.) Rechavem Zeevi, secretly flew to the French capital to interview the freed captives. Before passing through customs and the cavalcade of press each ex-hostage was questioned by anonymous men in neat suits who carried notepads and pencils. Addresses and telephone numbers were jotted down. A few hours later, as former captives joined their families and friends at welcome-home celebrations, ringing doorbells interrupted the moments of relief and happiness. Quiet men with tape recorders and notepads sat down in living rooms throughout Paris and pressed their polite hosts for any and every bit of information conceivable. "How many terrorists are there?" "Were they all Arabs?" "How did they address one another?" "What did their weapons look like?" "Did you notice any stores of ammunition or explosives?" "Did the terrorists guard you in shifts? Which gunmen guarded when?" "How many Ugandans were there?" "What did the weapons *they* were holding look like?" "What types of uniforms were they wearing?" "Did you notice any tanks or armored personnel carriers roaming about the airport?" "What did they look like?" "Where are the hostages sleeping?" "What is the mental state of the hostages, of the terrorists, of the Ugandan guards?" The information gathered was rushed back to Tel Aviv.

At 22:00 hours on the night of June 29, the second sleepless day of the ordeal, Chief of Staff Lieutenant General Gur broke into another all-night cabinet meeting in Jerusalem. Quietly he excused himself and walked gingerly toward Defense Minister Peres, moving the upholstered leather chairs so that he could speak quietly to his boss. He said simply, *"Le'Tzahal yesh optzia tzva'it"* ("The IDF has a military option"). Smiling, the usually lackluster Peres addressed a very somber Israeli government and offered the good news to the cabinet.

At a base somewhere in southern Israel additional hours of target practice were ordered, and the simulated deployment from the gigantic belly of a C-130 Hercules was honed to split-second precision. During one such midnight training regimen, as Yoni's stopwatch was finally measuring the needed speed, his communications officer informed him that Dan Shomon was on the line in his office. Yoni took the call, then left his modest office in haste, racing to the grounds where his men were assembled. *"Yala chevra, achshav be'retzinut!* ("Okay, guys, let's do it seriously now!"). The IDF was going to Entebbe* even though A'man's master soldier/spy, Major General Gazit, thought it would result in a full-scale Israeli-African conflagration.[16]

As Operation Thunderball slowly took form, encouraging developments continued to reach Israel. Intelligence was coming in from other unique sources as well. It was discovered that Entebbe Airport had been built by an Israeli contractor, and the blueprints of the terminal were on file in Tel Aviv. Immediately, a white Carmel Rom (a matchbox automobile produced in Israel and—unfortunately for many IDF officers—used as a staff car) rushed to the architect's office, and the plans were duly whisked to A'man HQ. Additional bits of invaluable HUMINT (Human Intelligence) were also providing enormous dividends. It was learned that a former IDF advisor to Uganda, Colonel (Res.) Burka Bar-Lev, had once forged a close personal relationship with the Ugandan strongman. Bar-Lev was immediately placed on a long-distance circuit to try and plead with his old friend for help of any kind. Idi Amin, a megalomaniac prone to acts of psychotic grandeur, rambled on about the plight of the PLO, the awesome might of the PFLP, and the glory of the African nation. He then agreed to apply some pressure to the hijackers, and he informed Bar-Lev that the terrorists would be broadcasting on Ugandan radio at 2:00 P.M. on July 1—less than ninety minutes before Wadi Haddad's ultimatum was set to expire, prompting the terrorists to execute the remaining Jews one by one.[17]

Bar-Lev's connection to Amin, it seems, was somewhat useful, as the Palestinians broadcast that the deadline was pushed back until 14:00 hours on July 4. Amin's control over the terrorists had also become apparent. A huge sigh of

---

*It has been rumored that in the early stages of the hijacking ordeal another contingency plan, quite separate from a rescue of hostages, was being considered in IDF HQ. The plan, a somewhat modified version of Operation Spring of Youth, called for Sayeret Mat'kal commandos to infiltrate Beirut and either kidnap or terminate the terrorist leaders responsible for the hijacking of Flight 139.

relief came over the office of Aga'm Commander Major General Adam. The window of opportunity for military action was now at hand.

The decision to rescue the hostages was a brave proclamation of a nation's resolve against terrorism. Yet political statements were nice in newspaper headlines or on billboards, not in a field of fire. The raid on Entebbe had by July 1 earned the James Bond–like code name of Operation Thunderball.* Brigadier General Shomron was named the operation's overall commander and was given a relatively free hand in choosing which units would go to Africa. Operation Thunderball was to be a nighttime raid with the sole overall objective of rescuing the hostages and bringing them to Israel safely. The assault party was divided into five groups and objectives:

• Force A: Commanded by Yoni** and Muki Botzer, Force A was the Sayeret Mat'kal component of the operation.[18] It would serve as the vanguard of the rescue effort, and its objective was to terminate the terrorists holding the hostages in the old terminal and secure the hostages until the remaining IDF units could facilitate their evacuation.

• Force B: Commanded by the conscript paratroop brigade's commander, Colonel Matan Vilnai (an ex-commander of Sayeret Tzanhanim and, at the time of this book's writing, the OC Southern Command), Force B

---

*For several years the actual designation of the Entebbe rescue remained shrouded in mystery—the operation owned names as diverse as Thunderbolt and Lightning Ball. At first the IDF computer came up with the dreary code name of Operation Gray Wave, but this was unacceptable to Shomron, who realized that a mission of such historical importance deserved a fitting title. Shomron ordered IDF HQ to press the keyboards once again, and the word *Kadur Ra'am* (Thunderball) appeared on the screen; naturally, such a title was acceptable to Shomron and his staff. After the raid, however, Operation Thunderball became "Operation Yonatan," in memory of fallen commander Lieutenant Colonel Netanyahu.

**Recent reports have indicated that IDF Chief of Staff Gur wanted Ehud Barak, not Yoni, to command Operation Thunderball.[19]

consisted of the very best officers and NCOs the paratroop reconnaissance force possessed. Colonel Vilnai handpicked each fighter for the task and chose only those soldiers whose past displays of courage and leadership would come in very handy at Entebbe. Force B's objectives were twofold: First, elements of the force were to fly in the lead C-130 with Yoni's men and jump out of the aircraft as it touched down and taxied toward the old terminal. Each reconnaissance paratrooper would carry a battery-powered beacon and position it alongside the existing runway lights, thereby providing the departing aircraft with illumination if and when the Ugandan authorities realized what was transpiring and shut off all electrical power. The Sayeret Tzanhanim fighters were then to race on foot a few hundred meters ahead toward the airport's new terminal building and interdict any Ugandan effort to interfere with the transpiring operation.[20]

• Force C: Commanded by the Golani Brigade commander, Colonel Uri Saguy (a former commander of Sayeret Golani and, at the time of this book's writing, the newly appointed A'man director), Force C was made up of the best NCOs and officers from Sayeret Golani and the brigade's Barak (Lightning) Battalion. They were to handle the evacuation of hostages and to see that they reached the awaiting C-130 transport in an orderly fashion. Elements of the Golani task force, along with portions of Matan Vilnai's paratroopers, were to remain behind and, utilizing several jeeps brought along for transport, rake an adjacent airfield with machine-gun and RPG fire, rendering the dozen or so Ugandan Air Force MiG-17 and MiG-21 interceptors useless. This was one of the more important objectives of the raid, and its assignment to the Golani Brigade was a sign of respect for the infantry brigade's epic performance during the 1973 War.

• Force D: Commanded by Major Shaul Mopaz, one of Lieutenant Colonel Netanyahu's most trusted deputies, Force D was the raid's heavy equipment section. Force D was armed with several armored personnel carriers, Soviet-produced BTR-152s captured from the Egyptians and Syrians during the 1967 and 1973 wars. Force D was to provide a protective ring around the old terminal insuring that any potential Ugandan counterattack would fail. According to many reports, Major Mopaz's force also consisted of American-made M113 APCs, but this has never been confirmed. The use of the BTR was meant to confuse the Ugandans—they were the same APCs the Israeli Ministry of Defense had agreed to give Idi Amin in the early 1970s, and they were prevalent in the Ugandan army's order of battle.

• Force E: The logistical command and control echelon of the raid consisted of the operation commander, Brigadier General Shomron. Although the IDF ethic of command is the "follow me" method, Shomron's task at Entebbe was to coordinate all the facets of the mission into a cohesive and speedy exercise. According to many foreign reports, Colonel Ulrich Wegener, the commander of West Germany's GSG-9 Border Guard antiterrorist commando force, was invited to and did in fact participate in the Entebbe rescue. Wegener dressed in IDF fatigues and tagged close to Shomron throughout the ordeal.[21]

As Yoni and Muki observed their unit's preparation for battle at a full-scale wooden mock-up of Entebbe Airport's old terminal in Sayeret Mat'kal's training base somewhere in southern Israel, both veteran officers realized that the thin line separating the hostages' safety from massacre was surprise. Yet the main problem was just how to obtain absolute dumbfoundedness! Although it was assumed that the terrorists were not expecting an Israeli commando raid, if PFLP paramilitary and terrorist training in Lebanon had been any good, the terrorists would surely be on alert against some type of action. The Ugandan perimeter also had to be overcome with speed and stealth. As the two men pondered their strategic dilemmas over a cartonful of cigarettes, it was decided to stress guile over firepower—deceit and genius over a frontal assault. In the IDF's battle-experienced and bloody history, the use of *sechel* (brains) had been the equalizing factor that allowed Israel to overcome numeric adversity for over twenty-five years, while at the same time minimizing battlefield casualties. *Sechel* would be desperately needed at Entebbe.

Operating on the assumption that the IAF would be able to land the first C-130 without any difficulty and without inviting unwanted attention, the remaining question mark for Yoni and Muki was how to bridge the few hundred meters separating the runway and the terminal without being discovered. Some officers argued that the mini-convoy of vehicles should floor the gas pedals once the C-130 touched down. But speed, in this situation, was a substitute for surprise. The distances were measured against acceleration, and a whole series of equations indicated that the terrorists would have almost a minute to react to the plane touching down before they were directly confronted. Almost a minute could mean scores of dead hostages.

One Mat'kal officer, however, was intrigued by the two visits Ugandan President Amin had paid to the hostages. Noting Amin's flamboyant style—and the fact that he wore a copy of IDF jump wings on his tailored uniform—the officer mentioned that it would be a good idea to masquerade the raiding party as Ugandans. With black ski masks, camouflage fatigues, and some luck, the Halloween trick might actually work. After all, it would not be the first time the IDF used disguises to fool an enemy. During Operation Chicken 53, a December 27, 1969, raid against an Egyptian radar base at Ras Arab where a top-secret Soviet P-12 surface-to-air radar was "borrowed," Na'ha'l paratroopers wore white uniforms that resembled the fatigues worn by Egyptian troopers. If it worked once, it might work again.

Yoni and Muki opted to expand on the original plan of trick-or-treat. "If we are going to dress up as Ugandans," Yoni pondered, "why not impersonate Idi Amin's entourage?" His visits to Entebbe were unannounced, and it was doubtful that any conscript Ugandan soldier manning the perimeter around the terminal would be insolent or foolish enough to try and stop the motorcade—or worse, try and impede it with a show of force. Third World armies belonging to dictatorial regimes operated through fear, and in Uganda, nobody was feared more than Amin.

After sifting through his intelligence files Yoni learned that Amin always traveled in a jet-black Mercedes-Benz limousine escorted by several camouflaged British-made Land Rovers.[22] Perfect! Muki went on a secure telephone line and rang up headquarters, demanding a black Mercedes 220D—a very odd request emanating from a usually sensible officer. Unfortunately, there was no such car in the IDF pool, although the request for several ex-Jordanian army Land Rovers was granted. Undaunted, Muki rang a friend who owned and operated a Tel Aviv car service, but the best his buddy could come up with was a *white* 220D. No problem! Muki requisitioned a few cans of Tambor black gloss paint from the base's supply sergeant, and Ugandan license plates—with Arabic numerals—were forged in the base's workshop.

The initial plan called for the commandos to wear Ugandan army uniforms. But it was later learned that Idi Amin did not trust his own army for his personal protection and employed Palestinians as bodyguards. The Palestinians, it is believed, were members of the PFLP.[23] Since the PFLP, based in Damascus and bankrolled by Syria, wore the Syrian army's unique vertical lizard pattern camouflage fatigues, so would the Mat'kal task force. After all, following the Arabs' 1967 and 1973 defeats, the IDF had placed several hundred—if not thousands—of these uniforms in stock. Impersonating Palestinians was a much easier task than putting on blackface; at least a dark mask would not interfere with the commandos' mobility and comfort. Nevertheless, elements of the Ugandan army did wear similar Syrian uniforms, and the danger of the commandos shooting one another in bursts of friendly fire was a dire concern. As a result, each Mat'kal commando wore a very "mysterious" top-secret identification device that would prevent such fatal mistakes from transpiring.[24]

Brigadier General Shomron was kept abreast of all developments every hour on the hour. On July 2, at 12:00 hours, the four force commanders (Yoni, Vilnai, Saguy, and Mopaz) presented their preliminary finalized plans to Shomron. The gathering was informal yet tense. Rank wasn't a factor at the exchange of brigadiers and colonels— all that mattered were promises of a successful execution of the raid. Shomron was, however, encouraged by the confidence of his task force commanders. They appeared deliberate in their predictions and conservative in their casualty assessments. Confidence would either be gloriously affirmed or disastrously shattered the following day, when the dress rehearsals were scheduled. The show would have to be good and convincing—in a special cabinet meeting, held behind closed doors in Jerusalem, the government of Prime Minister Rabin voted to open negotiations with the terrorists. After the 1973 earthquake, Qiryat Shmoneh, Ma'alot, the Savoy Hotel, and now Entebbe, Israeli capitulation seemed at hand.

July 2, 1976, 04:50 hours. Yoni's men had been training nonstop for nearly seventy-two hours. The commandos had worked hard and geared their disciplined mental states to the point that not going to Entebbe would have greatly disappointed them. At dawn's first light, however, it was time to put all the sweat and sore muscles to the test. On sweltering tarmac meant to simulate Entebbe Airport Yoni commanded another run of Operation Thunderball. With a whistle in his mouth and a megaphone in his hand, Yoni yelled *hikon* ("ready") and then the Arabic *y'allah*. The black Mercedes rolled off a ramp, followed by the two Land Rovers. Several officers sat in the backseat of the Mercedes clutching silenced Uzis and 9mm Berettas. Following the Land Rovers were fire teams running faithfully at full speed behind the motorcade with their weapons at the ready. Just outside the wooden mock-up the Mercedes stopped abruptly, and all the players leapt out in a mad dash; their onslaught was matched by the dance of their jumping across obstacles and pretending to fire their weapons. Yoni, clutching both his K'latch and his stopwatch with bitter strength, was anxious, but everything was going as planned. When he clicked his timepiece for the final for-the-record time, a huge smile erupted across his stubbled face. Time of the entire operation from touchdown to liftoff: fifty-five minutes![25]

Yoni knew, however, that his men could still shave a few seconds off the assault—a few seconds that might save lives.

Among the very small circle of leaders privy to the preparations, Chief of Staff Gur remained skeptical. Long-range airborne ops, after all, were foreign to the IDF. The only other time in IDF history that a similar feat was executed was in the opening hours of the 1956 Sinai Campaign, when the 890th Paratroop Battalion was parachuted into the Mitla Pass in the Sinai Desert. The eventual battle with entrenched Egyptian forces became one of the hardest fought, costliest, and most controversial in IDF history. At the time, Gur was commander of the 88th Na'ha'l Paratroop Battalion, the force that paid the heaviest price in the hellish gauntlet. This time, even though the means to bring the IDF to Uganda were more advanced than the 1950s-era trip to Sinai, Gur was adamant about ensuring the safety of the Israelis. A massacre of cut-off Israeli forces so far from home would not transpire now—not with the IDF under his control.

Gur's main concern was the IAF's ability to make a blind landing on a blacked-out runway. At 18:00 hours on July 2 Lieutenant Colonel S., the lead C-130's pilot, fired up his engines and then lifted off into a dark crimson Sinai sky. A few minutes later, the touchdown of the landing gear was smooth—smoother than an El Al jet landing at Ben-Gurion International Airport, one of the crew would sarcastically comment to the chief of staff. Gur, however, needed to be convinced one final time. After all, he would be facing the ultimate battle—selling the plan to the cabinet.

At 23:35 hours the final dry run was carried out. This time there was absolute darkness, and all five C-130s participated in the mock raid, as did all ground elements. At his vantage point atop a sandbagged wooden pillar Gur watched through his field glasses as the few hundred commandos, paratroopers, and reconnaissance infantrymen stormed the wooden mock-up of Entebbe. Nearly every movement had been rehearsed to perfection. Even Brigadier General Shomron's jeep, which was to land in the second C-130, raced from unit to unit in a well-timed shuttle of command and control. Finally Gur was satisfied. He found a secure telephone line and contacted Prime Minister Rabin. *"Heim Muchanim"* ("They're ready"), responded the chief of staff, *"heim muchanim!"*

Saturday night in Israel is usually a festive part of the week when restaurants are filled to capacity, cinemas are sold out for even bad movies, and the main streets of Tel Aviv and Haifa are bustling with strolling citizens eating falafel and sipping sodas. Yet there was supreme tension in the air that hot summer night—anxiety not felt in Israel since Yom Kippur day, 1973. Radios were turned on in every home, tuned to the news, hoping for any word from Entebbe. Very few Israelis believed that the post-1973 War IDF would be able to do anything, especially so far away from Israel's shores.

The Israeli cabinet met in an unheard-of Saturday emergency strategy meeting to decide whether or not to authorize the raid. The terrorists' deadline was less than twenty-four hours away, and unless the Israeli government stopped perfecting the art of indecision, the hostages would be doomed. In order to land at Entebbe at 23:00 hours the five C-130s had to lift off from Sinai no later than 13:00 hours. In Prime Minister Rabin's office Gur pleaded with the ministers for a green light. He spread out dozens of photographs, maps, and sketches illustrating exactly how the operation would be pulled off. Detailed briefing followed detailed briefing. Calm diplomacy was followed by frantic profanity. Consternation risked disaster.

Back at the base Yoni's men prepared their weapons and minds for the task at hand. His men were already dressed in their lizard-pattern fatigues, and their web gear was filled to capacity with magazines, grenades, and medical equipment. Since phone contact with the outside world had been cut off for security reasons, last-minute good-byes to loved ones were replaced by solemn moments of thought and the odd hour of reading, writing good-bye letters, or just plain sleeping. Many of the men attended Sabbath prayers for the first time since their bar mitzvahs, while others sharpened knives or fine-tuned their weapons' trigger mechanisms, making them all the more sensitive. The planes were on the runway, but permission to board the aircraft never came. "Hurry up and wait" was a dangerous order for a group of men who were about to face one of the most dangerous moments in their lives; self-doubt was an addictive commodity. *"Lama od lo ishru?"* ("Why haven't they yet given us the authorization?") was the opening line of countless conversations. From confident to anxious, the men were getting nervous.

Yoni knew the danger of the government's inability to show that it had a set of balls, and he contacted Shomron, who, in turn, contacted Gur. The situation was becoming desperate. Remarkably, the IDF chief of staff courageously ordered the fleet of C-130s airborne without government consent. Authorization would be received in midair.

"It's a go" was the word to Yoni. "It's a go!" Lieutenant Colonel Netanyahu checked his AK-47 one last time and then ordered his men into formation. His final speech was more of a subdued pregame pep talk than a last-minute briefing. Yoni reminded the fighters of the importance of the mission and emphasized to everyone that Wilfried Bose's *selektion* was not to be tolerated. It was Sayeret Mat'kal's task to remind the State of Israel and the world that Jews would no longer be separated for the slaughter. Yoni tossed his burning cigarette onto the tarmac and then said, *"Be'Hatlzacha!"* ("Good Luck").

At 13:20 hours the five C-130s lifted off from their bases in Israel. They took evasive flight patterns so as not to overfly a large city and arouse suspicion. Each aircraft carried nearly twenty thousand pounds over the normal rated capacity, and the trip to Ophir in Sinai, the final refueling and staging point, was bumpy and terribly uncomfortable. Many of the commandos—the most fearsome group of warriors Israel had ever produced—found themselves suffering from airsickness and vomiting into the side lanes of the cargo floor. The aircraft refueled quickly and continued toward the final destination—still without governmental authorization.

From the onset, the flight to Uganda was a hazardous one, and it appeared that Murphy's Law was haunting Operation Thunderball. First, the cabinet did not authorize the raid until after liftoff at Ophir. Second, the C-130s had to fly at low altitude so as to evade Egyptian and Sudanese radar. And third, a vicious electrical storm forced the flying armada to bank dangerously close to the frontier of Sudan, a nation with which Israel was still legally in a state of war and one with an extensive network of Soviet-supplied MiGs and SAMs. As the C-130s reached Lake Victoria the storm clouds were towering in a solid mass from ground level to forty thousand feet. There was no time to maneuver around it, and there was no route that would allow the lead C-130 to make its stealthy approach into Entebbe except straight through the hellish storm.[26] The turbulence was so bad, the vehicles barely held the strength of their harnesses, and men were flung about inside each aircraft's belly like pinballs flying off a bumper. Instruments were affected by the storm, and the cockpit windows were shrouded by an eerie blue light. One commando sitting beside the Mercedes wryly told a friend, "The IAF doesn't produce the best pilots in the world for nothing!" Entebbe would be reached on schedule.

At 22:54 hours a who's who of the Israeli political and military establishment gathered at IDF HQ in the Kirya, including Prime Minister Rabin, Defense Minister Peres, and Chief of Staff Gur. Over an amplified radio set they heard Major General Adam, flying above Uganda in a Boeing 707 C3 aircraft, utter an emotionless "Over Jordan," the code word that indicated that Lake Victoria had been reached. There was no turning back now.

The first C-130 touched down on Shoshana, the IDF code name for Entebbe's main runway, at 23:01 hours—

remarkably, only thirty seconds behind schedule! It came in directly behind a British cargo plane that—luckily for the Israeli task force—was also on schedule, and the runway lights were ablaze. It was as if the Ugandan radar operators did not even see the Israeli plane on their air traffic control radar screens, but that had been part of the top-secret game plan to ensure surprise. According to several reports, the Israelis, employing a team of Mossad agents with a secret device that jammed the Ugandan radar, had turned their screens into blank mysteries.[27] According to later reports, however, the IDF had managed to fool Ugandan radar using a device involving highly sensitive magnetic field technology; this device was invented by Dr. Gerald Bull, a Canadian ballistics genius who, according to foreign sources, was gunned down in Brussels by a Mossad hit team after helping Iraq obtain the Babylon super gun aimed at Tel Aviv.[28]

As Lieutenant Colonel S.'s Hercules touched down the aircraft's side doors were flung open, and paratroopers leapt onto the tarmac clutching their beacons. The C-130 was still taxiing at moderate speed; the paratroopers placed their battery-operated lights beside the regular runway strobes and assumed defensive positions, crouching on one knee and sweeping their assault rifles a full 360°, their all-encompassing field of fire meant to protect the slow and vulnerable C-130 carrying Yoni's men, the command team of Colonel Vilnai's reconnaissance paratroopers, and several of their fighters.

Before the lead aircraft came to a full stop its cargo ramp had already been lowered, and "Idi's" Mercedes and the Land Rovers were rolling toward the old terminal. The hundred-meter dash was on. The entourage, traveling at race-car speed, did not fool the two Ugandan soldiers standing guard just outside the building. One Ugandan soldier fled in panic, screaming wildly into the night, while the other readied his weapon for battle. Yoni fired several pistol rounds at one of the guards, and Giora, a veteran unit officer, fired at the other soldier; the subdued chirping of the silenced gunfire proved to be important, since it could not be heard inside the terminal. The gunfire from the speeding Mercedes, however, missed its mark by a wide margin. Seeing the possibility of a disastrous beginning marring any chance of success, an alert commando standing erect in the lead Land Rover grabbed the mounted FN MAG and fired a ten-round burst into one soldier's chest. The explosions of rounds detonating loudly announced the IDF's arrival. The terrorists would almost certainly be alerted by now. Surprise had been lost, and the triggers of over a dozen AK-47s were squeezed more tightly.

Realizing that their arrival had been announced with 7.62mm fire, Yoni ordered his men to leap from their vehicles and race the remaining few dozen meters to the old terminal. Muki led the assault. The first target he encountered was a Ugandan sentry standing alone and confused and fatally in the wrong place on the walkway outside the building. Still running at full speed, Muki lowered his K'latch to waist level and emptied a full magazine into the hapless guard. He jumped over the African's twisted body and continued toward the terminal. Changing magazines on the run, Muki was joined by his deputy officer, Lieutenant Amnon, and the two officers burst into the building together. Their men followed close behind. They found the hall fully lit and the hostages lying on the floor in a chaotic and bundled fashion. The only figures standing were the terrorists. Muki and Amnon fired short bursts at the heads and chests of the two Arab gunmen. The bullet-riddled bodies fell over several hostages, many of whom were already screaming, adding to the confusion. Kuhlmann's turn was next. As she attempted to raise her Czech machine pistol toward the commandos she was struck in the chest and head by a lacing blast of K'latch fire. Finally it was Bose's turn. According to popular legend, the German terrorist aimed his fully loaded AK-47 at a group of hostages and was about to pull the trigger, only to abort the slaughter when he gazed into the eyes of a Holocaust survivor he had befriended during the ordeal. A second later Bose was blown away by more than a dozen rounds of 7.62mm fire.

The four Flight 139 hijackers had been killed in less than fifteen seconds.[29] Immediately additional commandos from Yoni's force burst into the hall. Each fighter was equipped with a bullhorn, and they shouted, "This is the IDF! Stay down!" in both English and Hebrew. Several hostages jumped for joy at the sight of the rescue party and were tragically hit by the commandos' fire as they raced through the room in a mad dash to terminate the terrorists. Three hostages were killed.

Simultaneously with Yoni's action a squad led by Captain Giora's burst into the upstairs (second floor) departure lounge and VIP hall. It was known that the terrorists and Ugandan officers used these reasonably luxurious digs as their living quarters when not guarding the hostages. Giora led the assault two yards ahead of the remainder of his men. He kicked in the doors of the departure lounge and then raked the spacious room with a magazine-emptying burst from his AK-47. As he removed the banana clip to replace it with a fresh thirty-round load his second emptied another magazine of ammunition into the pockmarked walls for good measure. As they continued their purification of the upper floor two Ugandan soldiers appeared from behind a wall—they were firing their weapons wildly and screaming unintelligibly. Giora and his Number Two fell into firing position in a fluid motion that would have made any drill instructor proud, and they pumped several rounds into each of the Ugandans until it was guaranteed that they would no longer pose a threat to the operation.

Inside the VIP hall Captain Giora found his task of securing the building most difficult. Already there was a choking stench of cordite in the confined spaces from grenades the two-man commandos teams had thrown from room to room while assaulting the structure. Crouching in a low-profile defensive firing posture, Giora continued his quick search of the floor till two figures suddenly appeared in the background. They wore civilian clothes, appeared dazed, and, because of their rather light complexions, were at first believed to be hostages. Instinctively several of Giora's men approached the two, the Israelis nervously clutching their weapons as they closed ranks. They had orders to shoot at anything or anyone suspicious, but the thought of accidentally killing a hostage warranted extra—even life-threatening—care. As the tense confrontation came to a head one of the commandos noticed that the the two men were clutching round objects—Soviet-made F-1 fragmentation grenades—behind their backs. A., a sergeant in the unit whose full name is protected for security reasons, yelled *"Rimon!"* ("Grenade!") at the top of his lungs—a warning that ignited indiscriminate bursts of automatic fire from the covering teams. The two terrorists fell to the ground sharply. So did the grenades they were carrying. Giora's men also fell to the floor to avoid the fast-flying shrapnel. Seconds later the room erupted with an explosive thud, and several of Giora's men staggered outside, lightly wounded.[30]

A third squad from Giora's unit, deploying from the Land Rovers, attended to another portion of the building, where Ugandan soldiers were garrisoned. The battle was brief, yet very deadly. With speed and terminating firepower, over a dozen Ugandan soldiers were mercilessly gunned down in seconds, before they could mount even the slightest opposition. The commandos raced through the building with such lightning speed that the Ugandans did not even have the time to lock and load their weapons.

The liberation of the old terminal took only minutes. At its completion Muki went to confer with Yoni, who had remained outside to supervise elements of the assault. When Muki arrived he found his commander lying on the concrete floor just outside the building, attended to by the unit's doctor. A burst of machine-gun rounds from the adjacent control tower had ripped through Yoni's back.* Yoni's men, Muki later learned, immediately dragged him to shelter, where a team of medics and doctors courageously attempted to save his life. Yoni's men did manage to return immediate fire, which killed the Ugandan gunner, but the damage to

---

*Recently it has been suggested that Yoni was *not* killed by Ugandan fire, but rather by the AK-47 of Wilfried Bose in a face-to-face encounter.[31]

one of Israel's most capable soldiers had already been done. On the harsh African turf a hero of Israel lay mortally wounded.

For Muki, there was only one thing to do. Immediately, and with little emotion, he grabbed the radio and told Brigadier General Shomron, "Yoni has been hit. I'm assuming command. Over and out!"[32] Even though Yoni was a very close personal friend and a comrade in arms in operations and locations still classified by the IDF, the mission had to continue.

Sayeret Mat'kal's portion of Operation Thunderball lasted all of three minutes. With their K'latch rifles now slung over their shoulders the commandos helped gather the hostages and prepare them for evacuation. These men had readied themselves for a vicious and desperate battle, yet they were victorious in lightning time—a testament to their skill and to the minds of their commanders. Now, having beaten back death—at least for the time being—in 180 seconds, they politely helped children and old women fetch their belongings and directed them to the door. The most attended-to group of hostages was the stewardesses of Flight 139. Naturally, the commandos paid particular attention to the beautiful flight attendants they found lying on soiled mattresses, sitting in their bras and panties and frightened out of their wits! Muki realized that a potential conflict of interest was about to arise, and he sharply ordered his men away from the women and back to the mission at hand.

By 23:08 hours the four remaining C-130s had landed at Entebbe without incident. By the time the fourth aircraft touched down an alert Ugandan officer had shut off all electricity to the airport, including the runway. But it didn't matter. The beacons were working just as hoped, proving to be an invaluable and inexpensive element of the raid. The Golani and paratrooper elements had already deployed from their aircraft, and Major Mopaz's force of BTR-152s had touched down as well. Brigadier General Shomron's jeep—Operation Thunderball's mobile C3 nerve center—roamed across the tarmac from force to force, ensuring that all was proceeding with clockwork precision. Brigadier General Shomron supervised the operations (with a little help from Major-General Adam, flying overhead in the Boeing 707) with great calm and admirable cool. He organized his assets into effective cohesion. Operation Thunderball was ahead of schedule.

Major Mopaz's four BTR-152s raced toward the old terminal and constructed an APC ring of steel around the building. Several Ugandan soldiers approached the vehicles, believing them to be Ugandan, and were leveled by machine-gun bursts. Protecting the old terminal and the hostages was all-important, but a snag in the evacuation had developed. Fire from the control tower was increasing in intensity and accuracy. Several commandos were pinned down by the determined Ugandan machine-gun fire. Shomron ordered Mopaz's BTRs to destroy the tower. Two BTRs, their tracks clanking on the concrete ground, were moved into advantageous firing position. While several gunners laced the four-story tower with tracer fire, a squad of commandos emerged from protective armor cover and produced RPG-7 antitank rockets. They launched a deadly projectile—meant to penetrate 320 millimeters of armor plating—into the thin concrete and steel structure. The two rockets rose toward the target in a trail of fire and smoke, and the two warheads exploded a second later, causing the tower to erupt into a blinding ball of flame and a shower of tumbling debris and bodies.

With the control tower now silent, the ex-hostages were turned over to Colonel Saguy's Golani task force. Shomron and Saguy addressed the assembled group of tired and confused civilians and pleaded with them to proceed toward the C-130—which had moved to within fifty meters of the terminal—at a quick, calm, and controlled pace. Family heads were asked to count their own and ensure that nobody had gone astray. Captain Bacos was asked to do the same with his crew and his now very popular group of stewardesses. A few dozen of the Golani fighters stood a few yards across from one another in two separate lines and interlocked hands to form a human fence. Shomron's nightmare vision was a few hostages, bewildered in their dazed state and carrying belongings too heavy for their hungry bodies to hold, wandering into the middle of a firefight—or worse, into the hands of the Ugandans—and requiring IDF aid.*

As the evacuation proceeded and the wounded were carried on stretchers, Colonel Vilnai's paratroopers engaged the brunt of the Ugandan security detail around the new terminal. Sergeant Hershko Surin, a three-year veteran who was only twelve hours away from being released from active duty, was wounded in the pitched battle with the Ugandan forces, a fight that was fierce and at times conducted hand-to-hand.

As the battle raged, IAF technicians who had hitched a ride on the fifth C-130 were feverishly working on the fuel pumps that would transfer Idi Amin's fuel to the IAF armada. As they unloaded all the material, word came through from Defense Minister Peres via Major General Peled that the task force would be allowed to refuel in Nairobi. The Medical Corps Boeing 707 was already in Nairobi awaiting the seriously injured.[33] Entebbe would not have to be secured for another hour while the aircraft were rejuiced. This meant the operation's extremely high risk factor was greatly reduced and the probability of large-scale casualties seriously diminished. Shomron ordered Muki to expedite the retreat, and Lieutenant Colonel S., whose C-130 was patiently standing by with its engines on, was told to bring his ship closer to the freed captives. *"Y'allah . . . Nistalek mi'poh!"* ("C'mon . . . Let's get the hell out of here!")

At 23:59 hours the first C-130 ferrying the hostages, elements of the Mat'kal task force, and the seriously wounded was airborne, destination Nairobi. The fight at Entebbe, however, was far from over. As the engines of the first transport to leave Uganda roared overhead, firefights between Colonel Vilnai's paratroopers and Ugandan forces

---

*One hostage, seventy-five-year-old Dora Bloch, was taken to a Kampala hospital hours before the rescue raid and was subsequently murdered at the order of a vengeful Idi Amin.

were erupting all along the tarmac. The paratroopers' objective was not to destroy the airport or kill Ugandan soldiers for killing's sake. They had to keep any potential threat to the departing aircraft well out of their range, as well as deter the Ugandans from mounting a counterattack. A fundamental element in this strategy was played out by a combined force of jeep-borne paratroopers and Sayeret Golani infantrymen.

Following an order issued at the very last moment by Brigadier General Shomron, the commandos attacked the heart of the Ugandan air force, which posed a threat to the IAF armada. Israelis gunned down the planes on the ground with machine gun and RPG fire. Eleven MiG-17s and MiG-21s were destroyed as the PG-7 grenades ripped through the thin-skinned aircraft. The burning jet fighters created an immense fireball that illuminated the entire airport. As a result of the Ugandans' primitive communication infrastructure, the rest of the Ugandan air force could not be called up into the sky for the intercept.

At 00:40 hours* on the morning of July 4 the last C-130, carrying Brigadier General Shomron and a contingent of paratroopers and Golani rifleman, lifted off from the blazing airport. It was premature to celebrate victory, as the aircraft was still prey to ground fire or SAM launches. Shomron ordered that his men keep their web gear on and continue to clutch their weapons as if poised for battle even inside the aircraft, since the serious possibility remained that they could be shot down and forced to fight on African soil.[34] The mood inside the cargo hold was somber and tense until Kenyan airspace was entered and the miraculous victory assured. Thirty minutes later the six IAF aircraft and the top-secret C3 707 parked on a remote and highly secure stretch of runway at Nairobi. The seriously wounded were transferred to the hospital ship, and the hostages and commandos were given fresh milk and candies laced with large amounts of sugar, and once again placed on board their awaiting transports.

---

*At IDF HQ in the Kirya glasses of champagne were raised at exactly 00:41 hours.

Samuel M. Katz

Even though a miracle had been pulled off by the wily commandos, their mood was confused and sad. On board a C-130 the doctors had done their utmost to save the life of Lieutenant Colonel Netanyahu but failed. His body was covered by a coarse gray army-issue blanket, and a religious soldier in the unit chanted the Kaddish—the Jewish prayer for the dead—over the body of his fallen commander. Victory had been won, but for Sayeret Mat'kal and the State of Israel the price had been very high.

As the six aircraft returned to Israel—still over Sudanese and Egyptian airspace—Lieutenant Colonel S., a C-130 pilot, put on Galei Tzahal, the IDF's radio station, and heard an emotional report of the "daring, courageous, and miraculous operation in Entebbe." "Talk about field security . . . *shit,*" Lieutenant Colonel S. mumbled to himself. "How the hell did they know?" The BBC reporter in Kampala, the Ugandan capital, upon hearing the gunfire from Entebbe, had assumed that the Israelis had done something. The report that had begun to circulate was at first denied, then confirmed, and then denied once again. Finally it became fact throughout the world, and especially in Israel, where car horns were sounded in the midnight hours and dancing in the streets shattered the sleepy summer night's calm.

As the armada of aircraft entered Israeli airspace over the Red Sea and Gulf of Aqaba a demonstration of affection gathered in the resort town of Eilat to greet the high-flying aircraft. Following the traumatic 1973 War, the sight of flag-waving citizens joyous in a national victory was a welcome sight. Minutes later the C-130s touched down at an IAF base in southern Israel. The hostages were allowed to eat, wash up a bit, and shake off the horror and turmoil to which they had been subjected for the past week with a team of IDF psychiatrists before the short hop to Ben-Gurion International Airport, where friends and family were awaiting to participate in a frenzied national celebration of relief and joy.

Also at that remote portion of the desert tarmac Defense Minister Peres and Chief of Staff Gur greeted the returning

Mat'kal commandos. There was no celebration on board the aircraft, no back slapping. The commandos brought down the stretcher bearing Sergeant Surin and the body of their beloved commander. Peres asked Botzer what happened to Yoni. "He led from the front," Botzer replied tersely, "and was the first to fall."[35]

To the State of Israel, Operation Thunderball/Yonatan was Christmas and the Fourth of July all wrapped together in a national day of military redemption. The IDF was back to being its old self! The impossible was probable, and the world could rest easy because Israel was on the job. To the rest of the world Entebbe was a James Bond escapade beyond all logical comprehension. From Warsaw to Washington the world was in awe of the daring Israeli commandos—men who knew no fear and no limitations. The raid on Entebbe became a popular topic for television and film. In the dozens of quickly constructed celluloid "epics" Yoni was played by such stars as Richard Dreyfuss, and Dan Shomron can rest at ease knowing that he was portrayed on film by Hollywood tough guy Charles Bronson. An Israeli film, the most accurate of all, was made and utilized the services of Avraham Arnan as technical supervisor; according to several reports, Arnan threatened to walk off the set if the directors, "Golan and Globus," didn't portray the mission and unit accurately!

Sayeret Mat'kal had gone Hollywood, but the Hollywood image did not ease the loss of the unit's most heroic and perhaps most Hollywood-like figure, Yoni Netanyahu.

# NOTES

1. Major (Res.) Louis Williams, "Entebbe Diary," *IDF Journal*, 1986, 22.

2. Although the Arab-Israeli conflict is a regional one, the blood politics of the Palestinians' cause became an

international effort poised against the State of Israel. The PLO and its various factions have received financial, technical, and military support from the four corners of the world, including extensive KGB assistance from the U.S.S.R; military advisors from Cuba, North Korea, Vietnam, and East Germany; and, of course, funding from the oil-rich gulf states.

3. For the best and most accurate descriptions of Israel's covert military assistance to the Lebanese Christians, see Ze'ev Schiff and Ehud Ya'ari, *Israel's Lebanon War* (New York: Simon and Schuster, 1984), and Shimon Shiffer, *Snowball: The Story Behind the Lebanon War* (Tel Aviv: Edanim Publishers, Yediot Aharonot Books, 1984).

4. Edgar O'Ballance, *Language of Violence: The Blood Politics of Terrorism* (San Rafael: Presidio Press, 1979), 245.

5. Jillian Becker, *Hitler's Children: The Story of the Baader Meinhof Terrorist Gang* (Philadelphia: J.B. Lippincott Company, 1977), 17.

6. For the mention of an elite unit being summoned to Lod's Ben-Gurion International Airport, see excerpts from Shimon Peres's book *Diary Chapters* as syndicated in the June 30, 1990, magazine supplement to the Friday edition of *Yediot Aharonot*, 12. For the same elite unit being identified as Sayeret Mat'kal in various foreign sources, see Barbara Newman with Barbara Rogan, *The Covenant: Love and Death in Beirut* (New York: Crown Publishers, Inc., 1989), 16.; Christopher Dobson and Ronald Payne, *Counterattack: The West's Battle Against Terrorists* (New York: Facts On File, Inc., 1982), 92; and Leroy Thompson, *The Rescuers: The World's Top Anti-Terrorist Units* (New York: Dell Publishing, 1986), 158.

7. Christopher Dobson and Ronald Payne, *Counterattack*, 92.

8. Edgar O'Ballance, *Language of Violence*, 241.

9. Avi Valentin, "Kadur Ra'am," *Ha'aretz* Weekly Supplement, June 27, 1986, 4.

10. Naomi Levitzki, "Aluf Teflon," *Mosaf Hadashot*, July 21, 1989, 6.

11. Eilan Kfir, *Tzanhanim Ch'ir Mutznach: Tzahal*

*Be'Heilo Entzyklopedia Le'Tzava Ule'Bitachon* (Tel Aviv: Revivim Publishers, 1981), 190.

12. Baruch Ron, "Entebbe: Hayinu Sham," *Bamachane,* July 2, 1986, 9.

13. The cruelty that Brigitte Kuhlmann displayed to her captives was barbaric, yet her German-language tirades against the Jewish passengers were incredible and reminiscent of the Nazis' female guards in the death camps. In a now-famous incident, she verbally abused a Jewish passenger who had survived the death camps whose number was visibly tattooed on his forearm.

14. Avi Valentin, "Kadur Ra'am," 5.

15. "Gilu'im Chadashim Mi'Mivtza Entebbe," *Yediot Aharonot: 24 Shaot,* June 25, 1991, 10.

16. Shimon Peres, *Diary Chapters,* 16.

17. Major (Res.) Louis Williams, "Entebbe Diary," 25.

18. Christopher Dobson and Ronald Payne, *Counterattack,* 92.

19. "Yoni Lo Ratza Et Ehud Barak Be'Entebbe," *Ma'ariv Shabbat,* June 28, 1991, 2.

20. Baruch Ron, "Entebbe," 11.

21. Samuel M. Katz, *Follow Me!, A History of Israel's Military Elite* (London; Arms and Armour Press, 1989), 134.; and Rolf Tophoven, *GSG-9: German Response to Terrorism* (Bonn: Bernard & Graefe Verlag, 1984), 79.

22. *Ibid.,* 25.

23. According to Western intelligence sources, Idi Amin deployed highly experienced PFLP killers. This was not unique to his regime. In recent years several African leaders have employed Israeli-trained Lebanese Christian militiamen, Hizbollah members, and PLO gunmen as bodyguards.

24. Eilan Kfir, *Tzanhanim: Ch'ir Mutznach,* 195.

25. "Entebbe," *Bamachane,* 54.

26. Major (Res.) Louis Williams, "Entebbe Diary," 26.

27. Stewart Stevens, *Spymasters of Israel,* 381.

28. Jonathan Schachter, "Gerald Bull: Genius of Destruction," *Jerusalem Post International Edition,* September 15, 1990, 12.

29. Avi Valentin, "Kadur Ra'am," 11.

30. *Ibid.*

31. Billy Muskona-Lehrman, "Yoni Nifga Me'Esh Ha'Mechabel Ha'Germani," *Ma'ariv Shabbat,* June 21, 1991, 3.

32. Baruch Ron, "Entebbe," 12.

33. The fact that the Kenyan government provided such invaluable and remarkable, albeit covert, assistance to the Israeli operation indicates the high degree of secretly conducted intelligence and security cooperation enjoyed by the two nations.

34. Baruch Ron, "Entebbe," 12.

35. Shimon Peres, *Diary Chapters,* "The Unit Commanders Are Ready . . . ," *Yediot Aharonot,* June 30, 1990, 17.

# 9

## *From Beirut to Tunis*

*Mystery, Conjecture, Controversy, and Father
Holy War's Meeting with Destiny
April 16, 1988*

The IDF's raid on Entebbe proved to be much more than a
mere military operation, and even more than a breathtaking
and dramatic hostage rescue mission. It became myth. The
mystique of Operation Thunderball surpassed all military
reality and probability; for Sayeret Mat'kal, probably more
than in their participation in Operation Spring of Youth, the
foray into Uganda brought the unit forever out of its
self-imposed veil of secrecy. Even though in Israel the words
Entebbe and Sayeret Mat'kal have never appeared in the
same sentence, people knew. The world knew. The legend
of Sayeret Mat'kal and Entebbe were one and the same.
And in the wake of Entebbe, counterterrorist operations continued.

On the night of April 6–7, 1980, five terrorists from the
Iraqi-controlled Arab Liberation Front (ALF) slinked their
way past the security zone patrolled by the Christian/Shiite
militia of renegade Lebanese Major Sa'ad Haddad and cut
the barbed wire obstacles that separated Israel from Lebanon. Bypassing IDF patrols, electronic sensors, and mine
fields, the five-man squad ran a few hundred meters to the

gates of Kibbutz Misgav Am, a frontier collective long the target of PLO Katyusha and artillery harassment. Although such border settlements were protected by IDF and border guard patrols, the kibbutz also had heavily armed residents who manned posts throughout the compound; but the defenses proved to be ineffective. Well-trained attackers, the five ALF gunmen bypassed chance encounters with armed defenders of any type and headed straight toward the evening's objective: the nursery and a dozen sleeping children.

Initially units from the Golani Brigade had reached Misgav Am upon the terrorists' crossing of the fence; the electronic trip wire had been activated, and a state of disaster alert was declared throughout northern Israel. Patrolling units led by Bedouin trackers followed the terrorists' tracks, and once they were located, a tense standoff ensued. For the young Golani Brigade infantrymen protecting northern Israel, the terrorist infiltration was *their* failure —they had allowed a murderous squad to enter Israel and take a group of sleeping children hostage. For the IDF's top brass, the incursion into Misgav Am meant a long night of tension and anxiety ahead. The wheels of Israel's antiterrorist contingency planning were immediately set into desperate motion. The Golani OC, Colonel A., was immediately summoned, as was the OC Northern Command, Major General Avigdor "Yanush" Ben-Gal (commander of the elite and infamous 7th Armored Brigade during the 1973 War). The beeper of Chief of Staff Lieutenant General Raful Eitan also went off. For Raful, the incident had ominous echoes of past horror. Six years earlier, as OC Northern Command, he had been helpless as bureaucrats in Jerusalem more concerned about political careers than hostages in a schoolhouse in Ma'alot had allowed a situation to deteriorate to the point where a surprise rescue attempt became an impossibility. As the IDF chief of staff, however, Raful was determined to end the ordeal as soon as possible, with or without the government's green light. Without hesitation he summoned Lieutenant Colonel Uzi Dayan and his boys.[1]

From the onset of the hostage ordeal the assembled Golani force had attempted partisan attempts to free the sleeping infants on their own. A contingent from Sayeret Golani commanded by Captain "Gunni" Harnick* had also arrived and was preparing flak vests and Galil 5.56mm assault rifles for the rescue bid. At Captain Harnick's signal a flare was fired into the star-filled night's sky. Lieutenant Raz, a Sayeret Golani platoon leader, grabbed his Galil and raced into the two-story building, only to be met by a determined volley of AK-47 fire. The terrorists had barricaded themselves by piling overturned cribs against the main room's swinging doors, and children's beds were placed by windows to deter any assault through these openings. For the next fifteen minutes the terrorists fired continuous bursts of automatic and even RPG fire at the Golani recon infantrymen, who scurried behind small trees and fences to avoid the explosive offerings. The Israeli forces gathered around the building were reluctant to return fire, hoping to avoid harming any of the toddlers. The melee resulted in one Golani dead and five seriously wounded. It was decided to wait until morning before initiating any further action.

The arrival of Lieutenant Colonel Dayan's unit signaled that one way or the other the ordeal would be over soon. The commandos donned specially produced Kevlar bulletproof vests, body armor that was bulky around the chest and back but not restricting around the arms and shoulders; in the back of the vests designers had placed a pouch for a small, high-powered walkie-talkie that was connected to the commando's left ear by earphone. In any such assault it was realized that radio command, control, and communications needed to be maintained at all costs. Instead of the high-

---

*Major Harnick was killed on the night of June 6–7, 1982, on the first day of Operation Peace for Galilee, Israel's invasion of Lebanon, while commanding Sayeret Golani's assault on Beaufort Castle, a Crusader relic and PLO stronghold that dominated much of southern Lebanon and the Israeli Galilee from 717 feet above sea level.

velocity 5.56mm Galil or M-16 assault rifle, or the powerful 7.62mm K'latch the commandos favored, the assault force opted to use 9mm Beretta pistols and 9mm Uzi submachine guns—weapons whose ammunition was less likely to ricochet and hit one of the children. The commandos also wore khaki canvas Patauga boots with rubber soles that ensured greater traction and comfort than the standard brown leather jump boot.[2]

The assault plan was simple: Enter the building in an overwhelming display of firepower and then systematically eliminate the terrorists one by one. Attacking a two-story building severely limited available options—there was no room for fancy planning or the dramatic. There was no chance for James Bond theatrics here. Just get in, kill the bandits, and get the hell out. At the pre-assault briefing Lieutenant Colonel Dayan told his men that "barring the unexpected, the whole ordeal should take no longer than a couple of minutes." In retrospect, he would be off by only sixty seconds. Clearly, the mistakes of the failed Ma'alot rescue were engraved in the mind of each officer participating in the rescue bid's planning. Some of Dayan's men had taken part in that tragic assault and recalled the massacre with a vengeance.

H-Hour was set at 10:00 A.M. on the morning of June 7. By this time a wall of ambulances ringed the nursery, on call to see that any harmed innocents were rushed to medical care immediately, and also conveniently shielding the anguished parents from witnessing their children's rescue or death.

Slowly the commandos, supported by elements of Gunni Harnick's Sayeret Golani, inched their way along a neatly paved asphalt strip just outside the nursery's front door. Snipers ringed the tree line overhead, just to keep the terrorists honest and to keep them away from the doorway. In a froglike crouch the commandos advanced with their weapons nestled conveniently in their arms, their fingers firmly on the trigger mechanisms. Lieutenant Colonel Dayan deliberately counted off, "Three, two, one . . . zero . . . *fire!*" The commandos raised their bodies to an erect stance and then burst into the facility with weapons ablaze.

Lieutenant Colonel Dayan was the first to engage a terrorist —with a lone and extremely lethal head shot he killed a gunman doing a very good impersonation of a hippie and carrying an AK-47. Lieutenant Colonel Dayan was also the first to fall as a casualty. He suffered shrapnel wounds to the legs and chest from a Soviet F-1 fragmentation grenade tossed in his direction. Remarkably, Dayan continued to command the assault.[3]

The purification of the nursery was systematic. At close range the commandos attacked the defending gunmen; any shot that missed was followed by furious volleys from support teams of Uzi-toting commandos who followed in close pursuit. Once inside the nursery the commandos split ranks. Half the men threw themselves on top of the children, many of whom were covered with the blood and brains of terrorists hit by Israeli fire, trying to shield them from the barrages of unguided ordnance. The remaining commandos continued their mission with terminating firepower. Under heavy cover fire the children were quickly evacuated and brought far from harm's way.

The terrorists, however, stood fast. They gave as good as they got and responded to the assault with deadly fire of their own. Chaos ensued. The terrorists fired RPG antitank rockets through walls and doorways. The warheads exploded in deafening blasts and scorching fireballs; the smoke and debris were suffocating. Already there were six wounded Israelis, including soldiers from Sayeret Golani, and three of the terrorists were still alive. The battle was far from over.

Rallying his men, Lieutenant Colonel Dayan seized the initiative and led the advance in the brief seconds of quiet when the terrorists reloaded their weapons. A minute and a few hundred spent shells later, the call went out over the radio network, *"Ha'kol shaket . . . ha'kol nigmar!"* ("Everything is quiet, everything is over!"). It was not a total victory, however. One two-year-old-baby, a little girl, had been killed, as had a *kibbutz* worker; one Golani soldier had also died, and nearly a dozen other soldiers were seriously wounded.\* Lieutenant-Colonel Dayan received an honorary citation from OC Northern Command Major-General Ben-Gal for his decisive leadership while wounded, no less. Following the operation, Dayan petitioned Chief of Staff Eitan for the right to serve as Sayeret Mat'kal commander for an additional tour of duty. It was denied, and the wily commando genius returned to "tanks," and eventual service in Lebanon during "Operation Peace for Galilee."[4]

The role—if any—of Sayeret Mat'kal during the 1982 Lebanon fighting remains shrouded in mystery, speculation, and outright denial. Of course, there has been no official mention of the unit's participation in the Lebanon war, even though official histories of the Golani Brigade and paratroopers in the conflict have already been published. In fact, even rumors of Sayeret Mat'kal participation in several alleged operations deep behind Syrian lines remain Israeli state secrets of the highest order. In a fortieth-anniversary interview on IDF Radio, Raful Eitan, chief of staff during the Lebanon war, stated emphatically that there were countless operations in 1982 he hoped would remain classified forever. Nevertheless, there are conflicting though interesting mentions of Sayeret Mat'kal in Lebanon.

The most famous such report concerns Yasir Arafat's departure from West Beirut on August 26, 1982. After withstanding a hellish Israeli siege, Arafat had finally been forced from the Palestinians' most lucrative base of operations—the closest thing they had ever had to a state of their own. Realizing that his life was in danger (the IAF, with aircraft and RPV drones, had attempted to locate and terminate the symbol of international terrorism since 1965), Arafat took extraordinary precautions to ensure that the short trip between his Fakhani district HQ and his escape

---

\*In fitting revenge for the terrorist attack on Kibbutz Misgav Am, Captain Gunni Harnick's Sayeret Golani evened the score with the ALF. On February 22, 1981, the ALF headquarters in southern Lebanon, in the Christian village of El-Kfur, was assaulted by heliborne units of the Sayeret. It was known as Operation New Technology, and it resulted in fourteen dead terrorists.

vehicle, the Greek ship *Atlantis*, was not his last. He surrounded himself with dozens of heavily armed Force 17 gunmen and a human ring of Greek and U.N. officials, as well as the Greek and French ambassadors to Lebanon. Nevertheless, the wily PLO chairman's movements were monitored by the IAF's fleet of drones, as well as by scores of Sayeret Mat'kal snipers who kept Arafat's head in their high-powered sights.[5]

One Israeli sniper, in fact, came within a hair of placing a 7.62mm round through Arafat's *kefiyeh*-wrapped head. The range was perfect—a kill confirmed. The sniper clenched his right hand a fraction tighter around the mechanism of his M-21 7.62mm sniper rifle and placed his left eye directly at the scope. He almost pulled the trigger but at the last moment backed off and said "No!" He had not received the green light to terminate Arafat, and such an action would end the cease-fire and risk diplomatic embarrassment for Israel in a war that was already proving to be politically volatile.[6] According to popular legend, however, the sniper received the order not to fire from Raful, who just happened to be standing nearby.

Arafat boarded the *Atlantis* without incident and headed on to Tunis—the PLO's new base of operations—where he would join his two most trusted deputies: Security Chief Abu I'yad* and Operations Chief Abu Jihad. Tunis and the PLO would be featured prominently in the years to come. The PLO was beaten but not destroyed. Terrorism, like hatred and violence in the Middle East, would continue unhindered, even if it did not originate in Lebanon.

On April 12, 1984, a beautiful and vibrant spring day, four young Palestinian men, residents of the Gaza Strip, took their places on line to board the No. 300 bus line connecting Tel Aviv and the southern city of Ashkelon. In

---

*One of the most feared men in the who's who of the Palestinian revolution, PLO Security Chief Abu I'yad was gunned down in Tunis in January 1991 by an Abu Nidal Fatah Revolutionary Council suicide assassin over a policy dispute stemming from PLO support for Saddam Hussein in the Gulf War.

the days before the Intifada the sight of Arabs from the Occupied Territories milling about in Tel Aviv's chaotic central bus station did not arouse fear or suspicion. After all, the city's menial labor force was made up exclusively of Palestinians; the men from the Strip and the West Bank toiled with the city's trash, cleaned its busy thoroughfares, and did other work no self-respecting Israeli would do himself. They kept the cities of Israel going, and in the early evening hours they trekked back to their world before the night's curfew was firmly in place. The bus to Ashkelon was the first link on the long, roadblock-filled route back to Gaza.

The four men carried suitcases, looked somber, and were sweating profusely; they sparked suspicion, but when a nervous passenger approached a young IDF lieutenant about the two "Arabs" the officer was more concerned about a few moments of sleep than confronting two probable laborers. Thirty minutes into the ride the four men leapt out of their seats. The leader of the group raced to the front of the bus and held a very sharp butcher's knife to the driver's jugular, while the remaining members of his squad produced hand grenades and a case booby-trapped with a PG-7 antitank grenade. Miraculously, the driver managed to stop the bus and swing the hydraulic doors open, allowing a few horrified passengers the meager seconds required to escape. The terrorists regained control of the bus, however, and continued the speedy drive south—toward Gaza.

The passengers who had escaped immediately dialed 100 (the Israeli 911) and relayed the news of a frantic situation about to get worse to police operators. Police units in southern Israel were placed on full war alert. Vehicles and snake's-teeth-spiked roadblocks were set up; the Ya'ma'm was summoned and, according to foreign reports, brought by helicopter to an ideal ambush location near Gaza.[7] Seven kilometers down the road, at the Dir el-Balach junction, the bus, its tires already crippled by the road obstacles, encountered a force of Ya'ma'm sharpshooters that blew out what remained of its tires and forced it to a halt. The bus driver again proved to be courageous—he kicked out several side windows and allowed a few additional hostages to sprint to freedom. Once more the terrorists assumed control of the bus, and a tense standoff ensued. A legion of heavily armed Border Guards had already assembled and aimed their M-16 5.56mm assault rifles at the vehicle's windows, awaiting the order *"Esh!"* ("Fire!") It wouldn't come for a while. Through a megaphone the police hostage negotiators established a dialogue with the four terrorists, who demanded the release of five hundred jailed Palestinians in exchange for the lives of the hostages.

The seizure of the bus brought bitter emotions. The IDF's top brass assembled at the Dir el-Balach junction in haste to take control of the situation. All traffic in Israel, it appeared, was heading south. In the staff cars, jeeps, and choppers racing toward the Strip were IDF Chief of Staff Lieutenant General Moshe Levy; OC Southern Command Major General Moshe Bar-Kochba; and two men with unique experience in dealing with terrorist incidents, the A'man director, Major General Ehud Barak, and the chief Paratroop and Infantry Officer, Brigadier General Yitzhak Mordechai. The presence of so many generals and directors resulted in heated exchanges among the independent-minded military and intelligence men who offered their unique viewpoints on how the situation should be handled. One fact remained obvious: Israel would not negotiate with the terrorists and would certainly not acquiesce to their ludicrous demands. For good reason. At a nearby field a small group of heavily armed commandos arrived. They had been summoned by the Chief of Staff, and their arrival was low-key, kept far from the fray of press photographers and military policemen who lacked the security clearance to know of the unit's existence.[8]

According to foreign reports, a very tense tug-of-war developed between Brigadier General Mordechai and a senior Border Guard commander as to which unit—the Ya'ma'm or, it is believed, Sayeret Mat'kal—would be given the honor of rescuing the hostages.[9] Although one of the most important lessons learned after the Ma'alot massacre was that the police would handle all hostage-taking contingencies inside Israel proper, it was a ruling that was never put into practice; the 1975 Savoy Hotel incident and the attack on Kibbutz Misgav Am were handled by IDF units. The No. 300 bus incident would be no different. Although the border guard commander on the scene passionately pleaded for the green light to be given to the Ya'ma'm, the task finally fell to the elite IDF reconnaissance formation. It was argued that the IDF conscripts were younger, with fewer family ties to cloud their minds during the lightning assault.[10] Overall command of the rescue bid was handed to Brigadier General Mordechai.

With that dilemma settled, the only questions that remained were how and when. At 04:00 hours on the morning of April 13 Egged, the Israeli national bus line, sent an empty bus identical to the one seized nearly twelve hours earlier to Dir el-Balach so that the unit could perfect its assault techniques. Getting a bus was at least easier than temporarily borrowing an airliner. The vehicle was parked at a nearby field, far from outside view, and it was repeatedly assaulted until the time required to free the captives, from the first shot to the last hostage's exit from the bus, was refined to a matter of seconds. Security for the unit was so hermetic that what appeared to be a battalion-size force of paratroopers camouflaged the activities from view. Afterward the unit's commander, happy with the results on his stopwatch, ordered his men to check their gear one final time and jet into position.

At 04:43 the commandos struck. In perfect synchronization the brilliantly choreographed assault was under way with weapons ablaze. The first terrorist eliminated was sitting alone at the steering wheel; he was killed in a flurry of 7.62mm projectiles aimed in tight bursts at his head. A second terrorist, holding the booby-trapped PG-7 grenade, was cut down by an equally vicious flurry of automatic fire. He attempted to activate the grenade, but a few dozen rounds of K'latch fire prevented him from doing anything but falling to the ground in an anguished convulsion. During the melee the hostages began to escape—they leapt out the rear and front doors, racing into the dark night while crouching and shouting in relief and joy. Tragically, however, Corporal Irit Portugez, a nineteen-year-old female soldier returning home from the army, was accidentally killed by the commandos' fire. Her death marred the operation, which was otherwise performed with brilliant speed and exhilarating results. Rushed away from the scene to avoid publicity, the commandos all vowed revenge—but when, where, and against whom?

Those question, like many others, were answered exactly four years later, according to published reports, on the shores of a distant land.

The war in Lebanon affected the State of Israel in much the same way that Vietnam had the United States, inflicting a sense of division and moral self-doubt. The war began as an important act of Israeli self-defense with the goal of removing the Palestinian terrorist infrastructure from the northern Israeli frontier once and for all. Inevitably, however, political schemes of a pax Israel, together with the long-held dream of a Christian-controlled Levantine, led to the push into Beirut, full-scale war with the Syrians, and an eventual military quagmire. The Sabra and Shatilla massacres and the nearly four hundred IDF dead since the end of Operation Peace for Galilee were all by-products of this justified war gone too far. It was a time of madness in an already insane region.

Lebanon affected the IDF in a brutal fashion. Counterinsurgency operations against the Palestinians, Druze, and, ominously, Shi'ite Muslims in the years 1982–1985 removed the sense of duty and national survival from the egalitarian and apolitical Israel Defense Forces. A malaise overtook the once proud and mighty Tzahal in a period of self-doubt and neglect. In the IDF's vernacular it was known as the time of the *rosh katan* (small brain), when conscripts, NCOs, and officers showed little initiative in their daily tasks. They did only what they had been ordered to do, and the minimum at that! Even when the IDF did something spectacular, like the No. 300 bus rescue, it was marred by scandal and controversy. The two terrorists who had been seized alive by the commandos were first physically beaten by Brigadier General Mordechai and then seized by Shin Bet agents and murdered in a nearby field. The political fallout that ensued gripped Israel in much the same manner as the Watergate scandal had eroded faith in the office of the American presidency. The No. 300 bus incident had torn away the Shin Bet's coveted veil of integrity.[11]

Oddly enough, just as it appeared that Israel and the IDF had lost their touch in the execution of military and security policies, the PLO decided to take a bold and extremely dramatic military initiative of its own. It was an operation that once again illustrated el-Fatah's obsession with avenging Sayeret Mat'kal's Operation Spring of Youth. Had it succeeded, it would forever have changed the State of Israel.

The Ein el-Hilweh Palestinian refugee camp near Sidon, Lebanon, is one of the most wretched locations in the Palestinian diaspora. Rat-infested, immersed in desperate squalor, and locked in a permanent state of enforced poverty and hopelessness, Ein el-Hilweh was the frequent target of Israeli aerial attacks following acts of Palestinian terrorism. During the 1975–1976 Lebanese civil war its poverty-stricken hovels were systematically decimated by the pro–Christian Syrian army, which used ZSU-34 multiple-barrel antiaircraft guns to root out snipers. During Operation Peace for Galilee Ein el-Hilweh was the site of some of the war's most brutal fighting between IDF paratroopers and suicidal Palestinian defenders. Ein el-Hilweh was many things, but for the PLO it was a fertile breeding ground—a minor league where the scouts of various terror factions could observe the young talent and recruit men and women—with nothing to lose but their lives—to commit grand acts of suicidal revenge against Israel.

In early 1984 the PLO's deputy commander, Abu Jihad, traveled from Amman to Tunis, and then to Ein el-Hilweh to recruit a select group of men for a very special task. He needed a force of volunteers (families of recruited gunmen were rewarded with handsome "dowries" of foreign currency) who would be able to kill with zeal and die without thought or fear. The force had to be the embodiment of the hate and suffering the Zionist entity had perpetrated on the Palestinian people. After all, the operation he had conceived in his Amman office was meant to end the status quo in a bloody stroke. The unit he had gathered—twenty-eight men in all—was called the Holy Martyrs of Ein el-Hilweh.[12]

The twenty-eight Holy Martyrs of Ein el-Hilweh were transported to Annaba, Algeria, a major naval facility of el-Fatah's Force 17 where the force underwent intensive military training supervised by a senior naval terror officer responsible for, among other acts, the Savoy Hotel seizure. They were subjected to a long and arduous instruction, including infantry-style training, weapons proficiency, cold-killing, sabotage, explosives, high-speed driving, navigation, seamanship, and physical fitness; they were even taught the Hebrew language.[13] Toward the conclusion of their training they were addressed by Abu Jihad and Abu Tayeb, the Force 17 commander, and told that they were preparing for a historical mission against the enemy through either Lebanon, Sinai, or the Mediterranean. This operation was seen as so important for Arafat's PLO that for the last four days of their training Abu Jihad took over their instruction personally. He lectured the assembled martyrs on the possible interference they were likely to encounter from the IDF and how they should respond to it. He showed them photographs and videotapes taken by Force 17 intelligence operatives in Israel—mainly Western European tourists duped into working for the PLO—of Tel Aviv beachfronts, neighborhoods, and landmarks, including, ominously, the Kirya, the Israeli Pentagon.[14]

Considering the complexity of the terrorists' recruitment, covert training in Algeria, and extensive preparation, the target and planning were both spectacular and extremely complicated. The operation called for the terrorists to sail from Algeria to the Israeli coastline. At approximately 01:00 hours on D-Day the terrorists would lower their Zodiac rubber craft into the choppy Mediterranean waters and proceed toward an isolated beach at Bat Yam, a seafront suburb due south of Tel Aviv. In all there would be three Zodiacs carrying the twenty men finally selected for the arduous mission. Each rubber craft was laden down with two motors, fuel tanks, Warsaw Pact navigation equipment, AK-47 assault rifles, Tokarov pistols, RPGs, grenades, explosives, sophisticated communications gear, leaflets with the names of the 150 terrorists who were to be freed, and headache and seasickness pills.

The Zodiacs were to carry between six and seven terrorists each and to land two hundred to five hundred meters apart from one another. Upon ditching their Zodiac craft the men were to regroup and seize a bus the intercity drivers were known to park at a sand dune–filled lot. With a very detailed map of Tel Aviv at their disposal, the terrorists were to drive to the Kirya at approximately 09:00 hours on a Sunday morning, the time when many of soldiers were returning from their weekend leaves and a time when security at the sprawling facility was believed to be at its daily low. Also at 09:00, the defense minister met with the general staff at IDF HQ. Abu Jihad's plan called for the terrorists to break through the steel barriers of one of the Kirya's gates and, following a battle they were sure to win, seize the Israeli Defense Ministry and an adjacent building bristling with top-secret antennas.[15] Once inside the compound the heavily armed men—wearing bulletproof vests—would kill as many soldiers as possible and split into three groups. The first squad would seize the Defense Ministry's ground floor and defend it against counterattack; they would also disperse a few hundred kilograms of high explosives throughout the building, just in case. The second squad, consisting of the Ein el-Hilweh martyrs' best fighters, would take the defense minister and the general staff hostage. The third squad would race to the building's roof, which enjoyed a panoramic view of the entire city of Tel Aviv, and defend against a heliborne landing by IDF commandos; armed with RPGs and PK light machine guns, it was believed the IAF could land a force on the roof without suffering heavy losses.

The terrorists would receive their orders directly from Abu Jihad via Radio Baghdad, which reached Israel with great clarity. The terrorists were told that their return to an Arab capital would be with the 150 el-Fatah prisoners whose release their heroic action had helped to secure. It was an obvious lie. Abu Jihad was one of the PLO's more intelligent leaders. He knew that if his men were able to do the impossible and seize the who's who of Israel's military community, Israel would never release 150 prisoners and would never allow the terrorists and their hostages to leave Israel's shores alive. It was a suicide mission—one meant to expose Israeli vulnerability, place the PLO at its zenith, and receive the admiration and respect of much of the world as a result of the media blitz the suicide mission would receive. The mission's objective was the termination of the Israeli defense establishment—the assassination of the best minds and personalities the IDF had ever produced, from Defense Minister Yitzhak Rabin to the Territorial Command OCs. Had the daring gambit succeeded, Israel might have been permanently weakened.

On the foggy night of April 13, 1985, Abu Jihad boarded the S.S. *Attaviros,* a one-thousand-ton, sixty-meter ship registered in Panama, to supervise his master plan's embarkation into history. He joked with the captain and then saluted the Palestinian flag with his men. Within a few days his legions would be in Israel. D-Day was April 21, Israel's thirty-seventh anniversary. El-Fatah was about to give the Jewish state an Independence Day present that would never be forgotten.

At 23:15 hours on April 20, two hours before the rubber craft were to be lowered into the Mediterranean waters, the S.S. *Attaviros* was picked up by a sleek and fast nemesis to terrorist naval planning: the I.N.S. *Moledet* (Homeland), a Sa'ar 4 Class missile boat.

The commander of the *Moledet,* Lieutenant Colonel D. (the name is protected for security reasons), had been patrolling the Mediterranean and paying special attention to vessels traveling north from the Suez Canal. It was a busy maritime night, and there were twenty-five targets on the *Moledet*'s acquisition radar. Naturally it was too busy a workload for one missile craft to handle, so Lieutenant Colonel D., out of pure instinct, decided to encounter a slow-moving target heading north along the African coast. By fateful chance the *Moledet*'s commander had chosen the *Attaviros.* The I.N.S. *Moledet*—armed with Gabriel and

Harpoon SSMs (surface-to-surface missiles), a Vulcan Pha-
lanx 20mm radar-controlled antiaircraft system, and a
76mm gun—was 58.1 meters long and 7.8 meters wide and
could race on the waves at a maximum speed of thirty-two
knots.[16] The *Attaviros*'s maximum speed was only 11.5
knots. It was no contest.

The *Moledet* closed the gap on the *Attaviros* quickly,
coming from behind and gearing up for potential battle.
Lieutenant Colonel D. climbed to the bridge and slowly
raised his field glasses. The ship looked suspicious, with no
identifying flag, no proper cargo fastened on the deck, and
no visible crewmen. D. decided to scan the ship from a
different angle and ordered the *Moledet* but the *Attaviros*
foolishly attempted evasive maneuvers. D.'s suspicions had
proven to be correct. The vessel was labeled as an *"oniyat
fa'ha"* (hostile terrorist activity ship) and a Skunk, the
IDF/Navy's nickname for an enemy vessel. Battle stations
were sounded throughout the ship, and the thirty-two-man
crew donned life vests and raced to their posts. IDF/Navy
HQ in Tel Aviv was summoned immediately.

The inevitable battle was one-sided and deadly. Lieutenant Colonel D. approached the hulking *Attaviros* from a
ninety-degree angle of attack, which exposed its full profile
while only conceding the *Moledet*'s narrow silhouette. As
the *Moledet* prepared for action a flashing light was seen
emanating from the *Attaviros*'s deck—a terrorist had fired
an RPG at the IDF/Navy missile boat, but the warhead—
meant to destroy tanks, not ships—fell harmlessly short
into the turbulent waters. With the gloves off, Lieutenant
Colonel D. ordered the *Moledet* into action. First came
20mm tracer fire, and then—finally—authorization for the
fire-control officer to step on the trigger pedal and decimate
the terrorist mother ship with crisp bursts of 76mm cannon
fire. The *Attaviros* sank moments later while another IDF/
Navy missile craft, the I.N.S. *Mivtach* (Confidence), helped
the *Moledet* pluck survivors from the water.

In all, twenty Ein el-Hilweh Martyrs were indeed martyred, and eight wounded terrorists were pulled out of the
Mediterranean. They were brought to Tel Aviv and, when

questioned by A'man interrogators, "sang" like canaries. The entire makeup of their operation, from recruitment to the sea battle, was uncovered, as was the grandiose scheme of Abu Jihad. There was an unwritten, secret gentleman's agreement against targeting the top leadership of either side; working to assassinate Israeli Defense Minister Rabin was a fatal infraction of the contract. Since Abu Jihad, as the PLO's military commander, was in a loose way Rabin's counterpart, he was now considered fair game.[17]

Abu Jihad was born Khalil Ibrahim Machmud al-Wazir on October 10, 1935, in the town of Ramle, located a few kilometers south of Tel Aviv. He was the son of a baker. At the age of thirteen, during the 1948 War, the family fled to the political hotbed of Gaza, where young Khalil became involved in the student movement, forming clandestine cells of Palestinians opposed to the harsh Egyptian rule. The Palestinian defeat in the 1948 War would cause irreparable emotional pain for the young Khalil, who vowed to avenge his nation's moment of humiliation.

Khalil al-Wazir met Yasir Arafat in the 1950s when, together with Salah Khalaf (better known by the nom de guerre of Abu I'yad), he was an "exiled" Palestinian student enrolled in the University of Alexandria's philosophy faculty. The men would remain together for over thirty years. On October 10, 1959, Abu Jihad became Yasir Arafat's second-in-command upon the founding of el-Fatah, a military and political resistance movement that would try to destroy the State of Israel through armed struggle. In their spare time both Arafat and al-Wazir began to recruit Palestinians in Kuwait for their newly founded military resistance organization. Arafat worked as an engineer, while Kahlil al-Wazir taught at a primary school where his students learned the three Rs: reading, writing, and revolution. In 1963 al-Wazir moved to Algiers, where he founded the Kuwat al-Asifa (Storm Troops), the nucleus of el-Fatah's military wing. He went to the People's Republic of China, North Vietnam, and North Korea to receive guerrilla training and valuable military supplies.[18] After years of preparations and pan-

Arab support Abu Jihad masterminded el-Fatah's first act of armed resistance against the State of Israel. On January 1, 1965, a lone and courageous guerrilla named Mahmud Hijazi infiltrated into Israel and planted an explosive device along the National Water Carrier. To this day, January first is regarded as Revolution Day by Palestinian supporters of Yasir Arafat's el-Fatah.

In the twenty-three years to follow, Abu Jihad organized hundreds of operations against Israel, resulting in hundreds of Israeli dead and wounded; casualties on both sides resulted from Israeli retaliation to such attacks. He was behind the takeover of the Israeli embassy in Bangkok, Thailand, in 1972; he commanded Palestinian units that fought alongside the Egyptians and Syrians in the 1973 War; he staged a murderous June 1974 seaborne attack on Nahariya, the March 1975 seizure of the Savoy Hotel, and the deadly March 1978 Country Club massacre in which over thirty Israelis were killed. During the Palestinian Intifada (Uprising) Abu Jihad was involved in establishing a shadowy Palestinian government for the chaotic occupied territories, which would make the troubled lands totally ungovernable by the Israelis. His first move was to destroy Israel's elaborate network of informers in the West Bank and Gaza Strip by ordering the death of anyone even suspected of passing information to the Israelis. The perpetrators of Abu Jihad's policy were the soldiers of the secret armies allied to different PLO factions, which had grown out of the curfew-ridden territories. These were young men whose hopeless future turned them into zealous murderers.

And finally there was one final attempt by Abu Jihad to bring Israel to her knees.

On March 7, 1988, three heavily armed Force 17 terrorists crossed the border from Egypt and hijacked an intercity bus carrying workers from their homes in Beersheba to the nuclear reactor in Dimona. After prolonged and doomed negotiations the Ya'ma'm stormed the bus and killed the three Palestinians, but not before they managed to kill three of the hostages. The incident became known as the Bus of

Mothers massacre, and together with Abu Jihad's involvement in the Intifada, it was viewed as a turning point.

Although previously considered a symbol of terrorism throughout the world, by 1988 Yasir Arafat had become the archetypal Third World revolutionary succumbing to failure and age. Now he had become an accepted spokesman for his people and was widely viewed as a voice of moderation in the PLO. Such el-Fatah actions as the Bus of Mothers incident, however, exposed the fact that the group was still capable of gaining the international spotlight through the murder of innocents. The responsibility for action lay with Arafat's highly dangerous lieutenants. These were men who cared little for the frivolity of Third World conferences, United Nations tea parties, and—at the time—positive mentions in the Eastern Bloc press. They also paid little notice to the international diplomatic campaign that had given Arafat new life via the Intifada. Instead they saw themselves as soldiers, masterminds of a revolution in which the world was their battlefield and all the world's citizens legitimate combatants and casualties. Of all the men and noms de guerre now equated with terrorism, such as Abu Nidal and Ahmed Jibril, the man who chose for his calling card the name Abu Jihad (Father Holy War) was one of the best.

Much speculation exists as to the reason behind the decision to have Abu Jihad killed. Speculation will remain, since according to the official Israeli government line Israel was not responsible for his death. There was, of course, Abu Jihad's long history of murderous crimes, the failed seaborne raid against the Israeli Ministry of Defense, and the Bus of Mothers incident.

Given his record of spectacular operations in the past and the prospects for new and deadly operations in the future—together with the growing Intifada, which was raising the temperature of the Arab-Israeli conflict once again—it is believed that Israel made the fateful decision to assassinate Abu Jihad. Days before Sayeret Mat'kal embarked on one of its most spectacular operations, the usually close-lipped

A'man Director, Major General Amnon Shahak, made an ominous statement. He said, "I do believe that commando assault operations are highly successful. They have a strong deterrent impact on terrorists, and therefore I regard them as a highly important tool. I don't think that Tzahal has stopped thinking about them, or that we will stop conducting them."[19]

Indeed, the wheels were already in motion to validate Major General Shahak's prediction. It would prove to be a preemptive operation, since Abu Jihad was busy planning a notorious escalation in the blood level of hostilities. According to A'man intelligence reports, Abu Jihad was putting the final touches on a plan—the second phase of the Intifada—in which senior and highly talented IDF staff officers would be assassinated.[20] Yet the comments were mere window dressing, preparing the PLO leadership for the upcoming offensive. On March 10, 1988, the heads of the Mossad, the Shin Bet, and A'man met in the Kirya to discuss removing Abu Jihad. Shahak said that the IDF could remove the threats to Israeli security that had erupted in the past several weeks. Truly the Intifada was dire, but cross-border infiltrations like the Bus of Mothers incident were intolerable. Abu Jihad's death warrant had been signed. The IDF needed thirty days to get ready.[21]

For Israel, the most important detail of an assassination operation was deniability, an option that would serve as an escape hatch just in case an internationally embarrassing public outcry should stem from the killing of the PLO's number-two man. As a result, another pinpoint IAF air raid like the one on October 1, 1985, which destroyed Force 17 headquarters in Tunis, was out of the question. The Israelis wanted impact; they wished to strike a devastating blow right in the enemy's lair and to serve notice to other terrorist leaders that their lives were in danger, too. To succeed would require the best efforts of Israel's intelligence and military community in a combined and coordinated manner. For inspiration, Israel would only have to look back fifteen years to April 1973 and the legendary Operation Spring of Youth.

The killings of Black September's Abu Yusef, Kamal

A'dwan, and Kamal Nasser in Operation Spring of Youth were meticulous exercises and a fine example of special operations genius. Ironically, Operation Spring of Youth was the act that brought Abu Jihad to power when he was named Abu Yusef's successor as chief of el-Fatah military operations. Fifteen years later both Ehud Barak and Amnon Shahak would have the opportunity to refine a nearly picture-perfect operation in Beirut, as well as to correct that operation's odd twist of fate.

There was no doubt who would be executing the operation: the Chief of Staff's Boys, Sayeret Mat'kal.[22] There was, however, much work to be done.

In such a unique military operation, intelligence is obviously of paramount importance. When the PLO went into exile in Tunisia in August, 1982, after being expelled from Beirut by the IDF, the once-friendly confines of the North African nation had become a frontline enemy target. The two IDF military intelligence branches, A'man and Ha'man (Hebrew acronym for Heyl Ha'Mode'in, Intelligence Corps), intensified their intelligence-gathering efforts in Tunisia, as did Mossad.

By 1985 the Israelis had established an elaborate intelligence network in Tunis, including agents and operatives, safe houses and weapons caches. Their capabilities were so impressive that it has been reported that only eight minutes before the IAF F-16s were set to drop their ordnance on the Force 17 headquarters in Tunis on October 1, 1985, the IDF general staff was alerted that Yasir Arafat and Force 17 commander Abu Tayeb had just departed the complex. The IAF operations commander informed Israeli Defense Minister Yitzhak Rabin that Arafat and Abu Tayeb could be re-targeted, but the original battle plan was adhered to.

To complement the intelligence blitz, according to published reports, units from Ha'Kommando Ha'Yami began deep penetration operations in the Tunisian Mediterranean, mapping Tunisian beaches and possible landing sites. They surveyed the country's naval bases and seaborne detection capabilities and monitored the activities of the small Tunisian navy.[23] At the same time, small reconnaissance teams from Sayeret Mat'kal equipped with sophisticated communications gear made frequent deep penetration forays into Tunisia, conducting surveillance of roads, airfields, and various other targets, including the PLO headquarters in Hamam-Shat and the homes of top Palestinian leaders in the exclusive suburbs of Tunis. They conducted intelligence-gathering forays against other Palestinian targets and Tunisian troop concentrations and took extensive reconnaissance outings to monitor Tunisian military units stationed near the capital. To support this effort, all Tunisian and Palestinian signal communications were conveniently monitored by the IDF.

If one of the trademarks of Israeli special unit operations is the "follow me" ethic of command, then it comes as little surprise to discover that the Sayeret Mat'kal commander flew to Tunis on a commercial flight from Rome for a look-see of his own.[24] He was met at the airport by the leader of the six-man-and-one-woman Mossad team, which had been specifically flown into Tunis to do the groundwork for the Abu Jihad killing. (To avoid any security leaks or untimely and unlucky capture by the Tunisian internal security services, all Israeli agents were evacuated from Tunis prior to the operation.) They drove to Abu Jihad's home in the exclusive Sidi Bouseid suburb of Tunis and then proceeded to the landing site that had been chosen: a deserted, picturesque beach at Ras Carthage, near the ancient port city of Carthage and approximately forty kilometers north of Tunis.

In the first week of April 1988 a full rehearsal of the raid was conducted near the port city of Haifa, with the town atop Mount Carmel imitating the hilly confines of Tunis quite convincingly. A rough though accurate model of the Abu Jihad home was constructed at a nearby IDF ordnance base, with A Force—the vanguard team entrusted with the actual killing—supplied with a three-dimensional layout. Training for the hit was conducted at times when, according to foreign reports, superpower satellites would not be flying over Israel, and therefore hopefully would not discover the pre-raid preparations. After days of intensive, sometimes brutal training the Sayeret Mat'kal A Force blasted their way into a model of Abu Jihad's home, found and killed the elusive Father Holy War, and exited in extreme haste in an amazing twenty-two seconds.[25]

Although the operation depended on accurate intelligence obtained by the Mossad and Military Intelligence, the success or failure of the mission hinged on two other equally important components.

The approximately thirty- to forty-man force of Sayeret Mat'kal and Ha'Kommando Ha'Yami commandos was to be ferried to Tunis on four missile boats; these were four Sa'ar IVs, including the I.N.S. *Aliyah* and I.N.S. *Geula,* which carried helicopters. One of the boats would hold two AH-1S Cobra gunships for added fire support should the need arise. The other was outfitted with a full battalion aid station, complete with a surgery and an IAF Bell 206 helicopter able to evacuate serious casualties in haste. Also on board the mini-armada were Mossad communications and Tunisia experts, including Mossad's chief communications officer, who had spent years in deep cover in North Africa.[26]

Providing an aerial security blanket of ECM (electronic countermeasures) protection, two specially modified IAF Boeing 707s would fly in the skies over Tunis. One aircraft (international identification number 4X-007) would serve as an airborne reconnaissance and electronic warfare command and control center; it also ferried the head of Military Intelligence, Major General Amnon Shahak, as well as Nachum Admoni, the Mossad controller, and Deputy Chief of Staff Barak. The flight would be responsible for the coordination of all intelligence matters. The other Boeing 707 (international identification number 4X-497) would serve as a flying headquarters and ferry OC IAF Major General Avihu Ben-Nun. Nearby, two IAF flying tankers were positioned over the Mediterranean for refueling operations, while a flight of F-15s escorted them as aerial support. It was clear that Operation Spring of Youth was primitive when compared to the high-tech preparation involved in the Tunis raid.

On the ground the commandos would have to rely on their own well-honed skills. Each commando would wear a black Nomex coverall, ubiquitous khaki canvas Israeli-made Patauga boots, and Kevlar bulletproof vest. According to several reports, the commandos wore Tunisian National Guard uniforms for added camouflage. Although this report appears to be speculative, it is reminiscent of the Entebbe raid, for which commandos wore unique lizard-pattern camouflage fatigues to impersonate President Idi Amin's Palestinian bodyguards. To conceal their identities the commandos wore face masks as well as special night-vision goggles. Each fighter carried a personal miniature radio and emergency homing device—in case of separation from the main force or worse, capture—which was in constant contact with the flying control and command centers overhead. The force tasked with killing Abu Jihad carried silenced Uzi submachine guns (odd, since the Israelis generally employ captured Eastern Bloc throwaway weaponry, such as the AK-47, for such covert operations) and the Israeli favorite, .22-caliber Beretta automatics. The support personnel carried weapons with greater range, such as the Galil series of 5.56mm assault rifles and FN MAG 7.62mm light machine guns. These weapons were equipped with various high-power scopes, the IT AIM-1D I.R. laser aiming light, and the NVG-1 single-eye night vision goggles. In addition, each commando carried stun grenades for their shock value, as well as antipersonnel fragmentation grenades for the sheer killing power they possessed.

The Mat'kal task force, which was divided into four groups, also took with it, according to published reports, video equipment to record the mission for training's sake. The video camera, believed to be an M-2001 mini L.L.L. laser-augmented video camera produced by IT Lasers, is a low-light-level, high-sensitivity mini CCD video camera that can shoot clearly in light levels as low as .0001 footcandles. At seven kilograms it is both light and sturdy.

Under a veiled cloak of secrecy the missile boat armada departed the safe shores of Israel in early April and proceeded toward its date with destiny. It would be one of the most dramatic military statements ever to be made by the State of Israel.

The decision to proceed with the operation was, in fact, a brave one, considering that on April 14 French intelligence is believed to have warned the PLO that an impending raid on Abu Jihad was being planned by the IDF. Major General Barak counted on PLO overconfidence and Abu Jihad's disdain for airtight security (he was nicknamed the Wailing Wall by his Force 17 bodyguards, who complained of the scores of people who were allowed to visit him every day) when giving the green light for the mission. Abu Jihad believed that any attempt on a senior Palestinian leader's life would target Chairman Arafat, and since Arafat was in Bahrain at the time, Abu Jihad viewed the French intelligence reports as foolish. It would be a fatal mistake.

On April 15 the Israeli cabinet met to give its blessing to the operation or to forbid it. Foreign Minister Shimon Peres and Major General (Res.) Ezer Weizman (the IAF OC during the 1967 War), it was later learned, were vehemently opposed to the assassination of a top-level Palestinian figure, arguing it served no positive purpose. They were voted down by ministers from the right-wing Likud Party. The operation was on!

As darkness fell on the night of April 15, 1988, the armada of IDF/Navy missile boats rendezvoused just outside Tunisian territorial waters. The two Boeing 707s flew on civilian flight path Blue 21 between southern Sicily and northern Tunisia and blanketed the area with a thick ECM shield, which harassed Tunisian radar facilities and frustrated all communications traffic. Simultaneously Mossad agents on the ground in Tunis managed to tap into the local telephone lines and block calls that could have alerted authorities to the impending operation.

Two naval commandos entered the choppy Mediterranean waters and proceeded underwater toward the deserted beach, where they made contact with the awaiting Mossad team. The agents made coded contact with the flying headquarters hovering in the skies above, and the green light was given to dispatch the remainder of the heavily laden naval commando and Sayeret Mat'kal force. Five Zodiac craft were thrown into the water, and within moments the vanguard force of frogmen and four teams of commandos landed on the sandy beach.[27]

The naval commandos stayed behind, assuming defensive positions along the tropical palm-tree-lined beach, while the flotilla of Sa'ar IV-class missile boats retreated beyond the range of Tunisian coastal radar.

In almost a carbon copy of Operation Spring of Youth, the Mat'kal commandos were loaded into three rented vehicles (a Peugeot 305 and two Volkswagen minibuses) and driven toward Sidi Bouseid. The scenic area was a favorite among the PLO leadership; among Abu Jihad's neighbors were Abu el-Chol, el-Fatah's chief of intelligence, and Abu Massen, the man responsible for covert dialogues with Israeli left-wing politicians. The picturesque tree-lined streets were crawling with armed security personnel. Nevertheless, calm and an ECM cover blanketed Tunis.

Shortly after 0100 hours on April 16 the three Mossad vehicles arrived at the Abu Jihad household and linked up with the Mossad agents who had kept the house and neighborhood under constant and vigilant surveillance. Abu Jihad, however, was not at home, but attending a senior PLO meeting in downtown Tunis planning the assassination of an IDF general. With no choice but to sit tight the agents and commandos relied on their cool nerves to suppress the ever-flowing adrenaline. A Force remained in position around the Abu Jihad home, while the remainder of the force secured escape routes and defensive firing positions. To cover their identities the commandos and agents spoke to one another only in French and Arabic! Although the details of the raid remain highly classified, it is believed that the Mat'kal commandos selected for the mission were chosen for their language skills.

At 01:30 Abu Jihad's motorcade returned home. Anxiety was replaced by utter fear and tension as the commandos prepared their gear one final time and awaited the signal to enter the home. As he entered the front door his security guards parked the Mercedes and assumed defensive positions with their Beretta 9mm submachine guns and AKMS 7.62mm assault rifles. The Mat'kal plan was to kill Abu Jihad as he lay asleep in his bed, but the tireless PLO military commander continued to work, examining video reports from the Intifada. For nearly another hour the Israeli task force had to hurry up and wait.

Finally, at approximately 02:30 hours, the lights in Abu Jihad's second-floor bedroom were extinguished and the house immersed in a silent darkness. H-Hour was at hand.

As D Force deployed on the curbside approaches of Abu Jihad's house, C Force took up positions at all entrances, and B Force moved into assault position, a commando from A Force stealthily approached Abu Jihad's parked car and silenced the snoring driver with a lone shot to the head from a .22 Beretta automatic. A Palestinian guard was shot dead in a flurry of gunfire in Jihad's basement, and a Tunisian security guard was "silently" blown away as well.[28] The cast-iron doors of the house were blasted off their hinges using a virtually soundless and highly classified technique, allowing B Force to enter first and secure the basement and ground floor while A Force headed up the stairs toward the objective, meeting and killing a sleeping Force 17 guard in the process.

A Force assembled outside Abu Jihad's bedroom door. They raised their weapons and burst into the terror chief's bedroom with a sharp kick to the door. Abu Jihad had been alerted by the muffled noise outside his room and had managed to raise his sleepy head a few inches before his body was riddled with seventy-five bullets. Abu Jihad's wife, Umm Jihad (Mother Holy War), was lying beside her husband when the gunfire erupted but was unharmed by the Israeli force.

Slowly and calmly the commandos evacuated the scene, hoping to evade notice. With the heavily armed C and D forces securing the escape route, the commandos sped in their vehicles toward the Ras Carthage beach, taking ice-cold drinks for refreshing relief. They managed to reach the Ras Carthage beach without incident and were met by the nervous force of naval commandos that had prepared an effective defensive perimeter around the LZ. After ditching their vehicles on the beach in telltale fashion the commandos boarded their Zodiac craft and sped toward the missile boats, which—alerted to the success of the operation—had reentered Tunisian waters.

The Mossad agents proceeded directly toward the airport, where they boarded separate flights to various destinations in Western Europe, then switched to connecting flights for Tel Aviv.[29] Although they had participated in one of the more spectacular operations in the history of Israel's war against terrorism, they returned home nameless and unheralded.

The entire hit took an astounding thirteen seconds from the time the downstairs doors were blown off to the time the first commandos from A Force departed the house—better than in the dry run in Haifa. It was remarkable to consider that after all the hundreds of thousands of man-hours that had gone into the planning, pre-operational details, and logistical support procedures for the operation, it was over in a blink of an eye. The operation was a rousing testament to the skill of the Israeli intelligence agents who had laid the groundwork for the raid, and also to the Chief of Staff's Boys who executed it.*

Two days later, on April 18, the Israeli daily *Yediot Aharonot* reported that "the terminators of Abu Jihad had returned to Israel by sea." The armada of Sa'ar IV missile boats, covered by an aerial shield of F-15s and F-16s, had indeed reached the Israeli shore without incident. In fitting fashion, perhaps, the commandos they carried returned to Israel on the eve of remembrance services for the thousands of Israeli war dead and the civilian victims of terrorism.

Umm Jihad managed to take a split-second look at the attackers; oddly enough, she reported to the media that a

_____

*Indeed, many initially speculated that the Abu Jihad assassination could have been an "inside" job, but such suspicions were quickly dispelled by the emerging details of Israel's involvement. According to one anonymous Western intelligence source, "If the Palestinians or Syrians were behind the killing, half of Tunis would have been destroyed."

blond Israeli woman speaking French with an Israeli accent had worked with the commando team and had videotaped the killing. She also claims to have confronted the Israeli commandos and faced the wall, firing-squad style, to be martyred. She could not understand why the Israelis hadn't killed her and her daughter. Speaking in fluent Palestinian Arabic, one of the Sayeret Mat'kal commandos, it has been reported, told Abu Jihad's daughter to take care of her mother. During the earlier Beirut raid the Mat'kal commandos had killed Abu Yusef's wife as she attempted to shield her husband while he reached for his AK-47. Major Yoni Netanyahu was the officer who had killed Abu Yusef and his wife Maha, and it was a bothersome footnote to an otherwise successful operation; a repeat of the tragedy was to be avoided in Tunis at all costs. For propaganda purposes Umm Jihad stated that Abu Jihad had attempted to resist the Israeli force with a revolver he kept in his desk drawer.

What was actually found in Abu Jihad's drawer was a comprehensive list of hundreds of Palestinian terrorists operating in Western Europe and in Israel proper. The discovery of the list and countless other invaluable documents was an intelligence bonanza and a counterterrorist victory that in itself would rival the killing of Abu Jihad.[30]

Of all the Palestinian terrorist leaders killed since the onset of Israel's undeclared war against Black September in 1972, Abu Jihad was certainly the most important. The commandos of Sayeret Mat'kal had performed a remarkable feat, but they could not rest on their anonymous laurels. In Lebanon and Iraq new enemies to the State of Israel had emerged—enemies that required special attention only one Israeli force was capable of providing.

# NOTES

1. For a mention of Uzi Dayan as Sayeret Mat'kal's commander, see Yossi Melman and Dan Raviv, *The Imper-*

*fect Spies* (London: Sidgwick & Jackson, 1989), 200; for Dayan's unit being summoned to Misgav Am, see Emanuel Rosen, "Uzi: Ha'Klaf Ha'Chazak Shel Shoshelet Dayan," *Ma'ariv Sof Shavua,* February 5, 1988, 8, and Avi Battleheim, *Golani: Mishpachat Lochamim* (Tel Aviv: Golani Brigade Command/Ministry of Defense Publications, 1980), 226.

2. A description of commandos' top-secret equipment stems from published photographs taken at the hostage standoff.

3. Emanuel Rosen, "Uzi: Ha'Klaf," 8.

4. *Ibid.*

5. Although the account of the sniper belonging to the Chief of Staff's Boys cannot be confirmed (after all, Sayeret Mat'kal is only a legend), see Neil C. Livingstone and David Halevy, *Inside the PLO* (New York: William Morrow Company, Inc., 1990), 264.

6. Zeev Klein, ed., *Ha'Milchama Be'Terror: Ve'Mediniut Ha'Bitachon Shel Yisrael 1979–88* (Tel Aviv: Revivim Publishers, 1988), 70.

7. Samuel M. Katz, *Guards Without Frontiers: Israel's War Against Terrorism* (London: Arms and Armour Press, 1990), 86.

8. *Ibid.*

9. *Ibid.*

10. Michele Mayron, "Israel's Watergate," *Penthouse Magazine,* July 1987, 50.

11. For the best account of the Shin Bet affair, see Zeev Klein, ed., *Ha'Milchama Be'Terror,* 134–39.

12. Haim Raviah and Eilan Kfir, "The Objective: Massacre at the General Staff," *Hadashot,* April 23, 1988, 3.

13. Sigal Buchris, "Kashe Le'Ta'er Ma Haya Koreh Eilu . . . ," *Bein Galim,* April 1990, 47.

14. *Ibid.*

15. *Ibid.*

16. *Ibid.*, p. 60.

17. Neil C. Livingstone and David Halevy, "Israeli Commandos Terminate PLO Terror Chief," *Soldier of Fortune Magazine,* December 1988, 75.

18. "Father of the Holy War," *Jerusalem Post,* April 17, 1988, 5.

19. Yosef Argaman, "Ra'ayon Im Rosh A'man," *Bamachane,* April 13, 1988, 5.

20. Yochanan Lahav, "Abu Jihad Tichnen Lirtzo'ach Mefakdim Bechirim Be'Tzahal," *Yediot Aharonot,* April 19, 1988, 3.

21. Dan Raviv and Yossi Melman, *Imperfect Spies,* 26.

22. Gelen Frankel, "Hasifa: Kach Huchlat Ve'Butza'a Chisool Abu Jihad Al Yedai Tzahal Ve'Ha'Mossad," *Ma'ariv,* April 22, 1988, 4.

23. Gelen Frankel, "Hasifa," 4.

24. Neil C. Livingstone and David Halevy, "Israeli Commandos," 77.

25. *Ibid.*

26. *Ibid.*

27. Gelen Frankel, "Hasifa," 4.

28. Yossi Melman and Dan Raviv, *The Imperfect Spies,* 31.

29. Gelen Frankel, "Hasifa," 4.

30. "Yisrael Tafsa Be'Tunis Reshimat Sochnei A'shaf Ba'Aretz Ube'Shtachim," *Ma'ariv,* May 8, 1988, 6.

# 10

---

## *The Human Bazaar Is Now Open for Business*

---

*The "Abduction" of Sheikh Abdel Karim Obeid*
*Southern Lebanon*
*July 28, 1989*

Ever since the first men inhabited the desert sands, life has had a distorted value in the fanatic world of Middle Eastern currency. For in the tribal-minded world of the Near East, one's worth is measured not by individual accomplishments or intelligence—it is the price that one's live carcass can bring on the open market that determines one's value honor. In the Byzantine world of the Middle East modern military equation there is no human commodity more valued than the men and women who wear the olive fatigues of the Tzava Haganah Le'Yisrael. The Israeli soldier, after all, is worth more than his or her weight in gold to a wily national leader, terrorist chieftain, or reclusive guerrilla warlord wishing to hold the State of Israel and its army hostage. Israel's sensitivity about casualties is well known. Ever since 1948 and the battle of Latrun against the Jordanian Arab Legion, when wounded Israeli soldiers were left behind for the slaughter, there has been an unwritten IDF law stating that no soldiers—live, wounded, or dead—will be left behind on the battlefield. The enemies of the Jewish state are well-versed in this golden rule and realize that in order to secure the release of a live Jewish soldier—or even a corpse—Israel is willing to pay a thousandfold in released human currency, as well as handling fees in the millions of dollars.[1] In fact, since the IDF became an entity in the region over forty years ago, the value of human life has been one-sided and paid for with much blood and misery. Sometimes, however, the IDF finds itself in a position where obtaining the freedom of its men amounts to a Herculean challenge.

Just as this cruel human barter system has come to characterize the day-to-day existence of the Middle East, so have IAF air attacks against terrorist targets located throughout the maddening chaos that was once Lebanon. Beginning in 1970, Lebanon was the nerve center of the Palestinian military campaign against the Jewish state, and since that time it has been a natural target for Israel's retaliatory rage. The terrorist leaders were smart—very smart. By locating their headquarters, barracks, armories, and training facilities next to children's hospitals, UNRWA (United Nations Relief Works Agency) schools, and over-crowded refugee camps they made sure that any Israeli retaliatory action that killed a few dozen sleeping or crippled children (while at the same time obliterating a justifiable hostile military target) would be self-defeating in the ever-so-important public relations war. Terrorist leaders, especially Arafat, have reveled in the theater of mourning over the bodies of innocents killed in such attacks.

The Israeli government, however, have never allowed public opinion to deter it from actions it sees as vital to national security. According to the Israeli line made standard by the government of Prime Minister Menachem Begin, "The world doesn't have to love us . . . it just has to let us live in peace." The IAF would bomb terrorist targets whenever such action was warranted. Aerial action was warranted on October 16, 1986.

At an anonymous air base in central Israel a flight of two

IAF McDonnell Douglas F-4E Phantoms—for nearly twenty-five years the true workhorse and battleship of the Heyl Ha'Avir (Israel Air Force)—was being readied for action. It was midafternoon, a time when on an average day conscript soldiers would hang around the base canteen sipping sodas, eating candy bars, and trying to remain civilians at heart in the few brief moments their hectic work schedules allowed. As far as the mechanics, technicians, intelligence officers, and ordnance personnel were concerned, this afternoon *was* average—bloody average. Five-hundred-pound bombs were loaded onto hard-point pylons, air-to-air missiles were readied (their safeties gently removed), and the pilots—the Mach 2 drivers who delivered ordnance from the high heavens above hell—walked slowly from their lengthy briefing to a sun-baked tarmac. After the obligatory "Okay . . . thumbs up" from the chief ground crewman, the two F-4s raced for the skies in an afterburner-powered takeoff. Liftoff was both deafening and awe-inspiring. Within minutes the two aging aircraft would be high above the treacherous danger that is Lebanon.

From a few thousand feet high, Lebanon could very well be one of the most beautiful lands on earth. The sunset that turned that particular day into evening was absolutely breathtaking, from the sculptured mountains in the east to the shimmering sparkle of the Mediterranean in the west. Paradise at thirty thousand feet had surely been found, yet it would be fleeting. Down below, the reality that is Lebanon was about to kick in. As the two Phantoms approached the day's targets—a series of heavy gun emplacements and several fishing vessels used by the PLO to launch seaborne attacks against Israel in the sprawling Miyeh-Miyeh refugee camp, due south of Sidon—reality meant that the aircraft's menacing roar would alert a legion of antiaircraft gunners for the unavoidable split-second encounter. Experienced Palestinian gunners quickly removed the canvas covers from their aging Soviet 37mm antiaircraft cannons, and SA-7 Strellas were removed from armories and readied to lock onto the heat signature of the attacking aircraft. Realizing the reception they would likely receive—a routine risk of the job—the two Phantoms approached from the south in a mad-dash Stuka-like dive.

Within seconds the beauty of the Lebanese landscape existed no longer. The sight of plush pastures was replaced by the racing bursts of 14.5mm, 23mm, and 37mm tracer fire. Antiaircraft fire was emanating from the camp as well as the hills to the southeast; Shiite militiamen, the historic nemeses of the Palestinians, had entered the fray to destroy the common denominator in the hatred of Lebanon: the Israelis. Quickly ground fire grew in intensity and scope. The two IAF pilots, used to such incoming infractions in their aerial activities above the Levantine madness, continued their attack as planned. After all, out-chasing, out-smarting, and out-lucking enemy ground fire had become an IAF specialty, and the two Phantoms surpassed the threats launched their way, proceeding to prepare their bombs for the Palestinian gun emplacements and HTA (hostile terrorist activity) fishing vessels. Several bombs were dropped, but the lead aircraft incurred a most unfortunate mechanical glitch. A short-circuit on the bomb-release button caused an electronic malfunction that triggered the detonation of a five-hundred-pound bomb while it still lay on the hard-point pylon underneath the wing. The resulting fiery explosion engulfed the crimson sky and brought the Phantom to its flaming end as it cascaded down to earth.

Both the pilot, who, due to security considerations, is known simply as A., and the navigator, Captain Ron Arad, miraculously succeeded in ejecting from the midair inferno. Yet their slow glide to earth was a terrifying adventure; according to A., "It was like an old World War II movie. . . . I heard a loud *boom* and then 'deafening' silence. I was sure I was dead but I heard the ear-splitting bang of the explosion, the red flames and then humbling thoughts of mortality."[2] His mortality would, indeed, be secured.

After landing in an unforgiving ravine carpeted with flesh-piercing thorns, a badly bruised A. found himself dazed, confused, and pursued by hundreds of heavily armed men shouting in Arabic and praising Allah. A. was lucky.

The free-flying and daredevil crews of two AH-1S Cobra helicopter gunships courageously flew into the gauntlet of enemy fire and, after raking the encroaching Arab gunmen with deadly bursts of cannon and rocket fire, plucked A. to safety on the chopper's landing boards. His rather eventful journey back to Israel was meticulously protected by two airborne command posts (Bell 212 light transport helicopters) of the IAF's elite Aeromedical Evacuation Unit—a unit known for executing miracles and bringing abandoned and desperate soldiers back from harm's way.[3] A.'s story became legend.

So, too, did Ron Arad's saga, although he was not at all as fortunate. He, too, managed to eject from the flaming Phantom and managed to land on Lebanese soil without suffering physical injury. Yet instead of being picked up on the eagle's wings of an IAF helicopter gunship, Ron Arad found himself surrounded by swarms of heavily armed men, all wearing U.S. Army woodland-pattern camouflage fatigues and toting AKMS 7.62mm assault rifles.* From their close-cropped hair, green bandannas, and religious-inspired graffiti etched on olive canvas web gear, it was clear to Ron Arad that his captors were not pragmatic opponents, like so many of the Palestinian groups, nor were they merciful, like Walid Jumblatt's Druze army; they were not even confused Lebanese leftists who were struggling for one sort of revolution or another. These fighters were the warriors of Islam— zealous martyrs of the faith who were more than happy to sacrifice their lives in order to bring a Khomeini-like religious order to the entire Middle East. Initially, however, Ron Arad was "fortunate" enough to find himself in the

---

*Lebanese Shiite militiamen had obtained these American-produced uniforms through sheer guile and dominating victory on the battlefield. While the U.S. Marines were stationed in Beirut, Shiite militiamen managed to steal hundreds of such camouflage fatigues from wash lines; in fact, an Amal militia-owned laundry service even gained the contract for the marines' laundry; of course, most of the fatigues were never returned! Once the marine barracks were decimated by the suicide truck bomber, the Shiite guerrillas obtained the remainder of their uniforms from surrendering or killed soldiers in the Christian-dominated Lebanese army.

clutches of the Amal, the moderate Shiite militia run by Nabih Berri that was not as fanatic as Hizbollah.

The Shiite movement known as Amal was born out of the mysterious disappearance—and alleged murder—of Lebanese Shiite spiritual leader Musa Zadr in Libya in 1978. Outraged by their minority status and long neglected and abused in a Christian- and Palestinian-dominated Lebanese society, the Shiites began to arm themselves in the squalid slums of West Beirut and in the mountain villages of southern Lebanon. Oddly enough, Amal's principal military activities in the years between 1980 and 1981 were against Palestinian guerrillas; for years the PLO had turned the 200,000 Shiites of southern Lebanon into a frightened population of extortion and rape victims. So badly treated were the Shiites that when the IDF invaded Lebanon on June 6, 1982, to initiate Operation Peace for Galilee the advancing armored columns were openly embraced by the Shiites. Amal leader Nabih Berri ordered his men not to engage the Israelis, and even to surrender their arms to them should it be necessary.[4]

For the Israel Defense Forces, the loss of Ron Arad soon developed into a desperate situation quickly corroding into pure hopelessness. Although the IDF does its utmost to save any of its soldiers—from high-ranking officer to mess cook—captured by the enemy, a pilot was clearly a different story. Since the early 1950s the IAF had promoted itself as a service above and beyond the regular IDF. Its personnel were the best; in fact, the slogan used since 1963 to induce conscripts to volunteer to the pilots' course was *ha'tovim la'tayis* (the *best* for pilots). Beyond the fact that a navigator like Ron Arad was considered to be in a class by himself, and that a minor fortune had been invested in his extremely lengthy training period, IAF flight personnel owned a great deal of ultra-top-secret information—the actual flight strength of the IAF,* its tactics, and many of its planned operations and capabilities. Although all flight personnel undergo survival training and simulated interrogations, it is clear that a human being cannot withstand the brutal and

---

*The IAF has never officially published its exact order of battle.

sometimes sophisticated means employed by terrorists and the intelligence services of many Middle Eastern nations. More importantly, any information obtained from Ron Arad would be passed on to the Shiites' two principal backers in Lebanon: Iran and Syria. In fact, both Iran and Syria were determined to keep Ron Arad a POW and pressed their Shiite subordinates to make no deals. The Syrians, remembering Sayeret Mat'kal's daring Operation Basket of 1972, which eventually secured the release of captured IAF airmen, covered Amal troop movements in Lebanon and helped protect key Amal leaders and officers. Amal, too, realized that an IDF commando operation to kidnap a key Amal official or, worse, attempt to rescue Ron Arad was not out of the question. After all, the IDF had already been to Beirut on many occasions.

Days after Ron Arad's capture Amal leader Nabih Berri, who at the time of Arad's downing was the Lebanese justice minister, stated that he was more than willing to trade the Israeli airman for a few hundred Palestinian and Lebanese detainees in Israeli custody.[5] Unfortunately for Israel, Arad was no longer a prisoner of Amal—a somewhat pragmatic albeit bloody organization that was always willing to deal with Israel (in fact, it was even willing to trade the bodies of two IDF missing in action from Operation Peace for Galilee for four hundred Shiites in Israeli hands).[6] Within weeks of Arad's capture he was quickly hustled from southern Lebanon to the slums of West Beirut, and then to the Syrian-controlled Bekaa Valley. Arad was caught in the middle of an internal policy dispute within Amal's ranks as the moderates under Berri's tutelage were confronted by the radicals, led by Hassan Hasham and Mustafa Dirani, who pushed for an offensive and extremely bloody strategy of attacks against Israel. The radicals within Amal, realizing that Ron Arad was a political trump card, duly handed the IAF navigator over to another Shiite group that had become one of the dominant players in the Lebanese Russian roulette. Under cover of darkness and in absolute secrecy Ron Arad was transferred to the control of Hizbollah (Party of God). He was reportedly smuggled into Iran.[7] According to many Western intelligence experts, Hizbollah was the most terrifying and deadly terrorist phenomenon to emerge on the world scene since the explosive eruption of Black September in 1972.[8]

Of all the guerrilla groups the IDF has encountered in its nearly forty-three years of existence, Hizbollah has been one of the most bitter foes. Born in the Bekaa Valley town of Ba'albek, Hizbollah was the cover name for several extremist terrorist factions whose ideology was fundamentalist and Khomeini-istic; they were trained by Iranian clerics and revolutionary guards.* Its fighters, recruited from the slums of West Beirut—hopeless concentrations of squalor that made the nearby Palestinian refugee camps seem like exclusive suburbs—were indoctrinated into the art of hit-and-run warfare and martyrdom. Dying in battle with the hated Zionist—infidel—enemy secured one's place in paradise. Since Iran in essence created the movement, killing Americans secured one's entrance pass to heaven just as quickly as if an Israeli was butchered, and both interests became Hizbollah obsessions. Since the end of Operation Peace for Galilee, the Hizbollah legacy has been bloody. Among their most notable "achievements":

• The April 18, 1983, suicide car bombing of the United States embassy in West Beirut; 49 were killed and 120 wounded in this introductory attack.

• The ultimate bold move against Western interests in Lebanon: the October 23, 1983, suicide truck bombing of the U.S. Marines barracks at Beirut International Airport; 241 were killed and 40 wounded. Simultaneously, a suicide truck bomber smashed through the French MNF (multinational force) barracks in West Beirut; 74 were killed and 15 injured.

• The November 4, 1983, suicide truck bombing of the

---

*Hizbollah is also known as Islamic Jihad, Party of God, Revolutionary Justice Organization and Organization of the Oppressed, and Islamic Holy War for the Liberation of Palestine—a group made up of ex-PLO veterans converted to the fundamentalist Islamic movement.

Israeli military headquarters in Tyre, southern Lebanon; 30 IDF soldiers, Border Guard policemen, and Shin Bet agents were killed and 29 hurt.

• The September 20, 1984, suicide car bombing of the U.S. embassy annex in Beirut; 20 killed and 16 wounded.

• The March 10, 1985, suicide truck bombing at the Calf's Gate border crossing near Metulla in northern Israel; 13 IDF Ordnance Corps soldiers were killed and 12 wounded.[9]

Throughout the years 1982–1985 there were countless Hizbollah suicide attacks against IDF forces trapped in the Lebanese quagmire. Many fighters were females, some even children. With over three thousand fighters spread throughout Lebanon, especially in the southern area of the country near the Israeli frontier, the Hizbollah forces proved an elusive enemy to defeat, since they blended into the local Shiite population with great ease and confidence. Unlike PLO members, Hizbollah fighters did not wear uniforms or concentrate their arms and facilities in easily identified training camps. Often Hizbollah members took their secrets to the grave, since most attacks were suicide assaults. The inability of the IDF, A'man, Mossad, and Shin Bet to infiltrate this group and defeat it from within bred confidence. Confidence prompted the Party of God to undertake an ambitious operation that would surely strike hard at the IDF psyche. On February 17, 1986, they initiated a new and bold type of offensive: kidnapping.

Yosef Fink, twenty-three, from Ra'anana, and Rechamim Elshayach, also twenty-three, from Rosh Ha'Ayin, were part-time seminary students and part-time soldiers in the Hesder program (an institution that enables Jewish seminary students to split their military service between studies and combat units); the two served in the crack Giva'ati Infantry Brigade. During routine duty inside Israel's self-imposed twelve-kilometer security zone inside southern Lebanon, near the village of Beit Yahun, Fink and Elshayach were ambushed by over a dozen heavily armed gunmen as they protected a convoy of vehicles. No shots were fired as the gunmen, Hizbollah shock troops, used surprise and overwhelming numbers to subdue the two Israelis. The two IDF soldiers were beaten savagely and then dragged off to an awaiting vehicle. The IDF mounted an exhaustive search for its two missing soldiers; Bedouin trackers were deployed to follow bloodstains into the thick, mountainous woods, and heliborne forces searched without respite for any trace of the two soldiers. All came up empty, however. Fink and Elshayach had simply disappeared into the abyss of Hizbollah hideouts, villages, and tight-lipped supporters.

The IDF immediately attempted to open a channel of communications to the Shiite kidnappers, but all attempts to strike a deal ended in dismal failure. If Hizbollah was anything, it was extremely patient. The anger of the Shiite sect of Islam had been festering for nearly a thousand years, and it was in no hurry to give up such a valued commodity as two captured Israeli soldiers without causing Israel great pain and anguish. As was the case with the dozen or so Western hostages Hizbollah had seized, the three IDF captives would have to wait while a nation squirmed.

Israel, however, was determined to speed things up and take the equation on its own terms.

Militarily speaking, Israel had very few ways to place Hizbollah between a rock and a hard place. The IDF could and did place extraordinary military pressure on southern Lebanon, punishing known terrorists, their sympathizers, and their villages with harsh, vindictive treatment. This policy, known as the Iron Fist, was politically damaging and costly in military casualties, and it only increased the number of Shiite suicide attacks on IDF patrols. The IAF could have made a pinpoint strike against a key Hizbollah position in West Beirut, Ba'albek, or points beyond (targets in Syria and Iran could have been considered), but killing Hizbollah leaders wouldn't get Fink, Elshayach and, in late 1986, Ron Arad back alive; a selective air strike would likely have led to their executions, as Hizbollah spokesmen in Beirut warned Israel that any air attack against one of its positions would be answered with the summary murders of the three captives. Hizbollah, which operated along tribal lines, had to be encountered in a truly Byzantine manner in order for Israel to get its message across. The human bazaar would once again be open for business.

Kidnapping, in the Middle East's military way of doing business, is as fundamental a tool of a nation's defense policy as is the acquisition of tanks or the training of soldiers. Since the early 1950s, when Jordanian and Syrian patrols routinely seized lone Israeli sentries manning isolated border outposts, the IDF has made retroactive kidnapping a true art form. When on June 29–30, 1954, a Unit 101 veteran and paratroop NCO, Yitzhak "The Little" Jibli, was captured by Jordanian soldiers after suffering a leg wound, his release was secured weeks later by the paratroop's abduction of dozens of Jordanian officers.[10] When on December 9, 1955, a five-man paratroop and infantry squad was taken prisoner inside Syria while planting the ill-fated listening device atop the Golan Heights, its safe return to Israel was secured only after Sayeret Tzanhanim (supported by elements from the Giva'ati and Na'ha'l infantry brigades) captured twenty-nine Syrian officers near the Sea of Galilee. Of course, Sayeret Mat'kal had made a name for itself seizing enemy officers for purposes of barter during Operation Basket; even the unit's historic mission to Entebbe was an abduction of sorts. This time, too, according to foreign reports, the General Staff Reconnaissance Unit would be summoned to carry out this most delicate, undesirable, yet necessary of tasks.

On December 16, 1988 an IDF elite unit reported to be Sayeret Mat'kal entered the south Lebanese village of Tibnin, a few kilometers outside the security zone.[11] After a force secured an approach in and out of the town the commandos seized four individuals in a lightning strike on a building intelligence reports had isolated and identified as a Hizbollah stronghold. From here, however, reports of the operation remain sketchy and shrouded in military secrecy. It is known that two of the men captured by the IDF commandos were, in fact, released after proving they had nothing to do with terrorist activity, but two men were seized and brought back to Israel. One of the men detained is known to be Daud Qashfi, a senior military leader for the Believing Front, one of the principal terrorist factions operating under the Hizbollah umbrella in southern Lebanon; the second man is believed to be a senior operations officer in the Believing Front. The target of the sweep, it is believed, was the Believing Front's founder, Mustafa Dirani. Dirani, who was Amal's operations and intelligence chief at the time of Ron Arad's capture, was believed to have had personal custody of the IAF navigator, and after he defected to Hizbollah he took Ron Arad with him. According to published reports, Dirani managed to evade the IDF snatch squad by only a few hours.[12]

The IDF did not go public with the Qashfi capture, and neither did Hizbollah. Qashfi was a big fish, but the Hizbollah bait had yet to be taken; it appeared, according to an anonymous Western intelligence official, "that Hizbollah didn't care who was captured. . . . They weren't about to give up their hostages." Once again Israel went through the back-door channels of its intelligence services to try and strike a deal with Hizbollah, but the Shiite fundamentalists would have none of it. Reports even indicate that senior Iranian officials met in London with senior Israeli representatives, including the A'man director, Major General Amnon Shahak.[13] In retrospect, it was naïve of Israel to expect Hizbollah—an organization that takes hostages at will, sent suicide bombers to a glorified martyrdom, and in 1985 murdered eight Beirut Jews and then butchered their bodies in the city's streets—to play tit for tat. The capture of Qashfi was just revenge, considering that he was involved in the planning of the Fink and Elshayach kidnappings. Hizbollah was shrewd, cunning, and patient; it did not care if its own died in the enemy's hands. After all, that secured the *mujahadin*'s (holy warrior's) place in paradise. Israel was not able to play by such rules. The IDF was ordered to raise the ante.

Sheikh Abdel Karim Obeid had been a central figure in the Hizbollah terrorist network since 1983, according to Israeli intelligence sources.[14] The thirty-two-year-old

Iranian-educated cleric had been a zealous proponent of Shiite rights and Islamic fundamentalism in his south Lebanon village of Jibchit and had been the area's imam, or religious leader. A fiery speaker with a grand hatred for the West and Israel, Obeid frequently availed himself of the Western media when reporters daring to venture into Lebanon wished to typify the rage of Shiite Muslims by featuring the sharped-tongued cleric in their newscasts. Yet beyond his public image Obeid was a terrorist mastermind. Involved in every aspect of the day-to-day operations of Hizbollah in southern Lebanon, Obeid is also believed to have been behind many of Hizbollah's most notorious operations, including several suicide bombings of Israeli forces and the February 17, 1988, kidnapping of U.S. Marine Colonel William R. Higgins, who had been serving as an observer in UNIFIL (United Nations Interim Force–Lebanon); Higgins, it is believed, was held for a while in Sheikh Obeid's home. Obeid was believed to be Hizbollah's most important target outside of Beirut excepting Hizbollah's spiritual and political leader, Sheikh Sayyid Muhammad Husayn Fadlallah. In June 1989 the Israeli cabinet, by a vote of eleven to one, authorized Obeid's kidnapping. The operation would become a classic example of how an elite unit's speed, agility, and weapons proficiency could accomplish the nearly impossible.

Although it would be impossible for Israel to deny its role in the kidnapping of Sheikh Obeid, it has never acknowledged which unit was responsible for the operation. According to numerous foreign reports, however, only one force within the IDF could have pulled off such a masterful raid: Sayeret Mat'kal.[15]

Such an operation as the planned kidnapping of Sheikh Obeid from his home in Jibchit required a pinpoint strike in which the minimum of firepower would have to be employed and the attacking force would have to operate with little or no backup. As a result, the strike required *extremely* accurate intelligence. In this regard the IDF clearly had the upper hand. Not only had the IDF had free rein in Lebanon from 1982 to 1983, but during its withdrawal toward the border it had been in control of virtually all of southern Lebanon. All villages in the area were mapped out and listed; all pertinent information was noted, and the physical and geographic makeup was even videotaped for A'man's files just in case the IDF had to make a return visit in the coming years.[16] Israel also had the services of its three intelligence agencies, Mossad, Shin Bet and A'man, to compile data—SIGINT, ELINT, and HUMINT—on the targeted village, and the IAF could be called in for aerial reconnaissance.

Intelligence would have to be good. Jibchit was the military headquarters for the Hizbollah umbrella group known as the Islamic Opposition. Beyond the heavily armed Hizbollah units that roamed the city's teeming streets with heavy weapons and armored personnel carriers, nearly every one of Jibchit's eighteen thousand inhabitants owned a personal weapon—from a Tokarov pistol to a SVD sniper's rifle. Fearing an Israeli, American, or even Christian Lebanese attack, Hizbollah had protected every principal intersection in the town, with Koran-toting grenadiers manning checkpoints with RPGs and heavy machine guns. According to one diplomat in Beirut involved in the attempts to secure the release of Western hostages, "a stranger entering Jibchit is akin to a man dropping himself into an erupting volcano. . . . it's pure suicide!"[17]

If an attacking force were to succeed in making it through the streets of Jibchit, they would have to bypass the gauntlet of human firepower that protected Sheikh Obeid. His home, a four-story building on an unassuming street in the center of town, was surrounded by a legion of Hizbollah gunmen. Sheikh Obeid also employed nearly a dozen heavily armed bodyguards wearing bulletproof vests who followed his every move. He was an extremely difficult target.

After several delays caused by the government's desire to find a diplomatic solution to the hostage crisis, D-Day was finally targeted as July 29, 1989. Although details of the operation remain highly classified, the unit trained vigorously for the assault, running real-time obstacle courses through hastily assembled mock-ups of Jibchit and coordinating the attack from A to Z with all participating components. Training continued for nearly two months; according to reports, practice forays into enemy territory were mounted by the unit.[18] For such a risky operation nothing was—or could be—left to chance. The attack plan was conceived jointly by Chief of Staff Lieutenant General Dan Shomron and deputy Chief of Staff Major General Ehud Barak,[19] the two most brilliant and experienced minds in IDF special operations.

July 29, 1989. At 02:00 hours the residents of southern Lebanon were rocked out of their slumber by the thunderous bursts of Mach 2 flybys. The IAF was once again in business in the skies of Lebanon. The sonic booms were deafening and, to the untrained ear, sounded like a hellish bombing sortie. But the midair blasts were a mere illusion—a deafening and overloaded deception of sonic booms meant to disguise the muffled sounds of several IAF CH-53 heavy transport helicopters hugging the blackened earth and carrying a force of Mat'kal commandos.[20] The CH-53s were fitted, it is believed, with HALO, an advanced night-vision goggles/heads-up display system for safe nighttime nap-of-the-earth flight, produced by the Israeli high-tech master Elbit.[21] With the flight of IAF fighter-bombers buzzing overhead, the helicopters (some accounts list only one chopper, while others report as many as three) landed in a wadi, or dry river bed, two kilometers outside of Jibchit. One force remained behind to protect the aerial taxicabs while another force—armed, it is believed, with heavier weapons, including RPG-7s—prepared a defensive ambush around the strike force's route of retreat. According to several reports, Chief of Staff Shomron and Deputy Chief of Staff Major General Ehud Barak were among the soldiers remaining with the soldiers who secured the retreat route, in order to monitor the operation from the front lines.[22]

Ten minutes into the operation (the code name of which is still highly classified) everything was still going as planned. Sometimes, in the area of elite-unit operations, a good beginning is a hint of upcoming doom. The commandos, who in their training had overcome forced marches lasting hundreds of kilometers, had little difficulty in negotiating the two-kilometer path toward the eastern end of Jibchit. After all the briefings and preparations they had expected to fight their way into Jibchit, and as a result, according to eyewitness accounts, they carried a wide variety of weaponry, including AK-47 7.62mm and Glilon 5.56mm assault rifles and mini-Uzi 9mm submachine guns equipped with silencers and laser and infrared sights.[23] Yet the streets of Jibchit were deserted. The roaring sounds of swooping IAF bombers led many of the Hizbollah faithful who were tasked with the town's defense to find cover. With checkposts abandoned and only the crisp cries of barking dogs driven mad by the sonic booms heard in Jibchit's streets, the commandos entered the town unopposed. Moving through the town's narrow streets at a sprinter's pace, the commandos made their way to Sheikh Obeid's home, a four-story building easily identified by a huge hanging poster of the Ayatollah Khomeini. The kidnapping squad, wearing fatigues and special web gear assault vests specifically designed for shock attacks, readied their gear and grasped their weapons tighter, prepared for any eventuality.[24] The roar of the overflying IAF umbrella was still ripping through the night air, and the sheikh's Hizbollah guards were nowhere to be seen. The time to strike was at hand.

The commandos raced up the building's staircase in great haste. The sheikh's door was reached, but there was still no sign of bodyguards. As the commandos readied their weapons and grenades for a possible fight the team leader banged on the cast-iron door and in perfect Lebanese Arabic shouted, *"Iftah el bab!"* ("Open the door!"). When no reply was heard an explosive charge was placed by the door's hinges and lock and a short-action fuse set in place. Crouching in protective fashion, the commandos shielded themselves from the blast, which blew a hole through what remained of the door, and then burst into the apartment. Here the force split in two. With pistols and assault weapons raised the lead element raced into the living room and study, where they found a startled Sheikh Obeid, his uncle Ahmed Obeid, and a close family confidant, Majid Fahas, sitting around a coffee table.[25] While the three men were secured and prepared for transport, the second half of the raiding party secured Obeid's family (the exact size of the raiding party remains classified). His wife Mona, twenty-five, was tied to a chair, her hands and legs fastened with coarse rope, gagging tape placed over her mouth; Sheikh Obeid's five children were placed in a side room, secured and gagged as well. Attempting to protest their situation, Mona tried to free herself but could do nothing as her husband was dragged away blindfolded. The elapsed time was less than three minutes, and not a shot had been fired.

As the commandos rushed out of the building and into the street below to meet a small contingent of their own that had remained downstairs for protective cover, the beat of helicopter blades began to fill the sleepy town. IAF helicopter gunships began to swoop into position to provide aerial fire support should it be needed.[26] Sheikh Obeid struggled with his captors and was heard yelling in Arabic, "Kill me! I won't go with you!" His cries fell on deaf ears. From an adjacent doorway two flights below one of Obeid's bodyguards, Hussein Abu Zeid, glanced outside to see what was transpiring, but before he could attempt to intercede one of the commandos fired a lone shot into his head. According to several accounts, the Mat'kal commandos battled several of Obeid's Hizbollah bodyguards in a firefight.[27] Abu Zeid's family rushed to contact the local Amal commander, and within minutes a call to arms was sounded through the town's mosque minaret. A large force of heavily armed Shiite gunmen soon filtered into Jibchit's dusty streets in search of the Israeli attackers, but they were left with the sound of several helicopters flying by. In what appears to be a bravado-inspired tale of battle, many of the Shiite gunmen who raced into the town's darkened streets to engage the invisible Israeli commandos claim that their efforts were hampered by IAF helicopter gunships that strafed them with cannon and rocket fire. This cannot be confirmed, however.

The kidnapping operation was a brilliant military success; in the foreign press it was likened to the Entebbe raid and the IAF's destruction of the Iraqi nuclear reactor in 1981. It had been executed in less than thirty minutes, and

THE ELITE

in a move where one might expect casualties to be excessive
and indiscriminate, only one man was killed. The IDF
spokesman's office delayed serving up any announcement of
the operation until fourteen hours after the fact. Lieutenant Colonel Ra'anan Gissin briefed foreign correspondents
and, citing the military necessities behind the raid, stated
that Sheikh Obeid had been a fundamental element in
Hizbollah's planning and execution of terrorist operations
against Israel for several years.[28] Yet a few hours later the
true reason behind the lightning strike in southern Lebanon
was apparent. Through back-door negotiating channels Israel offered Hizbollah Sheikh Obeid and 150 incarcerated
Shiite guerrillas in exchange for Fink, Elshayach, and Ron
Arad; the fifteen Western hostages Hizbollah was holding
were to be included as well.[29] Sheikh Fadlallah's response
was bone-chilling in its clarity: a shadowy and mysterious
group calling itself the Organization of the Oppressed on
Earth vowed to execute Colonel William Higgins unless
Sheikh Obeid was immediately released. Days later they
circulated a gruesome videotape showing a dangling hostage
hanged by the neck. Shock waves were felt in Washington as
Hizbollah succeeded in placing the blame for Higgins's
murder on the Sayeret Mat'kal abduction of Sheikh Obeid;
Israeli intelligence reports, however, are adamant that Higgins had been dead for months, killed by excessive torture.[30]

The political fallout that followed Obeid's abduction and
the United States's assertion that Israel's unilateral action
might have led to the death of one of their hostages led many
military observers in Israel to ask the simple question, "Was
it worth it?" As of the early summer of 1991 not one of the
three hostages held by Hizbollah had been released. Militarily, however, the kidnapping reaped invaluable rewards.
Although Obeid might have been a firebrand preacher of a
holy war in his Jibchit lair, in Israeli hands—and under
careful pressure—he sang to his interrogators. Four A'man
officers fluent in Arabic were entrusted with his questioning,
and they uncovered information that ripped through
Hizbollah's veil of mystery, including planned operations,
proposed operations, and the vast and deadly Hizbollah
network.[31] A painful bit of information discovered in the

277

questioning was the fact that, according to Obeid, both Yosef Fink and Rami Elshayach had died while in Hizbollah custody. It was a self-defeating discovery that made nailing down a prisoner exchange a near impossibility. In the frantic march toward the peace talks in Madrid in 1991 the Israelis released hundreds of Shiite guerrillas in exchange for irrefutable proof that both Fink and Elshayach were dead. Of all the Israeli MIAs (including several held by other Palestinian factions since 1982), only Ron Arad is confirmed to be alive.

Yet perhaps one of the most important answers to the question "Was it worth it?" is to say that Sayeret Mat'kal's kidnapping of Sheikh Obeid was a loud and clear proclamation to each and every serving IDF soldier that the full force of his country would support him and do its utmost to secure his well-being and safety through any and all circumstances. It is a fundamental moral commitment on which the IDF was established and has flourished in the years since 1948. When a force like Sayeret Mat'kal is behind the statement, this fundamental commitment is seen as an ironclad guarantee.

As of the writing of this book, even though countless news reports have dropped hints about a possible prisoner swap, Sheikh Obeid still languishes in Israeli custody, as Hizbollah refuses to give up its Israeli hostages, releasing only the names of those confirmed dead (not their bodies) in exchange for Shiite terrorists held in Israel and by the South Lebanese Army. The end of this chapter remains, at the time of this book's writing, unwritten.

# NOTES

1. Israel's extreme sensitivity in obtaining the return of its fallen servicemen can best be seen in the fact that one of

the stumbling blocks preventing Israel and Syria from reaching even the most minor of accords is the question of Eli Cohen. Perhaps the greatest *known* spy in A'man/ Mossad history, Cohen was executed in Damascus on May 18, 1965. In every prisoner exchange, armistice discussion, or hint of possible peace talks, the return of Eli Cohen's remains has been placed at the top of the agenda. Realizing Israel's sensitivities, Nayif Hawatmeh's Democratic Front for the Liberation of Palestine, according to a report in the May 31, 1991, issue of *Hadashot*, was willing to trade the corpse of Sergeant Samir Assad, a Druze soldier kidnapped in Lebanon in 1983, for "hundreds" of Lebanese and Palestinian prisoners.

2. Elina'ar Ben Akiva, "Ha'Baita," *Biton Heyl Ha'Avir,* November 1986, 8.

3. *Ibid.,* 10

4. Zeev Schiff and Ehud Ya'ari, *Israel's Lebanon War* (New York: Simon and Schuster, 1984), 134.

5. Tzvi Alosh, "Manhig Amal: Echlif Et Ha'Tayas Be'A'atzirim Palestina'im Ve'Levanonim," *Yediot Aharonot,* October 19, 1986, 1.

6. Shapi Gabai, "Amal: Muchanim Le'Hachzir 2 Gufot Yisraelim Tmurat 400 Shi'im," *Ma'ariv,* May 20, 1990, 2.

7. Edwin Eitan, "Ha'Navat Ha'Shavu'i, Ron Arad Be'Yadei Ha'Iranim, Gilta Ra'ayato Be'Pariz," *Yediot Aharonot,* December 17, 1989, 1.

8. Even though Hizbollah is the group now holding Ron Arad, the IDF still holds Amal responsible for his welfare.

9. Zeev Klein, *Ha'Milchama Be'Terror Ve'Mediniut Shel Yisrael 1979-1988* (Tel Aviv: Revivim, 1988), 145.

10. Samuel M. Katz, *Follow Me! A History of Israel's Military Elite* (London: Arms and Armour Press, 1989), 40.

11. Avi Benihu, "Tzahal Chataf 2 Mefakdim Me'Irgun She'Beyado Kanireh Chayalim Yisraelim," *Al Ha'Mishmar,* December 18, 1984, 1-2; for mention of Sayeret Mat'kal's participation in the operation, see "Sayeret Mat'kal Heviah Et Manhig Hizbollah Be'Eizor Drom Levanon Le'Bikur Hatuf Be'Yisrael," *Yisrael Shelanu,* August 4, 1989, 2.

12. Douglas Davis, "Israel Kidnapped Top *Hizbollah* Man Before Obeid, Says U.K. Paper," *Jerusalem Post,* May 14, 1990, 10.

13. *Yisrael Shelanu,* "Sayeret Mat'kal," 2.

14. Drora Getlzer and Kenneth Kaplan, "Capture of Sheikh Was Held Up," *Jerusalem Post International Edition,* August 12, 1989, 4.

15. In the Israeli press, the top Israeli newspaper *Yediot Aharonot,* quoting the London *Daily Mail,* listed as the headline of its July 30, 1989, issue, "Sayeret Mat'kal Bitza Chatifat Ha'Sheikh Obeid" ("Sayeret Mat'kal Carried Out the Sheikh Obeid Kidnapping"). Another foreign source confirming the participation of Sayeret Mat'kal in the Sheikh Obeid kidnapping is Richard Layco, "Not Again," *Time Magazine,* August 14, 1989, 16.

16. Baruch Ron and Yair Zilbergleg, "Le'Hakdim Tmuna Le'Maca," *Bamachane Chu'l,* August 1984, 16.

17. Avi Benihu, "Pe'ula Ha'Chatifa Ushra Be'Kabinet," *Al Ha'Mishmar,* July 30, 1989, 1.

18. Ron Ben-Yishai, "Chatifat Shel Sheikh Obeid: Ha'Chatifa, Ha'Mivtza, Ha'Histabchut," *Yediot Aharonot: Shabbat,* August 4, 1989, 1.

19. Avi Benihu, "Pe'ula Ha'Chatifa," 1.

20. Richard Layco, "Not Again," 16.

21. In a recent catalog by Elbit Computers Ltd., Haifa, the HALO system is highlighted and its use for "special operations discussed."

22. As per eyewitness accounts on Lebanese TV as seen in Israel on July 29, 1989.

23. Danny Sadeh, "Iftach el Bab Tza'aku Ha'Chayalim Ve'Partzu Le'Beit Ha'Sheikh Be'Ekdachim Shlufim," *Yediot Aharonot,* July 30, 1989, 3.

24. *Ibid.*

25. *Ibid.*

26. Andrew Meisels, "Israelis Kidnap A Top Extremist," *New York Daily News,* July 29, 1989, 2.

27. Joel Brinkley, "Israeli Commandos Seize Leader of a Pro-Iran Group in Lebanon," *New York Times,* July 29, 1989, 5.

28. *Ibid.*

29. Jeane McDowell, "The Bazaar Is Open," *Time Magazine,* August 21, 1989, 23.

30. Andrew Meisels, "Why They Took the Risk," *New York Daily News,* August 3, 1989, 4.

31. Garry Lewis, "Obeid Gilah Be'Chakira Fink Ve'Elshayach Metu," *Yediot Aharonot,* August 13, 1989, 13.

# POSTSCRIPT

## The Years of Mystery, Myth, and Madness Continue

For the hundreds of thousands of Israelis who sat by their TV sets on Friday night, June 21, 1991, what they were about to see would be an absolute shock.

During the post-Sabbath news broadcast—usually reserved for stories of a religious minister embezzling government funds, a kibbutz or moshav experiencing financial ruin, or a weekend terrorist attack along the Lebanese or Jordanian frontier—a ground-breaking piece of journalism was about to be witnessed. The subject of the night's report was the Intifada, the three-year-old Palestinian uprising that had gripped the Gaza Strip and West Bank in ungovernable chaos. Yet instead of concentrating on the bad case of Palestinian fratricide that emerged from the uprising, or showing the IDF's inability to control the unruly mobs of masked youths, the topic of the Friday night documentary was top-secret. *Extremely* top-secret. A covert unit of the Israel Defense Forces was about to be exposed to the Israeli public and the world. Times had, indeed, changed.

The film was grainy, the images barely visible, but the overall picture was clear and mesmerizing. Two Palestinians, a man and a woman, were casually walking along an alleyway in a West Bank town, sauntering toward a white car and two young men leaning against it. In a split second the man and woman produced Beretta 9mm automatics, shed their disguises, and, in a brilliant move of "arresting choreography," pounced on the two men, subduing them with dazzling speed and whisking them off to an awaiting vehicle. Another scene—this time filmed at night with an infrared camera—showed several Arab men talking alongside a wall. Suddenly and out of nowhere a group of armed "Arabs" jumped them and threw them into a waiting van. The Arabs detained were all high-ranking members of terrorist cells responsible for fanning the flames of the Intifada; they were the hard-core faithful of various terrorist factions that instigated, intimidated, and murdered. The Arabs doing the detaining, however, were members of an elite IDF commando unit known as the Mista'aravim (Arabists)*—the newest special operations unit in Israel's war against the uprising.

As the film continued, the members of the unit were highlighted. They were shown donning Arab disguise, sticking Groucho Marx–type mustaches above their lips with vegetable paste and covering their uniforms and web gear with the black dresses usually worn by elderly Arab women. During the interview, of course, the identity of these soldiers was protected by mirrored sunglasses and face-covering *kefiyehs*. The film concluded with spectacular glimpses of the unit's training regimen. Wearing olive tank tops and canvas commando shoes or sneakers, the commandos were shown assaulting an obstacle course while firing non-standard-issue weapons, such as untraceable automatic pistols and mini-Uzi 9mm submachine guns.[1] The accuracy of their well-aimed volleys of automatic fire was uncanny and awe-inspiring; the targets, cardboard cut-outs, were decimated by thirty rounds of 9mm fire falling no more than

---

*The term "Arabists" was first used by a secretive handpicked intelligence unit of the Pal'mach that disguised its members as Arabs and then infiltrated them into the cold of neighboring Arab villages, capitals, and nations for intelligence-gathering forays.

an inch apart. The film concluded with a mock assault. As a group of commandos, still disguised as Arab men and women, raced up to a house with great speed, they produced their weapons and removed their costumes. Cocking their loaded weapons while leaning against the building's stone walls, the commandos synchronized their coordinated assault and then burst through the locked doors. According to the report, the Arabists had been operating in the field for an extended period of time and with the Shin Bet had brought about the capture of hundreds of suspects who had been involved in terrorist attacks.

That the unit existed at all came as no surprise to most Israelis, and especially not to the Arabs of the territories, since they had long been the victim of this unit's activities in the West Bank and Gaza. In fact, in 1989 and 1990, reports in the foreign media identified two covert elimination units named Shimshon (Samson), which operated in the Gaza Strip, and Duvdevan (Cherry), which operated on the West Bank. They were formed from the soldiers, all volunteers, of the most elite *sayerot* in the IDF's order of battle and, according to the foreign reports, were tasked with the destruction of the Intifada's leadership, given carte blanche to achieve this task.[2] Yet the IDF Military Censor's Office did its utmost to cover up the very *mention* of these two units, and that is what made the disclosure of the Arabists' existence so remarkable. They were not uncovered by a foreign news service, or even by Palestinian Arabs eager to tell the world of the unconventional means the IDF was employing to defeat a "legitimate" nationalist movement. The report was the work of the government-controlled Israel Broadcast Agency and was produced with the open assistance of the IDF spokesman's office and with the blessing of Chief of Staff Lieutenant General Ehud Barak and the OC Central Command Major General Danny Yatom, both Sayeret Mat'kal veterans.[3] Indeed, the report went on to claim that like the rumored-to-exist Samson and Cherry units, the Arabists unit was made up of the finest soldiers—all volunteers—from various reconnaissance formations, including, according to foreign reports, Sayeret Mat'kal. The Arabists' exposure to the Israeli public indicated that a new age had dawned for Israeli special and covert operations.

As happens with most issues in Israeli society, heated controversy followed the exposure of the Arabists. From former Defense Minister Yitzhak Rabin, who called the unmasking of the unit a disgrace that endangered national security, to the parents of soldiers serving in the Arabist unit, who stated that the unmasking of the unit put the lives of their sons in great danger, there was dissent. Major General (Res.) Avigdor "Yanush" Ben-Gal, commander of the elite 7th Armored Brigade during the epic Golan Heights battles of the 1973 War, was quoted as saying, "I'm shocked that Prime Minister Shamir, himself a veteran of Israel's secret services, allowed this material to be broadcast."[4] The fact is that neither Prime Minister Shamir or Defense Minister Moshe Arens was shown the film prior to broadcast. The decision to allow the controversial piece to be aired belonged solely to Barak. On the streets of Israel, security-conscious citizens asked themselves the simple question, "How could he [the chief of staff] allow such a breach of security to be shown to the world?"

Yet there was nothing new about the concept of disguising Israelis as Arabs to deter and destroy terrorist networks in the territories. In 1970–1971, when a Palestinian terrorist offensive in the Gaza Strip made the Intifada look like a schoolyard squabble, the OC Southern Command, Major General Arik Sharon, removed the large numbers of IDF and border guard units that had been sent to the Strip to quell the heavily armed and brutally prosecuted mini-uprising and replaced them with elite units, such as Sayeret Tzanhanim, Sayeret Golani, Sayeret Shaked, Sayeret Haruv, and, according to published reports, Sayeret Mat'kal.[5] These small-unit shock teams were dispatched into the forbidden zone of the casbah and refugee camp centers dressed, on many occasions, as Arabs, armed with non-issue weaponry, and equipped with accurate intelligence reports. By blending into the hostile environment they were able to watch and listen. When the time was right they responded violently by raiding hideouts, eliminating terrorist leaders, and causing havoc with the terrorists' morale. Although there were many other factors that led to Israel's victory in Gaza in 1971, the elite-unit presence was the deciding factor in rooting out a massive and unrelenting terrorist infrastructure. It was hoped that it would work the same way with the Arabist unit of the 1990s.

That the disclosure of this conglomerate of reconnaissance-unit warriors emanated from the office of Chief of Staff Barak was truly remarkable. IDF commanders and members of the top-secret club are secretive men who usually take many mysteries to the grave with them. They don't broadcast them on television. Yet the chief of staff's reasoning behind the decision to remove the veil of this new secret unit was to deter masked youth gangs of the territories from continuing their reign of terror against the IDF, Israeli settlers, and above all their fellow Palestinians.* Since the beginning of the Intifada, the masked youths had carried out merciless campaigns of intimidation and murder against any individual or family they suspected of collaborating with the Israelis. More Palestinians have been killed by their zealous brothers than by IDF troops. One of the exposed successes of the Arabists was the destruction of two of the uprising's most lethal armed mobs—the Red Eagles, a group of enforcers that takes its orders from Dr. George Habash's Popular Front for the Liberation of Palestine, and the Black Panthers, a termination squad under the control of Yasir Arafat's el-Fatah.[6]

In truth, there are countless reasons for the IDF to maintain another top-secret commando force for covert operations and countless reasons for its existence to be made—or not made—public. Yet perhaps Lieutenant General Barak's motive in this controversial episode is that he

---

*Some have speculated that one reason behind the decision to uncover the Arabists was to deter Jewish settlers from firing live ammunition at Arabs, since they might be aiming their licensed weapons at IDF troops in disguise.

wanted the rest of the IDF to use this newly publicized unit as an inspirational role model of self-sacrifice and sense of duty. It was a challenge to be emulated. Perhaps no man in the history of the IDF has as much understanding as to how a small group of highly talented and dedicated soldiers can set the tone for an entire army as Ehud Barak.

The IDF under Ehud Barak has assumed a cocky, arrogant, offensive, and—most importantly—unpredictable nature, much like the unit he called his own and then commanded for so many years. This is expressed in the decision to uncover the Arabists, and in the order to decimate Palestinian terrorist targets in Lebanon with massive air bombardments; the raids were meant to warn the various PLO factions that no trouble would be tolerated at the present, and certainly not in the future. In one such raid, in which the village of Shabaricha, north of Tyre, was targeted, the IAF missed a golden opportunity to terminate several major terrorist leaders when chief representatives of Amal, el-Fatah, the DFLP, and the PFLP arrived late for a top-secret meeting.[7] Clearly, the new IDF chief of staff is determined to keep Israel's enemies on their toes with all the forces—both conventional and covert—at his disposal.

One such enemy, of course, is Iraqi strongman Saddam Hussein. When the first Iraqi SCUD-B missiles began to land in Tel Aviv and Haifa during the opening hours of Operation Desert Storm, on January 18, 1991, speculation was that the IAF would retaliate with a precision air strike like the June 6, 1981, destruction of the Osirak nuclear reactor in Baghdad, or with a spectacular commando assault. Israel did nothing, however. As the SCUD-Bs continued to fall, and physical damage to Ramat Gan, a Tel Aviv suburb, neared the catastrophic, the belief was that the IDF would dispatch Sayeret Mat'kal to Baghdad in order to execute an Entebbe-type commando raid.[8] According to the report, Sayeret Mat'kal commandos would infiltrate Baghdad under cover of darkness and, with the assistance of deep-cover Mossad agents, eliminate numerous human targets; the operation would be conducted primarily by Iraqi-born Israelis.[9] According to Western intelligence officials, only Israel, with its superb military intelligence, commando warfare experience, and willingness to take risks, could pull off such a gambit.

Following the war, however, the true extent of Israel's retaliatory plans became clear, and they did involve commando strikes, although the words Sayeret Mat'kal were never officially mentioned. According to U.S. government officials, the Israelis, through Defense Minister Moshe Arens and then-Deputy Chief of Staff Major General Ehud Barak, told Washington that they planned to retaliate with massive air and land incursions into Western Iraq following the first of the SCUD-B attacks.[10] IDF commando teams would be heli-lifted into the Western Iraq region, and the H-2 and H-3 airfields in particular. The commando teams would conduct heliborne and jeepborne search-and-destroy forays against the mobile SCUD-B while IAF fighter bombers attacked fixed-site positions capable of striking at the Jewish state.[11] The Americans, however, urged Israel to stay out of the war and dispatched its own special forces unit to Western Iraq to remove the SCUD threat. Israel, however, has never surrendered its right to retaliate—somehow—against Iraq.

For Sayeret Mat'kal, the decade of the 1990s promises to be a time of decision. Lieutenant General Barak's general staff, the men responsible for activating the unit, is composed of the most brilliant special-operations veterans and minds the IDF has ever produced. The deputy chief of staff is Major General Amnon Shahak, a former Sayeret Tzanhanim officer; the A'man director is Major General Uri Saguy, a former commander of Sayeret Golani; OC Southern Command is Major General Matan Vilnai, a former commander of Sayeret Tzanhanim; OC Northern Command is Major General Yitzhak Mordechai, once OC Paratroop and Infantry Branch; and OC Central Command is Danny Yatom, a former comrade of Barak in Sayeret Mat'kal. It is clear that Israeli special operations in the years to come will expand in scale and scope. In 1991 a Druze Muslim was accepted for service in the Chief of Staff's Boys to become the first Israeli Arab minority soldier ever to make it to the ranks of Sayeret Mat'kal.[12] With one of its own as the IDF commander, the veil of anonymity has been peeled away from its top-secret status.

In his brief tenure as the IDF Chief of Staff Lieutenant General Ehud Barak has already become one of Israel's most controversial military chiefs. From the closing of the army radio station to implementing drastic budgetary cuts by sacking high-ranking officers, he has made it his mission to prepare the IDF for the next war—one that promises to be the deadliest ever waged in the Middle East. For the IDF to persevere it has only to look back at its past and the special men of the special forces who sacrificed much of their lives to perform the impossible above and beyond the call of duty. On April 1, 1991, Lieutenant General Barak's first act as the IDF's fourteenth chief of staff was to visit the military ceremony at Mt. Herzl, in Jerusalem. He paused at the graves of Brigadier General Avraham Arnan, Sayeret Mat'kal's founding father; Lieutenant Colonel Yonatan Netanyahu, the Sayeret Mat'kal commander killed at Entebbe; Captain Nechamia Cohen, a Sayeret Mat'kal officer who fell in the 1967 War during an operation that is still classified.[13] Finally Ehud Barak paused by the grave of another chief of staff, Lieutenant General David "Dado" Elazar, the IDF commander at the time of Barak's rule over Sayeret Mat'kal and an army commander who trusted the abilities of "his boys," using their services on numerous and spectacular occasions. Perhaps Barak was paying homage to a fine soldier of Israel, perhaps seeking inspiration. It is clear that Chief of Staff Barak will emulate his predecessor's policy and deploy Israel's top-secret commandos whenever and wherever in the world the need arises.

# NOTES

1. "Yechidot Chasha'iyot Ha'Poalot Be'Shtachim Nichsafu Le'Shidur Betelevisia," *Yisrael Shelani*, June 28, 1991, 4.

2. "The Shin Bet's Secret Drive," *Time Magazine*, August 29, 1989, 37; Danny Sadeh, "Ha'Ra'mat'kal: Ha'Chasifa Tesaye'a Le'Harta'a; Rabin: Ta'ut Chamura," *Yediot Aharonot*, June 23, 1991, 1.

3. Amos Gilboa, Yossi Levi, and David Lavi, "Tzamaeret Tzahal Ishra Ha'Chasifa; Horim Tovi'm Va'adat Chakira," *Ma'ariv*, June 28, 1991, 5.

4. Danny Sadeh, "Mi Tzarich Pirsum Kaze? Od Yichsafu Et Ha'Mossad Ve'Ha'Shabak," *Yediot Aharonot*, June 23, 1991, 3.

5. Roni Daniel, "Model 71," *Matara*, 1990, 26.

6. Amos Gilboah, Yossi Levi, and David Lavi, "Tzamaeret Tzahal," 5.

7. Shmayah Kidor, Shapi Gabai, and Yehuda Goren, "Heyl Ha'Avir Hi'Chmitz Chisool Rav Manhigai Ha'Mechablim Be'Levanon," *Ma'ariv*, May 24, 1991, 5.

8. Joshua Hammer, Douglas Waller, Jeffrey Bartholet, and Theodore Stranger, "Will Israel Hit Back?" *Newsweek*, February 11, 1991, 33.

9. *Ibid.*

10. Patrick Tyler, "U.S. Tells of Retaliatory Plan the Israelis Abandoned," *New York Times*, March 7, 1991, A1.

11. "Tzahal Tichnen Pshitat Kommando Ve'Mesokei Tkifa Neged Tilim," *Ma'ariv*, March 8, 1991, 1.

12. Emanuel Rosen, "Le'Rishona: Druzi Be'Sayeret Mat'kal," *Ma'ariv*, May 3, 1991, 3.

13. Danny Sadeh, "Ha'Ra'mat'kal, Rav-Aluf Ehud Barak," *Yediot Aharonot*, April 2, 1991, 8.

THE EXPLOSIVE AUTOBIOGRAPHY OF THE
CONTROVERSIAL, DEATH-DEFYING FOUNDER OF THE
U.S. NAVY'S TOP SECRET COUNTERTERRORIST UNIT
**SEAL TEAM SIX**

# ROGUE WARRIOR

## RICHARD MARCINKO
### WITH JOHN WEISMAN

**Available in hardcover from Pocket Books**

POCKET
BOOKS

480-01

## America's Fighter Aces Tell Their Stories

# TOP GUNS

### Joe Foss and Matthew Brennan

They were high-flying heroes who fought our wars, inspired the country, and left a proud legacy. Now, America's greatest living fighter aces tell their personal stories—many for the first time—in this extraordinary record of aerial combat from World War I through Vietnam.

Legendary WWII Marine ace Joe Foss and highly decorated Vietnam veteran and distinguished author Matthew Brennan bring together twenty-seven fighter pilots to create this astonishing volume of oral history. You are there, in the major theaters of four wars—in the cockpit.

POCKET
BOOKS

**Available in paperback from Pocket Books**

419-02